Are liberalism and perfectionism compatible? In this study Steven Wall presents and defends a perfectionist account of political morality that takes issue with many currently fashionable liberal ideas but retains the strong liberal commitment to the ideal of personal autonomy. He begins by critically discussing the most influential version of anti-perfectionist liberalism, examining the main arguments that have been offered in its defense. He then clarifies the ideal of personal autonomy, presents an account of its value and shows that a strong commitment to personal autonomy is fully compatible with an endorsement of perfectionist political action designed to promote valuable pursuits and discourage base ones. His study is a timely and original contribution to one of the most important contemporary debates in political philosophy.

Liberalism, perfectionism and restraint

Liberalism, perfectionism and restraint

Steven Wall

CAMBRIDGE
UNIVERSITY PRESS

PUBLISHED BY THE PRESS SYNDICATE OF THE UNIVERSITY OF CAMBRIDGE
The Pitt Building, Trumpington Street, Cambridge CB2 1RP, United Kingdom

CAMBRIDGE UNIVERSITY PRESS
The Edinburgh Building, Cambridge CB2 2RU, United Kingdom
40 West 20th Street, New York, NY 10011–4211, USA
10 Stamford Road, Oakleigh, Melbourne 3166, Australia

First published 1998

Printed in the United Kingdom at the University Press, Cambridge

Typeset in 10/12pt Times   [CE]

A catalogue record for this book is available from the British Library

Library of Congress cataloguing in publication data

Wall, Steven, 1967–
Liberalism, perfectionism and restraint / Steven P. Wall.
        p.   cm.
Includes bibliographical references.
ISBN 0 521 62411 8 (hardback)
1. Political ethics. 2. Liberty. I. Title.
JA79.W25   1998
320.51'3–dc21   97–27917   CIP

ISBN 0 521 62411 8 hardback

To my parents Jack and Nancy Wall

Contents

Acknowledgments

I owe my first and largest debt to Joseph Raz, who supervised my research while I was a graduate student at Oxford, and from whom I learned a great deal. I am extremely grateful to him for his trenchant criticism of earlier drafts of this book, criticism which helped me make my thoughts clearer and my arguments better.

I started thinking about some of the ideas in this book while I was a student at Columbia University, and I am delighted to have the opportunity to thank Robert Amdur, Julian Franklin and David Johnston for their help at this early stage. I am especially grateful to Robert Amdur, who supervised my work while I was at Columbia and who read and commented on several chapters of this book.

The book was written at Oxford, and a number of teachers and friends there provided valuable help. Adam Swift read an earlier draft of chapters 2–5 and gave me useful comments. A version of chapter 5 was presented at G. A. Cohen's research seminar in political theory in the Spring of 1996 and received very helpful comments from him and other participants in the seminar. Terry Price also criticized several drafts of most of the chapters in this book, and I am grateful to him for his generous help.

Brian Barry read an early draft of the entire book. His comments and criticisms saved me from a number of mistakes. Alan Ryan and Raymond Geuss read a penultimate draft, and I am extremely grateful to both of them for their valuable suggestions about how to improve it.

A contracted version of chapter 5 was published in *The Philosophical Quarterly*, and I am grateful to the editors for allowing me to use it here. I owe a debt of a different kind to the Institute for Humane Studies, which over the years has provided me with much-needed financial support. In particular, I would like to thank Walter Grinder, Christine Blundell and Leonard Liggio for their assistance.

Finally, I owe a special debt to Lynn Jansen. She not only commented on every chapter of this book, but provided stimulating friendship and unwavering support during the time in which it was written.

Introduction

Perfectionist conceptions of political morality have made something of a comeback in recent years. Long understood as opposed to liberalism, perfectionism has been depicted as hostile to personal autonomy and antithetical to pluralism. Lately, this depiction has been called into question. A number of political philosophers have attempted to defend a conception of perfectionism that is compatible with liberalism.[1] This book addresses the debate between these liberal perfectionists and their critics. It investigates whether the resurgence of perfectionism is well founded; and, if so, how congruent it is with liberal principles and ideals.

The issues

The main issue between perfectionism and anti-perfectionism centers on which one gives a better account of political morality. But what makes one account better than another?

Two answers suggest themselves. The first one concerns how well an account of political morality explains its subject matter; that is, how well it helps us understand political morality and how well it justifies substantive judgments supported by political morality. We can refer to this as the *justificatory force* of the account.[2] The second one concerns the substantive judgments about important political issues that the account yields or supports. We can refer to this as the *critical potential* of the account.

It would be, of course, a mistake to think that the justificatory force

---

[1] See J. Raz, *The Morality of Freedom*, T. Hurka, *Perfectionism* and V. Haksar, *Equality, Liberty and Perfectionism.*

[2] It might be thought that we can distinguish the explanatory power of an account of political morality (how well it explains its subject matter) from its ability to justify substantive judgments, and that I have collapsed the two with the broad phrase "justificatory force." But I believe that even if this distinction can be drawn, the two go together. The more we understand political morality, the better we will be at justifying substantive moral judgments in politics. If this is right, no confusion should result from using "justificatory force" as I define it.

and the critical potential of an account of political morality have nothing to do with each other. One reason for thinking that an account has justificatory force is that it yields or supports intuitively correct substantive judgments about important political issues. But while justificatory force and critical potential are clearly related, they remain distinct. This can be grasped by reflecting on the possibility that two accounts of political morality could support exactly the same substantive judgments about a wide range of political issues and yet differ dramatically in justificatory force. One account could do a much better job than the other in explaining and justifying the substantive judgments that both accounts support.

Much of this book is concerned with arguing that perfectionism provides a better understanding of political morality than anti-perfectionism. Liberal perfectionism, I will argue, has greater justificatory force than anti-perfectionist liberalism.[3] This conclusion is not threatened by the possibility that the best account of perfectionist political morality and the best account of anti-perfectionist political morality yield the same substantive political judgments. Such a happy convergence in critical potential would not show that both accounts were equally good.

This is worth bearing in mind, since perfectionists are sometimes taken to task for not being more specific about how their theories differ from anti-perfectionist theories with regard to concrete particulars.[4] The thought behind this complaint seems to be that until perfectionists can show that anti-perfectionist theories yield incorrect substantive judgments about concrete political issues their theories do not warrant serious consideration. Distinguishing the justificatory force from the critical potential of an account of political morality helps us see that this complaint is misguided.

Notwithstanding this point, in the concluding chapter of this book, I will discuss a range of public policy issues and I will show that (with regard to some of them) liberal perfectionism and anti-perfectionist liberalism point toward different political judgments. I will further argue that the judgments reached by liberal perfectionism are superior. This is intended to impart supplementary support for the claim that liberal perfectionism provides a better account of political morality than its anti-perfectionist rival.

A large part of my brief for perfectionism will consist in defending it

[3] By "liberal perfectionism" I mean a perfectionist account of political morality that holds that personal autonomy is a central component of human flourishing.
[4] See, for example, Rawls' general response to critics of political liberalism. "Reply to Habermas," p. 150.

from two general types of criticism. These two types of criticism are seldom distinguished, but it facilitates critical examination of them if they are kept apart. The two criticisms point toward two different levels at which perfectionism might be challenged. The first level is theoretical, the second practical.

Let me explain. It is sometimes argued that in formulating ultimate standards for judging political institutions and public policies we should not appeal to any controversial conception of the good. According to this view, we will get a better account of political morality if, when we formulate it, we bracket our understandings of what comprises a fully good life. So understood, this view is clearly incompatible with perfectionism. If it is sound, perfectionism must be rejected.

But the converse is not true. Rejection of this view does not thereby commit one to perfectionism. It is possible to believe that in formulating an account of political morality we should draw freely on our best understanding of what comprises a fully good life and yet reject perfectionism. This is possible, since an account of political morality so formulated might yield the judgment that when it comes to public policy the state should not intentionally favor any ideals of the good over others.[5] In other words, this account might come to the conclusion that the best way for the state to promote the good is for it to refrain from using its power to promote the good.

An adequate defense of perfectionism, therefore, must not only show that we ought to draw on our best understandings of the good life when formulating an account of political morality, but also show that when we do this we do not arrive at an account that rejects perfectionism out of hand at the practical level of public policy. I shall undertake just such a defense in this book.

A restriction in scope

Before outlining my argument, I would like to make it plain that I will be concerned with the political morality of *modern western societies*. I will not claim (or deny) that this political morality is binding on all people in all places. There are several reasons for restricting the scope of the argument in this way, but three in particular should be mentioned here.

First, the version of anti-perfectionist political morality that I shall be criticizing explicitly makes this same restriction. There is, moreover,

---

[5] To invoke Rawls' terminology, it is possible for an account of political morality to be both comprehensive and anti-perfectionist – a point noted by S. Mulhall and A. Swift, *Liberals and Communitarians*, p. 251.

good reason for it to make it. As we shall see shortly, this version of anti-perfectionist political morality relies heavily on the contractualist norm of reasonable rejectability. For this norm to yield determinate results, the range of people to whom it applies must be limited.[6] Given this, it makes perfect sense for proponents of this view to insist that their account of political morality applies only to modern western societies.

Second, the question whether moral norms in general and norms of political morality in particular are universally binding across all cultures raises large and difficult issues that I cannot address. In saying this I should not be understood to be endorsing any version of relativism. In this book, as much as it is possible, I simply want to leave this question open.

Third, in chapter 7, I will advance one argument about the value of personal autonomy that refers to the social forms that predominate in modern western societies. This argument presumes that the general character of these social forms is worthy of support, but I do not try to establish that these social forms are superior to all other social forms that either exist in other places or have existed in the past.

For these reasons, then, this book is concerned only with the political morality appropriate for modern western societies. Given this restriction, it may be helpful if I outline at the outset some of the distinguishing features of these societies. Six in particular can be singled out:

(1) geographic mobility
(2) technological and economic innovation
(3) familial and social mobility
(4) secularization
(5) pluralism
(6) a commitment to human rights

These six features are important constitutive elements of the social forms of modern western societies. Later I will discuss each one of them in more detail. For now it should suffice to point out that these features distinguish modern western societies from centralized tyrannies like the former Soviet Union, theocentric societies like some now found in the Islamic world, pre-industrial societies, and those societies which may have modern economies, but which suppress pluralism and do not respect human rights.[7]

---

[6] As B. Williams has pointed out, this is true because the norm crucially relies on shared beliefs and intuitions for its application. See *Ethics and the Limits of Philosophy*, p. 103.

[7] Not all societies that might plausibly be classified as modern western will exhibit each of these six features or have them to the same degree. But in assessing the argument of this book it may help to have in mind a paradigm case in which all six features are clearly present.

Outline of the argument

Now to the outline. The argument of this book unfolds in nine chapters. In the first chapter I present a general account of perfectionism. The purpose of doing so is, first, to make it more clear how the term will be used throughout this book and, second, to correct some common misperceptions.

After this introductory chapter, the book divides into two main parts. In Part II discuss and criticize (what I consider to be) the most important and the best-developed account of anti-perfectionist political morality. This is an account that receives its most rigorous expression in the recent work of John Rawls. Much of my discussion in Part I, accordingly, focuses on his work. However, I also consider a number of arguments advanced by others who share his general outlook.

Part I itself divides into four chapters. In chapter 2 I discuss the idea of restraint, an idea that lies at the heart of this account of anti-perfectionist political morality. Chapter 3 identifies and critically examines two prefatory arguments in favor of restraint. I term these the *pragmatic argument* and the *argument from political justification*. Picking up where this leaves off, chapter 4 discusses in detail Rawls' "democratic idea of toleration." I argue that this is a flawed account of toleration. Therefore, I conclude, it cannot be relied on to justify anti-perfectionism. Finally, in chapter 5, I analyze the idea of public justification and ask whether it provides any support for the idea of restraint.

The conclusion of Part I is that this version of anti-perfectionist political morality is unconvincing. I reach this conclusion not by showing that the account does not fit our considered judgments about important political issues, but by arguing that its central idea – the idea of restraint – is not rationally grounded.

Part II is the constructive part of the book. It seeks to show that perfectionism and liberalism are compatible; and that the best perfectionist theory is a liberal one. In chapters 6–8 I present an account of the nature and status of personal autonomy. This account provides answers to four questions: (1) What are the constituent elements of this ideal?, (2) What considerations account for its value?, (3) What standing does personal autonomy have in a sound account of political morality? and (4) What constraints does a proper respect for this ideal place on perfectionist political action?

My main conclusions are that personal autonomy is an ideal of special importance for people in modern western societies; that it, accordingly, warrants a privileged position in an account of political morality appropriate for these societies; and that, therefore, political authorities in these societies have duties to create and maintain social conditions that best enable their subjects to lead autonomous lives. I also conclude that a strong commitment to personal autonomy does not render impermissible (at least at the level of principle) perfectionist political action designed to favor valuable lifestyles, pursuits, options, etc. over base ones.[8]

The concluding chapter – chapter nine – brings the discussion down to earth by considering a range of public policy issues. Its goal is to give some indication of how the perfectionist views defended in this book might differ from anti-perfectionist views at the level of concrete politics.[9]

---

[8] As I will explain more fully in chapter 8 below, we can distinguish between two types of perfectionist political action. One type – call it Type (1) – covers political action intended to favor or promote personal autonomy. A second type – call it Type (2) – covers political action intended to favor valuable options over base ones. In chapters 6–8 I argue that a proper understanding of personal autonomy mandates Type (1) perfectionism and is compatible with at least some political measures that fall under Type (2) perfectionism.

[9] Although the parts of this book contribute to a single argument, they are to some extent separable. A reader could accept the critique of the bracketing strategy in Part I, but reject the account of personal autonomy in Part II. Likewise, a reader could accept the main arguments in Part I and Part II, but reject some of the policy judgments defended in chapter 9.

1   Perfectionism

There is not a clear, settled understanding of 'perfectionism' in contemporary political philosophy. The term is used to refer to different ideas and theories. Consider, for example, these three recent characterizations of perfectionist political morality.[1]

(a) Perfectionism is the view that a society "ought to arrange institutions and to define the duties and obligations of individuals so as to maximize the achievement of excellence in art, science or culture."[2]

(b) Perfectionism supports "the following standard of political evaluation: The best political act, institution, or government is that which most promotes the perfection of all humans."[3]

(c) Perfectionism is the view that "the state has the responsibility and the right to foster the good, the well-being, flourishing, and excellence, of all its citizens and to discourage them, even coercively, from at least some of the actions and dispositions which would injure, degrade, or despoil them, even some actions and dispositions which as such are 'self-regarding.' "[4]

These characterizations purport to tell us what is distinctive about perfectionism, but they emphasize different things.

The primary objective of this chapter is to present a general account of perfectionism that removes some of the ambiguities surrounding the term and makes it clearer how it will be used throughout this book. Working with this general account, the chapter also rebuts a number of common objections that have been raised against perfectionism.[5]

---

[1] Perfectionism can refer to an account of personal well-being, to an account of morality in general, to an account of political morality or to all of these. But since this book is primarily concerned with political morality, I use the terms "perfectionism" and "perfectionist political morality" interchangeably.

[2] J. Rawls, *A Theory of Justice*, p. 325.   [3] T. Hurka, *Perfectionism*, p. 147.

[4] J. Finnis, "The Legal Enforcement of 'Duties to Oneself:' Kant vs Neo-Kantians," p. 434.

[5] There are different ways of classifying political theories. I claim two virtues for the account presented in this chapter. First, it is general enough so that most writers traditionally described as perfectionist qualify under it. Second, it draws a clear contrast between perfectionist political theories and the regnant contemporary anti-perfectionist political theories which this book seeks to criticize.

Four claims

Perfectionism is committed to the general thesis that *political authorities should take an active role in creating and maintaining social conditions that best enable their subjects to lead valuable and worthwhile lives.* Clearly, this is a very general thesis.[6] Because it is so general it will be useful to supplement it by specifying some further claims perfectionists are committed to. Some of these claims clarify the general thesis; others add to it.

As it will be understood here, perfectionist political morality is committed to four claims. These are (1) that some ideals of human flourishing[7] are sound and can be known to be sound; (2) that the state is presumptively justified in favoring these ideals; (3) that a sound account of political morality will be informed by sound ideals of human flourishing; and (4) that there is no general moral principle that forbids the state from favoring sound ideals of human flourishing, as well as enforcing conceptions of political morality informed by them, when these ideals are controversial and subject to reasonable disagreement.

Taken together, these claims yield a modest account of perfectionism. In several respects, the account differs from the characterizations quoted above. It does not specify the content of perfectionist ideals, as does (a). Nor does it enjoin political authorities to "maximize" them, as suggested by (a) and (b). Nor, finally, does it prescribe how perfectionist ideals should be promoted, as (c) does in explicitly rejecting the harm principle. All these issues are important and at some point a perfectionist political theory must provide answers to them. But a general characterization of perfectionism should leave them open, permitting different perfectionist theories to resolve them in different ways.

Each of the four basic claims stand in need of explication. The first claim raises large and difficult issues. If there is at least one ideal of human flourishing that is sound and could be known to be sound, then it is true. But while this claim is not particularly contentious, it is a formidable task to give a perspicuous account of it.

What does it mean to say of an ideal of human flourishing that it is sound? The short answer is that such an ideal would realize or promote human interests, where human interests refer not merely to things that

---

[6] To get a sense of how general it is note that the following views all qualify as perfectionist: the Aristotelian view that the state ought to help people realize their supreme telos or end, the Millian view that the state ought to promote conditions that encourage the development of individuality, and the Marxist view that in a well-ordered political community private property would be abolished because it thwarts man's development as a "species-being."

[7] Ideals of human flourishing refer to pursuits, ideals, excellences or virtues that comprise a fully good life.

people happen to take an interest in, but rather to things that it would be intelligent or reasonable for them to take an interest in. This can be made clearer if we consider an ideal of human flourishing that is not sound. Think of the ideal that is realized by plugging into an experience machine and living a life of maximally pleasant experiences.[8] Most people believe that this ideal is not sound. They think that choosing to plug in would be a mistake, a failure to understand how one ought to lead one's life. Most people believe this because on reflection they agree with Aristotle that the good life is a life of activity.

I too believe that this view is correct. I mention it here for one reason. It nicely illustrates what is meant by the claim that an ideal of human flourishing is sound or unsound. Of course not all such claims will meet with the same measure of agreement as this one. But the question of whether an ideal is sound and the question whether most people think it is sound are obviously distinct.

To further clarify the notion of soundness as it pertains to ideals of human flourishing, I offer the following formulations (where X denotes an ideal of human flourishing).

(1) All things considered, there is reason to believe that X is sound.

(2) X possesses some property or set of properties which make it sound.

Those who accept (1) will also be inclined to accept (2); and vice versa.[9] But it is possible to accept (1) without having well-worked-out ideas about the metaphysics implicated in (2). For this reason, we should take (1) as primary. It is roughly equivalent to

(3) If a person had access to all relevant considerations and gave them proper weight in his or her deliberations, then he or she would believe that X is sound.

However, (1) and (3) should not be confused with

(4) If a person does not believe that X is sound, then he or she is unreasonable.

(3) does not imply (4) because a person may be insensitive to reasons without being unreasonable. That is, he may be unaware of, or incapable of appreciating the force of, various considerations even if there is nothing wrong with his general ability to deliberate rationally.[10]

---

[8] For discussion and criticism of this ideal, see R. Nozick, *Anarchy, State and Utopia*, p. 43, and J. Finnis, *Fundamentals of Ethics*, pp. 37–42.

[9] The truth of (2) does not entail (1); for it is possible that (2) is true, but that we have no way of knowing that it is true. But, typically, one would not accept (2) unless one believed that it could be known to be true.

[10] This point is well brought out by J. McDowell in "Might There Be External Reasons?", pp. 78, 81.

These formulations clarify what it means to say that an ideal of human flourishing is sound. They should suffice for the purposes of this book.[11]

Of course not everyone accepts the first claim. Some people believe that it does not make sense to say of an ideal of human flourishing that it is sound. Talk of soundness or truth, they think, is inappropriate in this context. Let us call this position *nihilism about the good*.[12]

This position poses a clear challenge to perfectionism. It undercuts most of the claims perfectionists make in defending their conceptions of political morality. This shows that a complete defense of perfectionism must include a theory of value. Yet despite its importance, no attempt will be made in this book to provide or defend a theory of value. The excuse for this omission is that such an attempt would take us far afield from the questions I want to address. Whether or not this is a good excuse, it must be conceded that the arguments in this book are vulnerable. They are based on the undefended assumption that it makes sense to say of an ideal of human flourishing that it is sound.[13] Fortunately, this assumption is not an especially precarious one; others have gone some distance toward supplying it with a satisfactory defense.[14]

One further point needs to be made. It is possible that the claim that some ideals of human flourishing are sound is true, but that no one is ever in a position to know which ideals are sound. In chapter 4 I will discuss the skeptical objection to perfectionism and I will give some reasons for rejecting it. For now, I will assume that there is at least one ideal of human flourishing that is both sound and known to be sound. This is all that is implied by the first claim.[15]

The second claim maintains that the state is presumptively justified in favoring sound ideals of human flourishing. Here the "state" should be interpreted broadly to include the political constitution of a society, its

---

[11] Thus, as I am using the term, soundness is not relative to an epistemic base. An ideal might be sound even if there were people who were justified in believing that it was not sound.

[12] It may be possible to be a nihilist about the good, but not about the right; hence, the cumbersome label.

[13] Someone might say: "It makes sense to say of an ideal of human flourishing that it is sound; but, in fact, no ideals are sound." The best response to this is simply to give one's arguments for why an ideal that one takes to be sound is indeed sound.

[14] See W. Quinn, *Morality and Action*, essays 11 and 12, E. J. Bond, *Reason and Value*, and J. Finnis, *Fundamentals of Ethics*, pp. 26–55.

[15] To be more precise, the first claim entails the rejection of the following three claims: (a) it does not make sense to say of an ideal of human flourishing that it is sound; (b) it makes sense to say of such an ideal that it is sound, but none in fact is sound; and (c) some ideals are sound, but no one knows which ones are sound.

political institutions and the policies of governments.[16] The claim does not hold that if an ideal of human flourishing could be shown to be sound, then *ipso facto* the state would be justified in promoting it through political action. It holds, more weakly, that there would be a presumptive case for such action. This leaves open the possibility that under some circumstances such action would not be wise. Nor does the second claim imply that if an ideal of human flourishing could be shown to be sound, then it would always be morally permissible for the state to promote it in whatever way it thought best. As we will see more clearly in subsequent chapters, there are moral limits to perfectionist political action, even when it serves ideals of human flourishing fully worthy of support.

The second claim, then, is a very weak claim; and it is worth pausing to emphasize just how weak it is. Many defenders of what has come to be known as the doctrine of state neutrality[17] could accept it. For instance, Charles Larmore, a leading proponent of the doctrine, concedes that it is permissible for the state to promote *shared* ideals of the good life.[18] Thus, he could accept the second claim.[19] Nonetheless, there may be some who would reject it. Let us call them *pure neutrality theorists*. They would claim that it is never morally permissible for the state to favor knowingly and intentionally some ideals of human flourishing.

Some people are pure neutrality theorists because they are anarchists. They believe that it is never morally permissible for the state to favor knowingly and intentionally some ideals of human flourishing because it is never morally permissible for the state to take any action at all. But a pure neutrality theorist need not be an anarchist. He or she could insist, first, that there is a sharp distinction between ideals of human flourishing and the requirements of political morality; and, second, that the state should only be in the business of enforcing the latter.

This brings us to the third claim. It denies that a sound political philosophy would cordon off political morality from ideals of human flourishing. Before trying to clarify what this means, I need to say a bit more about ideals of human flourishing and conceptions of political morality.

---

[16] For simplicity, I will often write as if the state were a government actively adopting policies or measures. But it should be borne in mind that a state, understood broadly, can favor some ideals by the way in which the constitution or political institutions of a society are designed.

[17] There are many different formulations of this doctrine. We need not discuss them here. But see chapter 2.

[18] C. Larmore, *Patterns of Moral Complexity*, p. 69.

[19] To know how strong this concession is we need to know more about what it means to say that an ideal is shared. Does this mean that everyone accepts it or, more weakly, that a large majority accept it? Larmore does not tell us.

Ideals of human flourishing consist of pursuits, ideals, excellences and virtues. They specify the ingredients of a fully good human life. There are a wide variety of such ideals. Some are comprehensive and rigorously worked out; others are relatively incomplete and not fully articulated. Some cover a wide range of human conduct; others concern one particular activity or one particular virtue. Some, like the Aristotelian ideal of the contemplative life, are substantively specific, prescribing particular activities and pursuits; others, like the Millian ideal of individuality, refer more to the manner or mode in which people lead their lives.

Moreover, some ideals of human flourishing are *person-relative* and others are not. A person-relative ideal applies to only one person. Its realization makes his or her life go well, given his or her particular talents, dispositions and personal history. In contrast, a non-person-relative ideal applies to people more generally. Its realization makes their lives go well.

Though they are sometimes derived from them, conceptions of political morality are not identical with ideals of human flourishing. They form a part of the larger enterprise of moral theory. Typically, conceptions of political morality are put forward as guides for political action. They consist of principles, rules and norms for evaluating political institutions and public policies and they include accounts of concepts such as justice, rights, obligation, authority and the common good. In short, conceptions of political morality supply criteria for distinguishing the morally justified from the morally unjustified exercise of political power.

The question the third claim raises is, should ideals of human flourishing inform conceptions of political morality? This is a complex question because it asks us to consider two different, but related, issues. The first issue concerns whether a sound conception of political morality requires the political promotion of some ideals of human flourishing. The second issue concerns whether an adequate account of concepts like justice, rights and obligation can be given without appeal to some ideal of human flourishing. The second issue is more fundamental than the first. To see why, return to the perspective of the pure neutrality theorist. As we have seen, he has a ready response to the first issue – it is never permissible to use political power to favor knowingly and intentionally an ideal of human flourishing. However, even if he is right about this, he still must put forward an account of concepts like justice and rights. And the second issue suggests that it may not be possible to do this adequately without appealing to some ideal of human flourishing. If this is right, then even if one does not let ideals come in the front door, they may enter from the back.

The idea that we can and should cordon off conceptions of political morality from ideals of human flourishing is a modern one.[20] It arose from the thought that persons naturally, and not unreasonably, embrace a wide variety of competing and conflicting conceptions of the good life; but that they, nevertheless, must agree on principles of political morality if they are to live together peacefully and productively. This provided the stimulus for the project of coming up with an account of political morality that is independent of and prior to contested ideals of the good. The project holds out the promise that if such an account could be suitably worked out, it could be accepted by all citizens, despite their commitments to conflicting ideals.

Perfectionism, as I understand it, rejects this project. The rejection can take one of two forms. On the one hand, it can be argued that all plausible conceptions of political morality are, in fact, informed by ideals of human flourishing, whether their proponents admit it or not. On this view, those who insist on a sharp distinction between ideals of human flourishing and conceptions of political morality fail to see the extent to which their own conceptions of political morality are informed by their own ideals.[21] On the other hand, it can be conceded that it is possible coherently to exclude ideals of human flourishing from conceptions of political morality, but maintained that doing so results in impoverished conceptions of political morality.

Both lines of argument drive to the same conclusion. We need not decide between them here. Both conclude that the effort to exclude ideals of human flourishing from conceptions of political morality is a mistake. In subsequent chapters I will provide my own arguments for this conclusion. But, for now, we need to get a better understanding of the proposed distinction and the issues that it raises.

No one believes that the state should actively promote every element of a fully good life. Some ideals cannot be effectively promoted through political action. For instance, romantic love is an important element of a rewarding human life, but it is hard to see how political authorities could effectively promote it. Other ideals, particularly person-relative ideals, have little or no role to play in political morality. The fact that some political action would benefit me, but no one else, is hardly a compelling argument in its favor. Nonetheless, there remains a wide range of ideals and excellences that could plausibly be thought to be relevant to politics. The perfectionist objects to the idea that there is a general rule which excludes their political promotion. Indeed, he or she believes that if they

---

[20] It is powerfully expressed in Kant's work. See "On the Common Saying: 'This May Be True in Theory, but It Does Not Apply in Practice.'"

[21] See V. Haksar, *Equality, Liberty and Perfectionism*.

are sound, and if they could be effectively promoted through political action, then there is a standing case for promoting them. However, it may be wondered whether anyone actually doubts this. Except for the pure neutrality theorist, who has a problem with the rejection of such a general rule?

This brings us to the fourth and final claim, which is really an extension of the third. We need to distinguish the perfectionist from those who are willing to let ideals of human flourishing inform political morality so long as those ideals are widely shared or not controversial. Recall that many who accept the doctrine of state neutrality have no objection to the idea that political morality should be informed by shared ideals of the good. They object only to the idea that political morality should be informed by *controversial* ideals.

To get a grip on this position, we need to know what makes an ideal controversial. Without going into too much detail, it can said that an ideal is controversial if it can be reasonably rejected by some citizens, given their epistemic situation and deeply held value commitments. This is still not clear, since it relies on an under-specified criterion of reasonable rejectability.[22] But the basic idea is not hard to grasp. There is a wide plurality of reasonable views about what are sound ideals of the good; and given this, if some of these ideals are intentionally favored over others by political action, then some people will have a reasonable complaint. Put slightly differently, a controversial ideal is an ideal such that if it informed a conception of political morality, that conception of political morality would be one that could be reasonably rejected by at least some who were subject to it.

This general view has roots in the social contract tradition where it has been assumed that a sound conception of political morality must be one that all parties could accept. In chapters 2–5 I will consider an important contemporary statement of this view and I will give my reasons for thinking that it does not succeed. Here I simply want to stress that this view supports the idea that there are principled moral reasons why no controversial ideal of human flourishing should either inform a conception of political morality or be enforced by political authorities.

This idea the perfectionist rejects. According to the fourth claim, he or she holds that there is no general moral principle that forbids the state from favoring sound ideals of human flourishing, as well as enforcing conceptions of political morality informed by them, when these ideals are controversial or subject to reasonable disagreement. In rejecting this idea, the perfectionist is not committed to the stronger view that whether

---

[22] In chapter 2 I specify this criterion in more detail.

an ideal of human flourishing is widely shared or controversial has no bearing on the question of whether it should be enforced by political authorities. The fact that an ideal of human flourishing is controversial may provide a reason in some contexts for not promoting it through political action, even if the ideal is sound. But this has to do with the wisdom or effectiveness of promoting it. It does not follow from a general moral principle which excludes controversial ideals of human flourishing from political morality.

This brings me to a final point. There is no reason why a perfectionist could not be a proponent of limited government. Indeed, it is possible for someone to accept the four basic claims characteristic of perfectionism and endorse what Mill called "the let-alone doctrine" – the doctrine that "governments can do no better than to do nothing."[23] As Mill observed, the let-alone doctrine gains its plausibility from the "manifest selfishness and incompetence" of modern governments. To the extent that perfectionists judge modern governments to be not up to the task, they need not endorse government action.

This would threaten perfectionism only if it were true that modern governments cannot, and could not be expected in the foreseeable future, to rule responsibly. This would show that perfectionist political morality is utopian, providing guidance for a world in which we do not live. But in the absence of such sweeping pessimism, perfectionism remains a viable view even if in some circumstances it is wise not to advocate the political promotion of some ideals of human flourishing.

Elitism

As I have been characterizing it, perfectionism delineates the form or shape of a political theory. It does not specify the substance. Different perfectionist theories fill in the substance by drawing on different ideals of human flourishing.

Still, the four claims discussed above are not devoid of content. Taken together, they distinguish perfectionist political theories from political theories that embrace value nihilism or value skepticism, political theories that follow Kant in sharply distinguishing the right from the good and political theories in the social contract tradition. In this section and the next I will discuss some claims that perfectionists are *not* committed to. This should further clarify the view.

One thing that has given perfectionism a bad name is that it is sometimes identified with political moralities derived from elitist

---

[23] J. S. Mill, "Essay on Coleridge," p. 218.

doctrines. Stated very generally, these political moralities hold that we ought to favor the excellence of the few over the needs and interests of the many. More precisely, they endorse one of the following two views.

(1) The flourishing of the excellent few matters; the flourishing of the many who are not excellent (or who do not have the capacity for excellence) does not matter or matters very little.

(2) The flourishing of everyone matters; but resources and opportunities ought to be distributed so as to promote excellence, even if this results in inegalitarian distributions.

Following others, I will call (1) the "superman version" of perfectionism.[24] Over the past century and a half, several writers, with varying degrees of enthusiasm, have endorsed it. These writers include, most notably, Nietzsche, but also the young Bertrand Russell and Hastings Rashdall.[25] For the most part, however, the superman version of perfectionism has no contemporary defenders. Perfectionist writers today argue that political authorities should take an active role in creating and maintaining social conditions that best enable *all* their subjects to lead valuable and worthwhile lives.[26]

For this reason, I will assume, rather than try to demonstrate, that the superman version of perfectionism is unsound. It is brought up here only to put it to one side. Since there is not even a *prima facie* case for thinking that all perfectionist theories must take the "superman" form, we should not, if we wish to give perfectionism a fair hearing, identify it with what is surely its least attractive version.

This still leaves (2). It is softer than (1), but it remains elitist. While conceding that the flourishing of all people matters, it insists that those with the potential to realize excellence (as specified by a particular conception of human flourishing) ought to receive additional resources and opportunities so as to make possible or to make more likely the realization of their potential. An example illustrates this view. A society that spends public money to foster scientific understanding because it believes that scientific understanding is intrinsically valuable might grant those who have talents for scientific research resources and opportunities that they would not have under a strictly egalitarian distribution.[27] Endorsing this use of public funds would commit one to (2).

Some perfectionists have endorsed (2). But notice that (2) does not

---

[24] See J. Griffin, *Well-being*, p. 60.

[25] See the quotations in J. Griffin, *Well-being*, pp. 60–64.

[26] See, for example, the quoted passages by Hurka and Finnis on the first page of this chapter.

[27] Egalitarians disagree among themselves over what is the best egalitarian distribution. But the reader should assume here that the egalitarian distribution referred to is the best understanding, whatever that may be.

follow ·from the four claims discussed above. Those claims direct the state to favor sound ideals of human flourishing. They do not direct it to promote excellence; for it is possible to promote excellence without promoting human flourishing. In the example just mentioned it might be the case that scientific understanding is intrinsically valuable and that it ought to be promoted irrespective of its contribution to human flourishing. This, however, is not a claim the perfectionist is committed to.

In light of this, point (2) could be revised so that the excellence referred to is excellence that promotes human flourishing or perhaps the flourishing of the species. This view is not clearly offensive. Indeed, it may even be a strength of perfectionist theories that they can accommodate it.[28] But it is still not a claim perfectionists must endorse. Some perfectionist writers are committed not only to the view that the flourishing of all people matter, but also to the view that in the good society resources and opportunities would be equally distributed.[29]

The lesson to draw from this should be fairly obvious. There is no conceptual connection between perfectionism and elitism. Whatever the merits of egalitarianism, it would be a mistake to reject perfectionism out of hand because of a strong commitment to equality.

Pluralism

There are other sources of distrust of perfectionism in contemporary political thought. Many are suspicious of it because they believe that it does not satisfactorily take account of the fact that people reasonably disagree over which ideals of human flourishing are worthy of support. They reject perfectionism because they see it as hostile to pluralism. According to the fourth claim discussed above, perfectionists reject the idea that there is a general moral principle that forbids political authorities from promoting controversial, reasonably disputed ideals of human flourishing. This appears to add some credence to the suspicion.

Before assessing whether the suspicion is well founded, we do well to get more clear about what "pluralism" means. Toward this goal, I will distinguish three claims, each of which could plausibly be construed as a claim about pluralism. The first claim is that people hold a wide variety of conceptions of human flourishing. They disagree about which ideals and excellences constitute a fully good life. The second claim is that reasonable people – people who are informed and make no mistakes in

---

[28] I argue that it is in chapter 9 below.
[29] This appears to be the view of L. T. Hobhouse, for example. See *Liberalism*, pp. 120–28 and *The Elements of Social Justice*, p. 109. Also see T. Hurka's discussion in *Perfectionism*, pp. 180–82 and M. Nussbaum, "Nature, Function and Capability."

reasoning – disagree about which ideals of human flourishing are best and worthy of support. The third claim is that there exist plural, incompatible and rationally incommensurable values.

These three claims are not identical. The first claim is a relatively straightforward factual claim. It is true, but it is not directly relevant to normative inquiry. It refers to what people believe, not to what they should believe or what they would believe if they were thinking clearly. The second claim is less straightforwardly factual. It is evaluative to the extent that it makes assumptions about the nature and limits of practical reason. But, if it is true, it may well have important implications for political morality. The third claim differs from the first two in that it refers not to the beliefs of people, but to the reality that underlies those beliefs. Accordingly, the third claim is more fundamental than the first two. If correct, it provides a (partial) explanation for them. Following others, I will call it the doctrine of value pluralism.[30]

Not only are these three claims distinct, they are also very broad. People who accept them can and do disagree about their content. For example, two people may both accept the claim that reasonable people disagree about which ideals of human flourishing are valid and yet disagree about the extent or pervasiveness of this disagreement. Likewise, they might both accept the claim that values are plural, incompatible and rationally incommensurable and yet disagree about how much and which kinds of plurality, incompatibility and incommensurability obtain. Finally, people may accept these claims, but differ over their significance for political morality.

The point I want to stress is that perfectionists are not committed either to the acceptance or the rejection, or any particular understanding, of any of these claims about pluralism. Consistent with their core commitments they can accept that people hold a plurality of views about the good life, that some people hold incompatible views without being unreasonable and that the world contains plural, incompatible and incommensurable values. And consistent with their core commitments, they can hold a variety of positions about the meaning and significance of these claims. The only position clearly ruled out by perfectionism is the value nihilist position mentioned above, but this position should not be confused with value pluralism.

Bearing this in mind, the suspicion that perfectionism is hostile to pluralism either is a mistake or is based on the thought that perfectionism does not adequately respond to or take account of the fact of reasonable

[30] Proponents of this doctrine include I. Berlin, *Four Essays on Liberty*, J. Raz, *The Morality of Freedom*, M. Stocker, *Plural and Conflicting Values*, and S. Hampshire, *Morality and Conflict*.

disagreement. One purpose of this book is to bring this latter thought into clearer focus and subject it to critical scrutiny. But right at the outset I want to emphasize that perfectionism, understood as a general view, is not committed to the idea that the state should use its coercive power to impose a single way of life on all its subjects. Nor is it committed to the idea that reasonable disagreement about the good life is impossible.

This should go some distance toward dispelling the suspicion that perfectionism is hostile to pluralism. It remains true that some perfectionist theories may be hostile to pluralism, but to infer that if some perfectionist theories are hostile to pluralism, then perfectionism in general is hostile to pluralism is to commit an obvious logical mistake.

To bring home this point, consider the following view: The best life for human beings is a life lived in a community which contains a maximal range of different ways of life and ideals of conduct. Diversity is always a plus in a political community; it always adds value and richness to the lives of those who live in it.

This view may be a bad one, but it cannot be faulted for failing to take account of pluralism and diversity. It celebrates them as the highest goods and it would direct the state to take active steps to foster and preserve the widest possible range of ways of life and conceptions of the good. More to the point at hand, the view is perfectionist.

Reflection on this view suggests that a commitment to the value and importance of pluralism bears no direct relation to the acceptance of anti-perfectionism.

Parochialism

As I explained above, value pluralism is a doctrine about the nature of value. It consists of a series of claims about the world.[31] These claims are either true or false. No attempt will be made in this book to prove that the claims are true.

Nonetheless, at certain points, I will assume that the claims are true. This assumption makes it possible to draw a distinction between two types of perfectionism: *universal perfectionism* and *parochial perfectionism*. These two types of perfectionism are distinguished by their justificatory rationales.

Universal perfectionist political action is justified, if it is justified at all,

---

[31] Broadly, the claims can be stated as follows: (a) There is more than one (non-derived) value in the world; (b) values compete and conflict in the sense that the realization of one may exclude the realization of another; and (c) at least some values are incommensurable in some choice-situations. These claims could be refined and broken down into a larger number of more specific claims. But these general claims capture the core of the doctrine.

because it promotes or contributes to the flourishing of all human beings. The justification for such action is not contingent on the particular commitments of people or the particular communities in which they live. The political action is universally valid or not valid at all.[32]

Not so for parochial perfectionism. It can be justified even if some political communities have no reason to undertake it. The reason for this is that the justification for parochial perfectionist political action makes essential reference to the particular circumstances of some people, circumstances which are not themselves necessary conditions for a fully good life. Parochial perfectionism is justified, if it is justified at all, because it promotes or contributes to the flourishing of a valuable, but not rationally required, way of life.[33]

To see the contrast between these two types of perfectionism more clearly consider these two justifications for a hypothetical political measure.

(1) "This measure ought to be passed because it is a good political measure. Every political community ought to adopt it. Failure to do so (when it could be done) is a blemish on the community."
(2) "This measure ought to be passed in our political community because it promotes a particular ideal of human flourishing. This ideal is a valid one for people living in our circumstances. Others, who live in very different circumstances, may have no reason to pass the measure."

The justification in (1) appeals to values and ideals that have significant weight for all people. For example, it might be held that all political communities ought to grant their members the freedom to express their religious views. Religious freedom, it might be said, is part of any fully good human life.

The justification in (2) is more modest. It appeals to values and ideals that have special standing for some political communities because of the social and economic conditions that predominate in these communities.

---

[32] This general description requires two amendments. First, it does not mention the distinction between form and content. Much political action that is universally justified must be described in general terms. This leaves considerable leeway for different communities to determine how to undertake it and in what fashion. Second, the description should not be read to deny that particular social and economic circumstances bear on the issue of how universal perfectionist political action should be undertaken.

[33] By "a rationally required way of life" I mean a way of life that all people ought to pursue if they have the opportunity to do so. This reveals why the distinction between universal and parochial perfectionism rests on the doctrine of value pluralism. For if this doctrine is correct, then it is possible that there are a variety of fully valuable ways of life, none of which is rationally superior to the others. But if the doctrine is incorrect, then we have good reason to believe that the only type of perfectionism that could be sound would be universal perfectionism.

For example, it might be held that self-reliance is an ideal of special importance for people who live in dynamic, highly mobile industrial societies, but for people who live in different societies it has less weight.

Universal perfectionism, then, is concerned with promoting values and ideals that are necessary components of any fully good human life. If there is only one kind of fully good human life, then all sound perfectionist political action is universal. But if there is a plurality of kinds of fully good human lives, and if some of these kinds of lives acquire special standing under some circumstances, but not others, then some sound perfectionist political action is parochial.

The possibility of parochial perfectionism shows how a political community could have compelling reasons to promote an ideal of human flourishing, even if that ideal did not represent a species-wide ideal. Accordingly, arguments that purport to establish that there is no fixed human nature or no universal human telos do not, even if successful, undermine perfectionism. At most, they show that some perfectionists claim too much for their theories.

Turn now to a final cluster of issues.

Political morality and institutional design

Political theorists concern themselves not only with questions about the content of political morality, but also with questions about institutional design. The two sets of questions are related, but remain distinct. People who agree about substantive political morality can still disagree about which political institutions are best for their political community.

This simple point needs to be remembered when assessing the plausibility of perfectionism because it is sometimes claimed that perfectionism conflicts with democratic assumptions.[34] In a democracy all are on equal footing. No one has special authority to dictate what is and what is not in the common good. But this, it is claimed, conflicts with the perfectionist assumption that some ideals of human flourishing are sound and that some could come to know this while others did not.

It is important to see that this claim is confused. It runs together the issues of political morality and institutional design. Even if perfectionists believe that some people have views that are closer to the truth than others, they are not (generally) committed to the view that those who have knowledge about political morality ought to have disproportionate political power. In other words, perfectionists are not (generally) committed to either Platonic philosopher-kings or Millian plural votes.

---

[34] I thank Brian Barry for bringing this objection to my attention.

This is fully consistent, since the later commitment concerns political procedures, while the former concerns the content of political morality.

In this regard, it is worth noting that it would be intelligible for someone to have no firm views about institutional design. Such a person might have strong views about the content of political morality. He or she might have a theory that tells us which political actions and outcomes are best, but might concede that he or she has no idea about which form of government is best or what type of political procedures would best implement the correct political morality in his or her political community. It is harder to conceive of the mirror image of such a person. This would be someone who had no views about substantive political morality, but who had strong views about which form of government and which political procedures were best. The reason for this asymmetry is that when we think about questions of institutional design we typically consider the results that would likely be engendered by different possible institutional schemes. If we had no views about substantive political morality, it would be difficult to pass judgment on these schemes.

Still, some might believe that judgments of this sort could be made by appealing solely to process-oriented considerations. They might hold that we do not need to consider issues of substantive political morality in order to judge different political procedures and institutions because we can make these judgments by asking which procedures are fair or which institutions treat people with equal respect or something along such lines.[35] Of course these judgments themselves are judgments of political morality. They rely heavily on moral ideals, but it could be said that these ideals are different in kind from the ideals of substantive political morality. And it could be further said that they do not draw on ideals of human flourishing. They apply to the process of political decision-making, not to its results.

Call this the *process-centered view*. It is a view perfectionists reject. They are committed to the general thesis that political authorities should take an active role in creating and maintaining social conditions that best enable their subjects to lead valuable and worthwhile lives. This thesis presupposes that political institutions are to be judged in part by their results. Put differently, perfectionists hold that political institutions are instruments for serving the goals of substantive political morality. Call this the *results-priority view*.

The objection that perfectionism conflicts with democratic assumptions might now be reformulated. It might be argued that the results-priority view clashes with a strong commitment to democracy, for on the

---

[35] See the discussion of proceduralism in C. Beitz, *Political Equality*, pp. 75–96.

results-priority view democratic government is only contingently justified. It is justified, if and only if, it is the best available means for advancing the goals of substantive political morality. And, it might be further argued, this is inconsistent with a strong commitment to democracy, since a strong commitment to democracy should allow that democratic government has intrinsic, as well as instrumental, value.

This reformulated objection fails. The results-priority view does not imply that process-oriented considerations could not have intrinsic value. If one rejects the process-centered view, then one must accept that political procedures are to be judged in part by the substantive results they are likely to yield; but it does not follow that one must discount process-oriented considerations altogether. If this is right, one can accept both the results-priority view and the view that democracy has intrinsic, as well as instrumental, value.

So perfectionists can agree that democratic political procedures have intrinsic value.[36] This raises the question of exactly how much weight these considerations should have *vis-à-vis* other considerations, such as results-based considerations. The name given to the results-priority view suggests that results-based considerations take priority, but it is not necessary to make this suggestion more definite here. The only point I am seeking to establish is that perfectionists can acknowledge the intrinsic value of democratic procedures.

This prompts the opposite objection: "If perfectionists can be strong democrats like the rest of us, then the view loses its distinctiveness and theoretical interest." The response to this objection comes in two parts. First, as I mentioned above, questions of institutional design are not identical with questions about the content of political morality. So even if perfectionists fully endorse democratic political procedures, they may differ from anti-perfectionists in their views about what democratic majorities ought to do or what it is permissible for them to do. Second, a strong commitment to democracy does not settle all questions of institutional design. In thinking about issues such as representation, the composition of the political agenda, and the nature and scope of constitutional restraints on legislative decision-making, perfectionists will draw freely on their views about substantive political morality.

Both points undermine the objection. They show that even if it were

---

[36] For example, it might be true that political procedures are to be assessed in part by their expressive meaning. Democratic procedures express a view of citizens as equal participants in the political life of their community. The institutional expression of this view might be valuable. If so, there is no reason to think perfectionists could not accept it. This may have been Rousseau's view. See *The Social Contract*, book 1, 8–9 and book 2, 2–3.

true that "we are all democrats now," perfectionism would retain its distinctiveness.

One final issue that concerns institutional design warrants attention. It is sometimes claimed that perfectionism should be rejected because it does not take proper account of the fact that the good of individual people should not be identified with the goals and commitments that they have at any given time, but rather with their "continuing status as a rational agent able to adopt and modify these goals."[37] To see how this point has critical force against perfectionism recall that perfectionists seek to promote through political action sound ideals of human flourishing. Accordingly, they presume that they know what are and what are not sound ideals. But this presumption seems to run counter to the recognition that we are fallible beings who make mistakes and that we have a continuing interest in living in conditions that allow us to revise and modify our beliefs and commitments.

If this is right, then, it might be thought, perfectionism should be rejected not because no ideal of human flourishing is sound or because no one could come to know that some ideals were sound, but because it overlooks the fact that all of our judgments are fallible. Since they are fallible, it is a mistake to try to seal our values and ideals into the future by promoting them through political action.[38]

This line of thought establishes two points. First, in designing political institutions we have good reason to ensure that they can be revised without too much difficulty if future evidence or reflection warrants doing so. Second, in designing political institutions we have good reason to ensure that individuals live in conditions that allow them to reflect on their way of life and modify or abandon it if they come to believe that this should be done.

These two points conflict with some perfectionist theories. They also impose limits on justified perfectionist political action. However, it would be a mistake to conclude from this that they discredit perfectionism in general. Perfectionists can acknowledge that most, if not all, of our judgments are fallible. They also can draw the appropriate lessons from

---

[37] T. M. Scanlon, "Rawls' Theory of Justice," p. 171. See also A. Buchanan, "Revisability and Rational Choice."

[38] This point is often overstated. From the fact that our judgments are fallible, we are not entitled to infer that it is likely or probable that we will change our minds about what ideals are worthy of political support. As Richard Arneson has noted, "adult individuals do after all tend to stand by their present values; values are more likely to change at the margin than by a radical conversion experience." Moreover, it may be possible to estimate the probability of error and this could be taken into account in the decision about whether it would be wise to promote an ideal through political action. For the quote from Arneson, see "Primary Goods Reconsidered," p. 439.

this acknowledgment. They can agree that institutional schemes should be revisable and that individuals should be given opportunities to reflect on and modify their understandings of human flourishing.

Taking these points into account still leaves room for perfectionist political action. Just how much room it leaves is a matter taken up in Part II of this book.

Part I

The rejection of the bracketing strategy

Having clarified perfectionism, I now will examine in some detail its strongest rival. This is a version of anti-perfectionist political morality that I will term the *bracketing strategy*. The distinguishing feature of the bracketing strategy is the claim that citizens in modern western societies have compelling moral reasons to exercise a special type of restraint.

Chapter 2 clarifies the nature of this restraint and distinguishes several understandings of it. Chapters 3–5 then consider and reject the main arguments in its favor. The examination of these arguments will strongly suggest that no convincing case has so far been made to justify the claim that citizens in modern western societies act wrongly if they do not acknowledge the type of restraint recommended by the bracketing strategy.

Since its distinctive feature is not rationally grounded, I will conclude that the bracketing strategy lacks justificatory force and that, therefore, we ought to reject it. This negative conclusion provides indirect support for the substantive perfectionist views defended in Part II.[1]

---

[1] Naturally, there are other alternatives to perfectionism. But I will limit my discussion to what I consider to be the best-developed alternative. In Part II some further anti-perfectionist arguments will be discussed.

2   The idea of restraint

Citizens in modern western societies often justify their political action by claiming that what they advocate is for the good of their societies or that it promotes ideals and values that will help their fellow citizens lead valuable and fulfilling lives. Sometimes these claims are well founded, sometimes they are false and sometimes they are rationalizations of self-interest or group bias. But, irrespective of their merits, these claims are often dismissed. In response to them it is said that it is not the business of governments to promote controversial visions of the good society or to act on particular conceptions of what it is that makes a life valuable and fulfilling.

Many different arguments can and have been made in defense of this response. But of late the argument that has become the most influential appeals directly to the "fact" of reasonable pluralism. This is the claim that in modern western societies there exists a multitude of conflicting, irreconcilable and reasonable religious, moral and philosophical doctrines. Taking this "fact" as a permanent feature of these societies, the argument seeks to establish that it is unreasonable or inappropriate to use political power to advance controversial conceptions of the good society or to promote controversial ideals or values. Naturally, this claim leads proponents of the argument to search for a conception of politics that all parties could reasonably accept, despite the beliefs and ideals that divide them.

Let us call the general statement of this argument the bracketing strategy. In chapters 3, 4 and 5 I will examine critically several different arguments that try to show that when we encounter reasonable disagreement the right thing to do is to step back from our differences and build an account of political morality on a commonly accepted core of moral beliefs. I will contend that all of these arguments share a similar structure and that all of them suffer from the same general defect. Since none of them succeeds, I will conclude that we have good reason to reject the bracketing strategy.

But first, in this chapter, we need to clarify the distinguishing feature of the bracketing strategy. In all of its versions the bracketing strategy rejects the idea that it is permissible for citizens to use political power to impose controversial ideals and values on their fellow citizens. However, as indicated above, people often want to use political power to advance their ideals and values. Believing these ideals and values to be sound and worthy of support, they naturally seek to give political expression to them. Thus, the bracketing strategy demands a special type of restraint. It asks citizens to refrain from doing what they believe they have good reason to do.

This demand has appeal because it is thought to be a proper response to the fact that in free societies men and women inevitably will disagree about the nature of the good life and the good society. But it raises a number of puzzling questions: Why should citizens refrain from doing what they believe they have good reason to do? How could the fact that others disagree with them have any bearing on the soundness of their views? And, if such disagreement has no bearing on the soundness of their views, why do they have reason to refrain from promoting them?

Of course we know all too well that people are often mistaken in believing they have good reason to do what they want to do. Sometimes, as mentioned above, they are mistaken in thinking the values and ideals they wish to promote are sound. In this case, if they come to see that they are mistaken, they should no longer want to promote them through political action. People do not believe, at least when they are thinking clearly, that they have a claim to impose values and ideals on others irrespective of whether or not those ideals and values are sound.[1] But it is often hard to know whether one's ideals and values are sound. We are often unsure whether our beliefs about the good society and the good life are correct, particularly when those beliefs are met with reasoned dissent; and because of this uncertainty we may conclude that we should not use political power to impose them on others. We may think that in such matters it is wise to err on the side of caution.[2] So to see the nature of the restraint that is called for by the bracketing strategy it will help to look at matters from the perspective of what I will refer to as the *model citizen*. The model citizen is a person who has good reasons for believing that his or her ideals and values are sound, has a good measure of confidence in

---

[1] It is true that some communitarian writers argue that citizens do not need to establish the soundness of the ideals they wish to promote. It is enough, they argue, if these ideals are widely accepted in the community. See, for instance, P. Devlin, *The Enforcement of Morals*. This argument is subject to a number of serious objections. But I will not discuss it here. For relevant discussion, see J. Waldron, "Particular Values and Critical Morality."

[2] For instance, people may think that it is worse to impose unsound ideals on others than it is to fail to impose sound ideals.

these reasons and has a strong desire to promote his or her ideals and values through political action precisely because he or she believes they are sound. We can add that the model citizen also considers the costs of imposing those ideals on others. He or she asks questions like: Would the imposition unjustifiably infringe the autonomy of others? Would it cause too much suffering? etc. And he or she will not impose those ideals if he or she believes for good reason that such promotion would do more harm than good.[3]

The reason why it is helpful to take up the perspective of the model citizen is that this is the person the bracketing strategy must address. If it can demonstrate that he or she should show restraint, then *a fortiori* it can demonstrate that all citizens should show restraint. Alternatively, if there are no decisive reasons for the model citizen to show restraint, the bracketing strategy fails.

The idea of restraint, however, is fairly complex. Since it is the distinguishing feature of the bracketing strategy, it is worthwhile to spend some time clarifying it. To get a sense of what restraint requires we need to distinguish several different understandings of it. Defenders of the bracketing strategy often point with pride to the historical example of Locke's argument for religious toleration as the model of restraint. In response to the plurality of conflicting beliefs about religious practice, Locke, as is well known, argued for a limitation on the scope of legitimate political authority: "The jurisdiction of the magistrate . . . neither can nor ought in any manner to be extended to the salvation of souls."[4] This suggests that restraint concerns the legitimate scope of political authority. Policies and institutions which are subject to reasonable disagreement should not receive political support. Citizens should just take them off the political agenda.

But this is by no means the only understanding of restraint. A second one refers to the idea that citizens should not intend or aim to promote controversial ideals and values through political action. According to this view, it is permissible to promote controversial ideals and values through political action insofar as the political action is not designed or intended to advance those ideals and values. This understanding of restraint is based on the familiar distinction between intending to bring about a given state of affairs through one's actions and merely foreseeing that one's actions will bring about that state of affairs. Let us consider an example. Suppose David and Mary both believe that their government

---

[3] I will not say much about the content of the model citizen's views until Part II of this book. Here I use him or her as a foil to the bracketing strategy.

[4] John Locke, *A Letter Concerning Toleration*, p. 17. However, the restraint Locke advocated applied only to the coercive exercise of political authority.

should stop giving public money to organized religion, but David believes this because he thinks that it will help bring about a more secular society which is, on his view, a better society. In contrast, while Mary believes that David is correct about the probable consequences of withdrawing government support, she supports this measure because she thinks government support for religion is inconsistent with the shared democratic values of her society. On the second understanding of restraint, Mary shows it, but David does not. Thus, on this understanding, what is significant is not just the action taken, but the conjunction of the action with the reasons for which it is taken.

Finally, a third understanding of restraint refers to the idea that citizens should refrain from appealing to certain types of reasons and considerations in justifying their political action. In particular, it is sometimes claimed, citizens should refrain from basing their political arguments on reasons or considerations that are not publicly accessible or on ideals and values that are controversial. This suggests that restraint concerns the types of arguments and modes of reasoning to be employed in political debate. On this third understanding of restraint, it is the presentation of arguments in political debate, rather than the political action undertaken or the motives upon which the political action is based, that is fundamentally important.

To sum up: the idea of restraint can refer to the *results* of political action, the *intentions* of political actors or the *types of arguments* political actors make in political discussion. On the basis of these understandings, we can formulate three corresponding principles of restraint.

(1) Citizens should refrain from political action which, in fact, promotes controversial political results.
(2) Citizens should refrain from acting with the intention to promote controversial ideals and values through political action.
(3) Citizens should refrain from basing their political arguments on reasons or considerations that are controversial or not publicly accessible.[5]

Proponents of the bracketing strategy do not always distinguish these three principles. So we need to ask which one or ones they would accept on reflection. There are good reasons for rejecting the first principle. Despite its rhetorical appeal, it will not stand up to careful scrutiny. This can be seen by considering a simple, but telling, example. A government can permit or prohibit the practice of abortion. It cannot do both and it cannot do neither. It must come down on one side or the

---

[5] I deliberately state this principle in broad terms because it is often stated that way by its proponents. We will see in chapter 5 that from this broad principle it is possible to formulate more fine-grained principles, some of which are more plausible than others.

other.[6] Assuming abortion is a controversial practice in a given society, its citizens will have no choice but to promote controversial political action. Some may wish to promote the legalization of abortion and others may wish to promote the prohibition of abortion. Either way, they will violate the first principle of restraint. This shows that the principle is practically unworkable.[7]

It might be objected that I have moved too quickly in rejecting this principle. There is an important distinction that I have overlooked, the distinction between what the state actively does and what it merely allows to happen. The first principle of restraint, it may be thought, should be interpreted to apply only to the active promotion of controversial political results. Understood in this way, the first principle would seem to favor the minimal state. If everything that is controversial is to be taken off the political agenda, there may be little that is left on it.[8]

But this distinction will not rescue the first principle. To see why it will not, we need to clarify the idea behind the phrase "what the state merely allows to happen." To say that political authorities allow something to happen is to say that those authorities permit their subjects to act in ways that bring it about. The permission granted by the authorities to their subjects can take different forms. We can distinguish three types of permissions: active permissions, inactive permissions and weak permissions.[9] An active permission is granted when the political authorities permit some action that was previously legally forbidden or required. They announce that henceforth citizens have discretion to do or not do

---

[6] Strictly speaking, for this to be true we need to further specify the example. There are of course many possible legal schemes for regulating abortion. Most schemes prohibit some abortions and permit others. But the example could narrow its focus to what might be called the standard case: mature adult women who wish to have an abortion to terminate an unwanted pregnancy. The focus could be further narrowed by stipulating the time frame of the pregnancy. Given these stipulations, it is true that a choice must be made one way or the other.

[7] In saying that the principle is practically unworkable I do not mean to say that it is never wise to take a controversial question off the political agenda. For example, some issues may be so divisive that if they are ruled on by the legislatures or the courts they will effectively bring civil government to a standstill. With this in mind, one might conclude that effective government is more important than a correct resolution of this particular issue. (On this line of thought, see S. Holmes, "Gag Rules.") But this does not alter the fact that taking an issue off the agenda is itself a controversial political action, a point amply illustrated by one of Holmes' central examples – the handling of the slavery issue in the pre-Civil War United States.

[8] Hayek developed this line of argument in his classic critique of centralized economic planning. See F. A. Hayek, *The Road to Serfdom*, esp. pp. 42–53.

[9] In drawing these distinctions I follow H. L. A. Hart, "Legal Rights" and G. H. von Wright, *Norm and Action*, pp. 85–90. The terms "active permission" and "inactive permission" are taken from Hart, who took them from Bentham. The term "weak permission" is taken from von Wright.

the action. An inactive permission is granted when the political authorities declare that some action previously not legally forbidden or required is permissible. The inactive permission clarifies the legal status of the permitted action. Both active and inactive permissions need to be distinguished from weak permissions. Weak permissions exist when the political authorities have remained silent about the actions in question. They have neither forbidden, required nor expressly "permitted" them. The important point about weak permissions is that they can exist without the political authorities making a judgment about the normative status of the actions that are permitted. The same is not true of active and inactive permissions. Applied to the abortion issue, the act of aborting the fetus is actively permitted if the state has previously forbidden it (or required it), but now declares that it is permissible for women to choose to have or not have an abortion. The act is inactively permitted if the state has not previously forbidden it (or required it), but now declares that it is permissible for women to choose to have or not have an abortion. And the act is weakly permitted if the state remains silent about its legal status.

Once these distinctions are drawn, it is harder to maintain that when the state merely allows things to happen it is not promoting controversial political results. For if it actively or inactively permits controversial actions, then it is making an authoritative judgment on their normative status. It is declaring that the actions in question are properly left to the discretion of individual citizens. But this declaration itself is a controversial political action. The first principle of restraint rules it out. Thus understood, the first principle of restraint cannot instruct us to take controversial political issues off the political agenda; for this action itself constitutes controversial political action. The first principle of restraint forbids its own application.

But perhaps this conclusion is too strong. It might be argued that the state should remain silent about controversial political matters. It should neither actively nor inactively permit them. It should only weakly permit them. It then could be argued that a well-ordered state is one in which all controversial political actions are weakly permitted. To achieve this goal political authorities would out of necessity have to take some controversial political action. They would have to revoke some previous active permissions that had been granted, cease granting inactive permissions that concerned controversial political actions and rescind all laws that make controversial actions obligatory or forbidden. But, it could be said, the goal would, in principle, be reasonably coherent. It could inform the application of the first principle of restraint.

On this view, the distinction between what the state actively promotes and what it merely allows to happen is re-interpreted as the distinction between what the state actively or inactively does and what it weakly permits. It can be said that when the state weakly permits controversial actions, such as the act of abortion, it is not violating the first principle of restraint because it is not making any judgment on the normative status of the actions that are permitted. So to speak, it keeps its hands clean.

This view could be rejected if it is true that political authorities have a general duty to protect the interests of their subjects. This duty would imply that when important moral issues are at stake, political authorities have derivative duties to find out which actions should be forbidden or required and which should be permitted. These duties, it could be said, come with the possession of political authority; for the political authority is justified only if it is exercised in the interests of those subject to it.[10] Thus, in failing to consider the moral status of these actions the authorities would be neglecting their general duty. If this is correct, then this duty is in conflict with the first principle of restraint. It would provide a reason for rejecting the principle.

This objection is powerful, but it presupposes a certain conception of political authority. A proponent of the first principle of restraint could dodge it by defending a different conception of political authority, one that does not tie the justification of political authority to any duties about protecting the interests of subjects. Let us, then, consider another more damaging objection to the idea that the state can weakly permit controversial political actions. Once the moral status of an action is called into question, there is pressure for the state either to forbid it, require it, or actively or inactively permit it. In this context it is very difficult for political authorities to avoid taking a stand on the normative status of the actions that are permitted. The reason for this is that when some citizens believe that some permitted action is morally impermissible they will in all likelihood try to prevent others from performing it. When this occurs, the state faces a dilemma. It either can intervene and help those who are attempting to perform the permitted action or it can stand by and do nothing.

Suppose it stands by and does nothing. This would mean that its citizens would be permitted to do the action, but that they would have no right to do it. The state would not prevent them from performing it; but it likewise would not prevent others from interfering with its performance. The permission to do the action would be like the permission one

---

[10] The existence of this duty (if it does in fact exist) explains why it is possible for a voluntary association, say the American Council of Churches, to decide not to take a stand on the abortion issue while it is not possible for the state to do this. For the state, unlike the American Council of Churches, has a duty to protect the interests of all of its citizens.

has in the state of nature. One would be permitted to do it, but everyone else would be free to prevent one from doing it. This is a logical possibility. There is no contradiction in a political order that weakly permits all controversial actions and lets it citizens struggle over whether the permitted actions will or will not be performed. But logical possibility is one thing, practicality another. It is hard to think of anyone who would be happy with this arrangement.

Suppose the state grabs the other horn of the dilemma. It intervenes and helps people perform the permitted actions (or it takes the other side and forbids them). When it does this, the weak permission becomes more than a weak permission.[11] The state is no longer silent about the permitted action. It now uses force to ensure that its subjects can perform the permitted action. In doing this, the state engages in controversial political action and it violates the first principle of restraint. If this is correct, then the first principle of restraint is not feasible. It must be rejected because the restraint it demands is not a viable option.

Consider now a last-ditch effort to save the first principle of restraint. It might be argued that when the state intervenes to help people perform the permitted action it does not have to take a stand on the normative status of the action. It can simply protect and enforce the non-controversial rights of its subjects. These non-controversial rights, it might be said, form a "protective perimeter"[12] around the agent which permits him to engage in controversial actions. For instance, the state might protect a woman's right to property, her right to contract, her right to free movement, her right not to be assaulted, etc. as she goes to the abortion clinic. But there is an obvious problem with this response. Protective perimeters are not air-tight. There is absolutely no reason to think the obligations imposed on others by one's non-controversial rights are sufficient to protect one's ability to perform all the morally significant weak permissions.[13] It is much more plausible to believe that the weakly

---

[11] This point is suggested by von Wright. "If a permission to do something is combined with a prohibition to hinder or prevent the holder of the permission from doing the permitted thing, then we shall say that the subject of the permissive norm has a *right* relatively to the subjects of the prohibition." *Norm and Action*, p. 89. This right cannot be granted without a consideration of the normative status of the permitted action.

[12] See H. L. A. Hart's discussion of liberty rights and protective perimeters in "Legal Rights," pp. 171–72.

[13] As all lawyers know, rights require specification and adjustment. Thus, political authorities might try to tailor the specification and adjustment of non-controversial legal rights so that all morally significant weak permissions received sufficient protection. But this would rightly be seen as an act of bad faith. On the one hand, the state would be saying that it is silent on the normative status of the permitted actions. On the other hand, it would be scrupulously adjusting and specifying legal rights in order to ensure that the permissions were protected.

permitted actions would be weakly protected. Those who wished to obstruct them could with sufficient ingenuity find ways to do so without violating non-controversial rights. The state of nature struggle would resurface in the interstices of the protective perimeters.

We ought to conclude, then, that when controversial moral issues are at stake the state cannot realistically avoid controversial political action. Here its failure to act is as significant as the action it takes; and since some set of legal rights and protections must be enforced, there is no way to avoid promoting controversial political results. This shows that the distinction between what the state does and what it merely allows to happen will not rescue the first principle of restraint.

I have spent a fair amount of time on the first principle of restraint, not because it has many defenders in the philosophical literature, but because it has significant rhetorical force when invoked in public discussions of controversial issues. Proponents of the bracketing strategy benefit from this rhetorical force. It contributes to the persuasive appeal of their arguments. I have wanted to make it crystal-clear that this rhetorical force is not deserved.

Let us turn now to the second and third principles of restraint, principles which do have a fair number of defenders in the philosophical literature. Do they run into similar problems? They do, unless we introduce further considerations. As I have described them, the principles of restraint exclude controversial beliefs, ideals and values. But this presupposes that there is some body of non-controversial beliefs, ideals and values. These non-controversial beliefs, ideals and values, it is sometimes said, are drawn from the shared public culture of the society. If it is possible to specify completely the rights and entitlements of all citizens by referring only to these shared elements, then it may be possible to avoid the problems that the first principle of restraint runs into. Suppose, for instance, that we can derive a woman's legal right to have an abortion from this shared set of beliefs, ideals and values; then, even though the enforcement of this right might still be a controversial political result, citizens could affirm it without intending to advance any controversial ideals or values. Likewise, citizens could argue for it in public without appealing to controversial beliefs or publicly non-accessible information.

However, it may well be doubted that the shared set of beliefs, ideals and values in modern western societies will be robust enough to answer the abortion question in particular, much less provide answers to all questions concerning the rights and entitlements of its citizens. It may turn out that some issues cannot be resolved by appeal to these shared elements. If so, with respect to these issues, the second and third principles of restraint would not be action-guiding. They would exclude all options. But even if this were so, it would not necessarily undermine their force. They could still serve as valid guides for political action in all cases in which they did yield results. Given, then, certain modest assumptions about the shared public culture of modern western societies, both the second and third principles of restraint can be shown to be coherent, practically workable principles.

The arguments that we will consider in the next three chapters often invoke both principles. But it is worth pointing out that there is no necessary connection between them. Acceptance of principle (2) does not entail acceptance of principle (3). Citizens can support non-controversial ideals and values through political action and make political arguments for them that appeal to reasons or considerations that are controversial or publicly non-accessible. Such action would violate principle (3), but not principle (2). Similarly, acceptance of principle (3) does not entail acceptance of principle (2). It might be difficult to aim to promote controversial ideals and values through political action without referring to them in political argument. But it is possible to do so, as our earlier example of David suggests. David aims to promote a secular society, but he could do so by appealing to shared democratic values.

Several further clarifications are in order. The principles of restraint,[14] as we have seen, rely on a distinction between the controversial and the non-controversial. But what is the basis of this distinction? It was suggested above that non-controversial beliefs, ideals and values might be drawn from the shared public culture of a society. But this cannot be a sufficient condition, for controversial beliefs, ideals and values may also be drawn from the shared public culture. They may, as it were, grow out of that shared culture. Nor can these non-controversial beliefs, ideals and values be said to be universally accepted. The existence of one person in a society who denies that human life has value would not show that the belief that human life has value is a controversial belief in that society. Universal acceptance is clearly too stiff a criterion for non-controversiality.

Matters are helped somewhat if we say that non-controversial beliefs, ideals and values are those that no *reasonable* person in the society could reject. But this calls for a specification of the criterion of reasonable rejectability. Broadly speaking, two interpretations of this criterion can be distinguished. The first one holds that a belief, ideal or value can be reasonably rejected if it is inconsistent with right reason. This is the classical understanding of reasonable rejectability. Not infrequently, when people advance a theory as true they think that no reasonable

---

[14] From now on the principles of restraint refer to the second and third principles only.

person could reject it. Rejection of the theory, they believe, constitutes an intellectual mistake.[15] But this is not the only interpretation of reasonable rejectability. According to a second understanding, a belief, ideal or value can be reasonably rejected if it is inconsistent with a person's deeply held point of view. We can call this the *contractualist understanding* of reasonable rejectability.

Given the motivation behind the principles of restraint, it is not hard to see that the classical understanding of reasonable rejectability will not do. If ideals and values are non-controversial when they could not be reasonably rejected, and if reasonable rejectability is understood to mean in accord with right reason, then any ideal or value that was in accord with right reason could not be controversial no matter how many people actually rejected it. This would make nonsense out of the principles of restraint. We do well, then, to work with the contractualist understanding of reasonable rejectability.

This understanding clearly stands in need of further clarification. I have said that, according to it, a belief, value or ideal can be reasonably rejected if it is inconsistent with a person's deeply held point of view. This makes reasonable rejectability a purely personal matter. Political justification, however, is not purely personal. It is addressed to others. So if the contractualist understanding of reasonable rejectability is to be relevant to political justification, it must be modified.

Toward this goal, let us say that a belief, value or ideal can be reasonably rejected if it could not be accepted by all people given their deeply held points of view and given their need and desire to come to an agreement on principles to regulate their political life.[16] This assumes that all people have a compelling interest in coming to agreement with others on principles to regulate their political life. This is one interest that they share, despite their different deeply held points of view.

Do they share any further interests? Most proponents of restraint believe that they do. They believe that at some deep level people accept a common conception of the person or some set of shared fundamental values.[17] These shared interests make it possible for them to converge on principles of political morality that all could accept without giving up

[15] A prominent and instructive proponent of the classical understanding of reason is Plato. For him, correct understanding is criterial for reasonableness, e.g. it is not possible for a person to be both wrong and reasonable. See *The Republic* and see C. Taylor's discussion of this point in *Sources of the Self*, pp. 121–24.

[16] Compare this with T. M. Scanlon's formulation of reasonable rejectability in "Contractualism and Utilitarianism," p. 110, and with Nagel's remarks on political legitimacy in *Equality and Partiality*, pp. 33–34.

[17] See J. Rawls, *Political Liberalism*, and S. Scheffler, "Moral Skepticism and Ideals of the Person."

their deeply held points of view. To be sure, not everyone accepts this idea. Some believe that diversity runs too deep in modern western societies for talk of shared ideals and values to make much sense.[18] We do not, however, need to settle this issue here. I will assume, for the sake of argument, that there are significant shared interests among people in these societies.[19]

Working with this assumption, it is possible to give a more precise account of the distinction between the controversial and the non-controversial. We can say that a belief, value or ideal is controversial if it does not satisfy the criterion of reasonable rejectability and we can add that this criterion is satisfied if (a) the belief, value or ideal could be accepted by all people in the political community given their compelling interest in coming to agreement with others on principles to regulate their political life and (b) it is a part of, based on or derived from deep, shared commitments. Conversely, we can say that a belief, value or ideal is non-controversial when it does satisfy the criterion of reasonable rejectability so described.

I do not mean to imply that this is the only possible way to specify this distinction. One might say, for example, that non-controversial beliefs, ideals and values are those beliefs, ideals and values that a preponderant number of reasonable members of the political community would accept on reflection. And then one might try to refine this by asking a host of further questions – How substantive is the notion of reflection? How informed must the reflection be? How many people are a preponderant number? etc. But the above account of the distinction between the controversial and the non-controversial is the one relied on by the most influential proponents of restraint; and it is the one that will be most relevant to the critical discussion of the bracketing strategy in chapters 3–5.

Notice, moreover, that this account of the distinction is congruent with our earlier rejection of the first principle of restraint. Political results can be controversial in the sense that they are subject to reasonable disagreement, but non-controversial in the sense that they can be justified by reference to values and ideals that all persons could reasonably accept. The reason for this is easy to grasp. Even if people share a common set of beliefs, ideals and values and even if it is possible to justify a particular

---

[18] See J. Tully, *Strange Multiplicity*.
[19] T. M. Scanlon has coined the phrase "non-unanimously held normalized standards of value" to characterize values which can be taken as "fair starting points for justification" even if there are some people who do not accept them. (See "The Significance of Choice," p. 71.) This may be another way of stating the thought that it remains meaningful to talk of shared interests even when we do not have unanimity.

political end by reference only to those shared elements, people's controversial beliefs, ideals and values will often drive them to different conclusions about the justifiability of the political end. This is where the principles of restraint come into play. They enjoin citizens to put aside their differences and not try politically to promote controversial ideals and values or appeal to them in public political argument.

This demand highlights an important feature of the principles of restraint. To the extent that citizens recognize and act on them, it should, other things equal, be easier to achieve a rational consensus on political questions. It is this feature which undoubtedly gives the principles their strong appeal. For if a rational consensus were achievable in politics, then the exercise of political power would be accepted by all. No one, save the irrational and the unreasonable, would have a complaint. That would be no small achievement, and I shall come back to this feature when I examine whether or not citizens have good reasons to accept the principles of restraint.

Here we can just note some further points. A rational consensus in politics does not require or mandate the exclusion of all ideals from political action. The political promotion of non-controversial ideals and values, for instance, would not threaten or disrupt the consensus. This is sufficient to show that the principles of restraint, as I have described them, do not, strictly speaking, exclude the promotion of conceptions of the good. Nor are the principles, strictly speaking, neutral principles.[20] They permit citizens to promote (and intend to promote) some ideals and values through political action at the expense of other ideals and values. What they rule out, as I have emphasized, is the intentional political promotion of *controversial* ideals and values (which could not be justified by reference solely to non-controversial beliefs, ideals and values) or the justification of political ends by appeal to controversial or non-publicly accessible beliefs, ideals and values.

Thus far I have spoken rather loosely of political ends or political questions. But these too require some clarification. It is an important matter which types of political ends or questions the principles of restraint are meant to apply to. A natural answer is "all of them." On this view, if restraint is valuable, it ought to be shown in all cases in which political issues are at stake. But many have felt that this is asking too much.[21] Citizens, they contend, need not show restraint in all cases.

---

[20] For a discussion of the different versions of neutrality, see chapters 5–6 in J. Raz's *The Morality of Freedom*. Also see J. Rawls, *Political Liberalism*, pp. 191–94, and R. Arneson, "Neutrality and Utility."

[21] See J. Rawls, *Political Liberalism*, B. Barry, *Justice as Impartiality*, p. 161, and C. Larmore, *The Morals of Modernity*, p. 126.

It is sufficient if restraint is forthcoming when questions of "constitutional essentials" or "basic justice" are on the table. Questions such as these concern the fundamental issues of political morality such as the assignment of liberties and rights and the distribution of basic resources. The principles of restraint, on this view, do not apply to non-basic political issues. To distinguish these two views let us call the first one *comprehensive restraint* and the second *narrow restraint*.

If narrow restraint is to be a plausible view, then some account must be given of the distinction between constitutional essentials[22] and other political matters. Such an account should provide answers to two different sorts of questions. First, it should tell us how to determine when a given political issue is an issue of constitutional essentials and when it is not. In other words, it should provide a reasonably clear criterion for making the relevant classifications.[23] Second, it should propound some rationale for the distinction. This rationale should explain why the principles of restraint apply to some political questions, but not to others.

So far no proponent of narrow restraint has provided such an account. As it stands, the proposed distinction between constitutional essentials and other political matters is both vague and ambiguous. This is a point that I shall return to in later chapters.

Finally, it is necessary to stipulate who the principles of restraint are meant to apply to. Judges, legislators, administrative officials or the citizenry as a whole are all possible candidates. Moreover, given different institutional roles and responsibilities, the principles of restraint might apply with greater or lesser force. In what follows I will interpret the principles of restraint as guides for action meant to apply to all citizens. This will free us from the need to discuss the different institutional roles and responsibilities of the judge, the legislator and the administrator. The principles of restraint, as they will be understood here, are general

---

[22] I shall use the term "constitutional essentials" as a shorthand for constitutional essentials and/or basic justice.

[23] It might be thought that we could just rely on common sense to make these classifications. Some matters are clearly matters of constitutional essentials; for example, the right to religious freedom. Other matters are clearly not matters of constitutional essentials; for example, traffic regulations. But common sense only takes one so far. Consider the following list of political issues: abortion rights, capital punishment, drug enforcement legislation, public funding of the arts and rules governing the finance of democratic elections. None of these issues falls clearly on either side of the line between constitutional essentials and other political matters. Moreover, proponents of narrow restraint disagree amongst themselves over some of these issues. For example, Barry believes that abortion is not a constitutional essential (*Justice as Impartiality*, pp. 90–93) while Rawls believes that it is (*Political Liberalism*, pp. 243–44.)

principles meant to apply to all citizens participating in the political affairs of modern western societies.[24]

Proponents of the bracketing strategy maintain that the principles of restraint inform an ideal of democratic citizenship. The degree to which they are recognized and respected is one important measure of what it means to be a good citizen. As we shall see, different arguments in support of the bracketing strategy have different implications about how this ideal of democratic citizenship can best be realized. But all the arguments endorse the ideal and all are committed to the claim that citizens in modern western societies have weighty moral reasons to accept the principles of restraint in either a comprehensive or narrow form.

---

[24] Sometimes I speak of the principles of restraint applying to the "state." This assumes that the principles *do* apply to legislators, judges and administrative officials. Nevertheless, as indicated above, I wish to avoid consideration of the different institutional roles and responsibilities of public officials. Such consideration would needlessly complicate the issues I want to discuss.

3 Political liberalism and the bracketing strategy

We are now ready to take a closer look at the bracketing strategy. The bracketing strategy starts with a simple idea: to justify a conclusion to a person we need to start with premises he or she can accept. It then extends this simple idea to political justification: to justify a political conclusion to all citizens we need to start from premises all of them can accept. If the citizens in a political community hold a multitude of incompatible moral, philosophical and religious views, we are led naturally to the demand that political justification proceed from a set of shared beliefs, ideals and values. To meet this demand citizens must bracket their differences and search for common ground.

In one form or another, a number of contemporary political philosophers defend the bracketing strategy.[1] But it has received its most rigorous expression in the recent work of John Rawls. By focusing on his work, we can best bring out the problems with the strategy in general. Yet while the focus will be on Rawls, I intend to reach a general conclusion about the bracketing strategy. Accordingly, in discussing him, I will (particularly in chapter four) draw freely on the work of others who are sympathetic to his views. This will allow me to supplement his arguments where they are undeveloped or not fully spelled out and to anticipate possible responses he could make to my criticisms. In this way, I hope to give the bracketing strategy a fair run for its money.

This chapter will consider two initial arguments that Rawls puts forward to support the bracketing strategy. In a sense, these arguments are prefatory to the more important arguments to be considered in chapters 4 and 5. But it will be helpful to consider them here on their own terms; and, hence, to get them out of the way before tackling the more important arguments.

Since Rawls' work is intricate and subtle, I begin this chapter by briefly discussing some of its main features. Before considering Rawls' specific

---

[1] Prominent examples include: T. Nagel, *Equality and Partiality*, B. Barry, *Justice as Impartiality*, C. Larmore, *Patterns of Moral Complexity*, and B. Ackerman, *Social Justice in the Liberal State*.

arguments, we need to familiarize ourselves with his terminology and we need to make it plain that he does indeed accept the principles of restraint discussed in chapter 2.

Rawls' political liberalism

In *Political Liberalism* Rawls puts the following question to his readers: "how is it possible for there to exist over time a just and stable society of free and equal citizens who still remain profoundly divided by reasonable religious, philosophical, and moral doctrines?"[2] The answer he gives to his own question is that such a society is possible only if it is regulated by a conception of justice which could gain the free and willing support of adherents of all the reasonable religious, philosophical and moral doctrines in it. To do this, he tells us, the conception of justice regulating the basic structure of the society must be the focus of an "overlapping consensus." That is, it must be a conception of justice that could be accepted by all reasonable people, irrespective of their particular religious, philosophical and moral views.[3]

This obviously calls for some explanation as to how an overlapping consensus could come about and how it might work. To provide this Rawls introduces a vital distinction, the distinction between a comprehensive and a political conception of justice.[4] The thought behind the distinction is "that to succeed in finding [an overlapping] consensus political philosophy must be, so far as possible, suitably independent of other parts of philosophy, especially from philosophy's long-standing problems and controversies."[5] This is no simple task. At least as it has been traditionally understood, political philosophy is political *philosophy*. It is unavoidably embroiled in philosophy's long-standing problems. To satisfy this unorthodox requirement a conception of justice must be, Rawls tells us, limited in content and scope. It must not address a large number of subjects and it must seek to avoid presupposing or committing itself to values and ideals that are not widely shared. By recognizing these limits, a conception of justice strives to be a "freestanding" view. It strives, in other words, to free itself from all disputed metaphysical,

---

[2] J. Rawls, *Political Liberalism*, p. 47.

[3] Rawls claims that such a consensus could include all of the main historical religions as well as the philosophical doctrines of Kant, Bentham, Mill and others. See *Political Liberalism*, pp. 145–46, 168–72.

[4] Rawls contrasts political liberalism with comprehensive doctrines. To describe this contrast I prefer the terms "political conception of justice" and "comprehensive conception of justice." But nothing turns on this terminology.

[5] J. Rawls, *Political Liberalism*, p. 172.

epistemological and moral doctrines. Assuming such a conception could be suitably worked out, it would be a political conception of justice.

But if a conception of justice is to be freestanding and if it is to avoid committing itself to larger philosophical claims, then from where is it going to get its content? Would not a free-standing conception of justice be a vacuous conception? Rawls does not think so. He suggests that a political conception of justice is derived or worked up from the "fundamental political ideas viewed as implicit in the public political culture of a democratic society."[6] These fundamental political ideas constitute the common ground of the society.[7] They make it possible, or so Rawls believes, to construct a conception of justice that does not refer to controversial ideals.

The contrary to a political conception of justice is a comprehensive conception. Rawls defines a comprehensive conception of justice as one that "includes conceptions of what is of value in human life, as well as ideals of personal virtue and character, that are to inform much of our nonpolitical conduct."[8] Thus comprehensive conceptions of justice draw freely from philosophical and moral doctrines. Arguably, all conceptions of justice prior to Rawls' conception have been comprehensive.[9] The comprehensiveness of a conception, however, is a matter of degree. Rawls suggests three primary dimensions along which it can be gauged. First, there is what can be called the *scope dimension*. This refers to the number of subjects a conception of justice addresses.[10] Second, there is what can be called the *articulation dimension*. This refers to the degree to which the virtues, values and ideals of the conception are rigorously articulated and rationally ordered. And, third, there is what can be called the *controversiality dimension*.[11] This refers to the degree to which a conception presupposes or consists of controversial beliefs, values and ideals. Reference to these three dimensions allows Rawls to draw a further distinction between "a fully comprehensive" and "a partially

---

[6] Ibid. p. 223.

[7] Rawls often characterizes these fundamental ideas in terms of a shared conception of the person as free and equal and a shared conception of society as a fair system of cooperation. See *Political Liberalism*, p. 149.

[8] Ibid. p. 175.

[9] Including, perhaps, the conception of justice defended in J. Rawls' *A Theory of Justice*.

[10] A political conception addresses a narrow range of subjects. Principally, these include (a) the specification of basic rights, liberties and opportunities; (b) the assignment of priority to these basic rights, liberties and opportunities over considerations of general welfare or perfectionist value; and (c) the fair distribution of adequate all-purpose means (J. Rawls, *Political Liberalism*, p. 223).

[11] It is not always clear what Rawls means by controversial. In the context of his work the most natural interpretation of controversial is "subject to reasonable disagreement." I propose that we understand this idea in terms of the contractualist understanding of reasonable rejectability as explained in chapter 2.

comprehensive" conception of justice; the former scoring high along these dimensions, the latter scoring low.[12] Good examples of fully comprehensive conceptions of justice include those provided by religious doctrines such as Catholicism. It is much harder to identify good examples of partially comprehensive conceptions of justice. Rawls gives no examples; but perhaps the contrast is reasonably clear.

Assuming the distinction between a political and a comprehensive conception of justice stands up, how does it help Rawls explain the possibility of an overlapping consensus? His main argument is relatively straightforward: only a political conception of justice could form the basis of an overlapping consensus. This is true because comprehensive conceptions, whether full or partial, could not reasonably be expected to command reasonable agreement among all the adherents of all the different religious, philosophical and moral doctrines likely to be found in a modern western society. Their comprehensiveness marks them as unacceptably sectarian. Still, this does not show that a political conception could do much better. After all, the demand that a conception of justice be acceptable to all reasonable people in the society is a stiff demand. It is not clear how any conception of justice could meet it. Undaunted, Rawls insists that a suitably worked out political conception is up to the task. In describing how it might work he invokes the metaphor of a module:

[T]he political conception [of justice] is a module, an essential constituent part, that fits into and can be supported by various reasonable comprehensive doctrines that endure in the society regulated by it.[13]

The module metaphor is indeed instructive. It shows that to be successful a political conception of justice must be capable of fitting into each reasonable comprehensive doctrine in the society regulated by it. However, and importantly, it need not fit into each comprehensive doctrine in the same way. Rawls stresses that citizens can decide for themselves how "the public political conception [of justice] all affirm is related to their own more comprehensive views."[14] Thus, a political conception of justice can be the focus of an overlapping consensus, despite the fact that different people accept it for different reasons. For instance, a philosopher might accept it because he believed it was correct

---

[12] This is not very precise. It is clear from the text (*Political Liberalism*, pp. 13–14, 175, 152) that Rawls distinguishes these three dimensions and that he believes a fully comprehensive conception scores high along all three; but he tends to group all three dimensions together and so does not tell us whether a conception that scored high along some dimensions and low along others would be classified as fully or partially comprehensive or how we might make such classifications.

[13] J. Rawls, *Political Liberalism*, p. 12.   [14] Ibid. p. 38.

according to the best philosophical account of morality and a Protestant minister might accept it because he believed it was correct according to the best interpretation of Christian scripture.[15]

Still, to function as a module, to be capable of fitting into each citizen's comprehensive view, the political conception of justice must have a certain content. This content, Rawls says, consists of two basic types of values, the values of political justice and the values of public reason. The former underlie substantive principles of justice derived from the shared fundamental ideas implicit in the political culture. The latter are norms or guidelines that are to govern the presentation and application of these substantive principles. Both types of values are important. Careful attention to them reveals that Rawls is committed to the principles of restraint.

The values of political justice define the substance of a political conception of justice. Reference to them is necessary in formulating principles of justice to regulate the basic structure (e.g. the main political, economic and social institutions) of a society. Since these values define the substance of a political conception of justice, citizens must appeal to them – and them only – in working out conceptions of justice for their society. Otherwise, the conception of justice they work out will be comprehensive and, *ipso facto*, incapable of being the focus of an overlapping consensus. Given that the attainment of an overlapping consensus is, on Rawls' view, the only way to achieve justice and stability in modern western societies, it follows that, on his view, citizens in these societies act wrongly if they try to advance controversial ideals in formulating conceptions of justice. It should be clear that this commits Rawls to the second principle of restraint.[16]

The values of public reason supplement the values of political justice. They provide guidelines for political discussion. In particular they specify what types of information, modes of reasoning and appeals to authority are acceptable in defending and applying a political conception of

[15] For this to work citizens must judge that the value of adhering to a political conception of justice generally overrides their more sectarian values that conflict with it. Rawls claims that the political liberal "hopes" that citizens will do this (see J. Rawls, "Reply to Habermas," p. 147). The question we are asking in this and the next two chapters is whether citizens have compelling reasons to do this. We need to answer this question in order to know whether the political liberal's hope is rationally grounded.

[16] Rawls identifies his view with the view that the state should be neutral with respect to controversial comprehensive doctrines. Thus, he writes that a political conception of justice "hopes to satisfy neutrality of aim in the sense that basic institutions and public policy are not to be designed to favor any particular comprehensive doctrine." (*Political Liberalism*, p. 194). Neutrality of aim, as he describes it, requires that the state not "do anything *intended* to favor or promote any particular comprehensive doctrine rather than another, or to give greater assistance to those who pursue it" (Ibid. p. 193).

justice.[17] The point of these values is to establish a common framework for political deliberation, one that is acceptable to all reasonable citizens. The common framework allows citizens to debate competing political conceptions of justice and to apply them to particular political issues in ways all could reasonably be expected to endorse. But to do this the framework needs to impose limits on acceptable political argument. Specifically, it requires citizens to appeal only to "political values," "presently accepted general beliefs," "the forms of reasoning found in common sense" and "the methods and conclusions of science when these are not controversial."[18] Thus, the values of public reason exclude appeal to non-political values, controversial information, controversial ideals and non-public modes of reasoning in political argument. It should be clear that this commits Rawls to the third principle of restraint.

The content of a political conception of justice, then, is fixed by respecting the principles of restraint. Compliance with them makes it possible to construct a conception that all reasonable people could accept. Taken together, the principles express the Rawlsian ideal of democratic citizenship: "to live politically with others in the light of reasons all might reasonably be expected to endorse."[19]

One final point deserves mention. Does this ideal of democratic citizenship commit Rawls to comprehensive or narrow restraint? Rawls indicates that he wishes to limit restraint to political questions that concern "constitutional essentials and basic justice." But, as I pointed out in chapter 2, he does not provide a clear criterion for distinguishing these fundamental matters from less fundamental ones. Nor does he answer the question he himself raises; namely, why not extend restraint to other political questions as well?[20] This presents a potential problem. Citizens who wish to promote controversial ideals through political action might plausibly claim that this can all be done at the less fundamental level. Provided they do not restrict basic liberties, they are free to promote their ideals and values. Disagreements about whether citizens could permissibly promote controversial ideals, then, would boil down to disagreements about whether the issues under consideration

---

[17] Rawls also says that the values of public reason include certain political virtues like civility, tolerance and reasonableness. (Ibid. p. 194)

[18] Ibid. p. 224.   [19] Ibid. p. 243.

[20] Rawls is not at all clear on this matter. He advances three different positions on the question of whether citizens should show restraint when non-basic political questions are at stake. First, he is agnostic, asserting that such matters can be worked out later after the fundamentals have been taken care of (ibid. p. 215). Second, he is cautiously committal, claiming citizens "may properly vote" their comprehensive views when constitutional essentials and basic justice are not at stake (ibid. p. 235) And third, he claims much more affirmatively that it is often "more reasonable" to go beyond political values when resolving these less fundamental questions (ibid. p. 230).

were matters of constitutional essentials or basic justice. In the absence of a criterion to resolve such disputes, the application of the principles of restraint to these cases would be indeterminate.[21]

Notwithstanding this problem, one I shall return to later, we should interpret Rawls as favoring narrow over comprehensive restraint.

The pragmatic argument

The above summary was brief. It was not intended to be a comprehensive exegesis of Rawls' work. Rather, the objective was two-fold: to introduce some of the terms and concepts Rawls uses and to show that his commitment to a political conception of justice commits him to the principles of restraint, at least when questions of constitutional essentials and basic justice are at stake. We are now in a position to consider the arguments he advances in defense of that commitment.

Let me start by noting that Rawls' argument could be interpreted as one that is advanced by an observer. Surveying the wide variety of incompatible comprehensive doctrines in a modern western society, an observer might come to the conclusion that all parties ought to seek principles that all could accept. Given their intractable differences, he might reason, their best response is to bracket controversial views and seek common ground. In this way, they could arrive at a serviceable conception of justice for their society.

Yet despite its surface appeal, this judgment would likely be dismissed by many citizens in these societies. As a judgment from the perspective of an outsider, it simply would not address the issues that divide them. Reflective committed participants in the political life of modern western societies would have no trouble recognizing that compromise is sometimes necessary, but many of them would resist the suggestion that the content of political morality is determined by it.

I will assume, then, that if Rawls is to defend his commitment to the principles of restraint, he will need to take up the perspective of a participant in a modern western society. From this perspective, we can ask, what reasons might justify restraint? In posing this question we need to keep in mind the point noted earlier. That is, when thinking about

---

[21] Rawls often defends political liberalism by stressing the fact that political power is "coercive." It is this feature of political power that gives rise to the demand that we make sure that we can justify its exercise to all reasonable people. (See also C. Larmore, "Political Liberalism," p. 349, and T. Nagel, *Equality and Partiality*, p. 159.) But political power that is exercised when constitutional essentials are not at stake can still be coercive political power. So the distinction between coercive and non-coercive exercises of political power will not draw the same line as the distinction between constitutional essentials and non-basic political matters.

justifying restraint we need to think of the model citizen, e.g. the person who has good reasons for believing that her ideals and values are sound, has a good measure of confidence in her reasons and has a strong desire to promote them through political action because she believes they are sound. To justify the principles of restraint, Rawls needs to show that there are good reasons for the model citizen to accept them. If he can show this, then *a fortiori* he can show that all citizens ought to show restraint.

There is no one master argument that Rawls puts forward to justify the principles of restraint. He makes his case in different ways by appealing to different considerations. As a result, his readers must engage in some detective work to track down all the arguments he relies on. We do well to look at these arguments one at a time and then at the end of our investigation ask ourselves whether they add up to a convincing case. In this chapter and the next two this is the method I adopt.

In *A Theory of Justice* Rawls made much of the idea that we all have strong reasons to value stable social cooperation, for stable social cooperation not only helps us achieve our individual ends, it also lets us share in the diverse accomplishments of others. This suggests a pragmatic argument for restraint. Suppose it turns out that we can only have a decent and stable system of social cooperation if everyone recognizes the principles of restraint. This would provide citizens with a powerful reason to acknowledge the principles, provided they had assurance that their fellow citizens would acknowledge them as well. Sometimes Rawls gives the impression that he believes this to be the case for modern western societies. For example, he instructs us to recognize "the *practical impossibility* of reaching reasonable and workable political agreement in judgment on the truth of comprehensive doctrines, especially an agreement that might serve the purpose . . . of achieving peace and concord in a society characterized by religious and philosophical differences."[22] If Rawls is right on this point, he is close to clinching the case for restraint. He will have shown that all citizens have compelling reasons to recognize the principles of restraint – the goods of peace and concord surely provide compelling reasons. In most circumstances, it is better to compromise than exchange bullets.

But Rawls does not give arguments for this bold assertion. Nowhere does he demonstrate that comprehensive or partially comprehensive conceptions of justice could not serve the purpose of achieving peace and concord. No doubt it is true that there are some comprehensive concep-

---

[22] J. Rawls, *Political Liberalism*, p. 63 (emphasis added).

tions of justice in our society that, if enforced, would lead to widespread social strife. But from the fact that some comprehensive conceptions of justice would be practically unworkable it obviously does not follow that all would.

Notwithstanding this, suppose there are some political and social conditions that would make Rawls' pragmatic argument true. Imagine a society with many competing groups of roughly equal size and power, each with their own well-worked-out system of ideals and values. Imagine further that the groups are at one another's throats so that the political situation is extremely volatile. Under these conditions, it might be true that a political conception of justice would be the only type of conception that had a prayer of establishing social peace and concord.[23] Surely, under these dire conditions, the model citizen would acknowledge that she has compelling reasons to show restraint.

Yet, even if this is conceded, it does not get Rawls to the conclusion he needs. Under these unfavorable conditions, the model citizen would show restraint, but she would show it for the wrong reasons. She would show restraint because it would be the best option open to her. According to her values, it would be better than any realistic alternative. But Rawls has given us no reason to think that the model citizen would not look forward to the day when conditions improve and she would have better options. When, and if, conditions did change for the better, the model citizen would no longer have a compelling reason to accept the principles of restraint. Happily, she would put forward her favored conception of justice.[24] Thus, her commitment to restraint is contingent and unstable.

This is not acceptable to Rawls. He is keen to distinguish a political conception of justice from a mere *modus vivendi*.[25] Under some social conditions the need to compromise with others may provide citizens with compelling pragmatic reasons to accept the principles of restraint. But Rawls insists that citizens have not only pragmatic reasons, but moral

[23] Even under these conditions there might be workable alternatives to the bracketing strategy. For example, the society might adopt a version of the "millet system" used in the Ottoman Empire. Under this system, different groups tolerate one another; but they do not share the same principles of political morality. Each group is allowed to enforce its own ideals, and each group allows other groups to do the same. For discussion of this alternative, see W. Kymlicka, *Multicultural Citizenship*, pp. 156–58.

[24] It might be objected that the model citizen having first adopted the principles of restraint for pragmatic reasons might come to value them intrinsically. I do not dispute that this is a psychological possibility. But the model citizen, as I am describing him or her, looks to see if there are good reasons to show restraint and is not under the influence of irrational psychological mechanisms.

[25] Other proponents of the bracketing strategy are equally keen to draw this distinction. See, for example, C. Larmore, "Political Liberalism," pp. 346, 358–59 fn14.

reasons as well. To make this absolutely clear he claims that citizens should continue to show restraint even if the "relative strength of their view in society [should] increase and eventually become dominant."[26] But while this point does indeed distinguish a political conception of justice from a mere *modus vivendi*, it is puzzling for two quite different reasons. First, if a comprehensive view does become dominant in a society it can claim with some plausibility that its ideals and values are shared. At a certain point its ideals and values simply become a part of the public political culture of the society and, at that point, they cannot be excluded from political action by the principles of restraint. (I grant that it is a difficult matter to determine when this point has been reached.) Second, this claim shows that the pragmatic argument about the practical impossibility of comprehensive conceptions of justice simply drops out of the picture. Rawls' argument is not that we should not embrace a comprehensive conception because it will not work; but, rather, that we should not embrace it even when it is clear that it would work.[27] The task remains, then, of showing that citizens in general, and the model citizen in particular, have good moral reasons to accept the principles of restraint.[28]

The argument from political justification

Let us turn, then, to a second argument. In assessing Rawls' work it is hard to avoid confronting methodological issues entirely. Rawls puts forward not only an interpretation of liberalism, but also a method for determining moral reasons with respect to basic questions of political morality. The method is what he dubs "political constructivism";[29] and he contends that its full significance comes into view once we grasp how it is connected to the "need for a democratic society to secure the

[26] J. Rawls, *Political Liberalism*, p. 148.

[27] Following Hobbes, some modern writers have argued that morality, at bottom, simply consists of pragmatic self-interested considerations. See, most impressively, D. Gauthier's *Morals by Agreement*. If this line of thought is right, then the pragmatic argument is the only argument that could provide moral reasons for citizens to show restraint. Like many others, I do not find the Hobbes/Gauthier argument convincing. But since it has been criticized extensively by others, there is no need to take it up here. See B. Barry, *Theories of Justice*, pp. 241–54, and D. Braybrooke, "The Social Contract Theorist's Fanciest Flight Yet."

[28] It may seem unfair to attribute this argument to Rawls and then refute it. As we have seen, Rawls himself is aware of its limitations. Nevertheless, Rawls does appeal to this argument from time to time, relying on it to buttress his case for restraint.

[29] Rawls is careful to distinguish "political constructivism" from "moral constructivism." The former is concerned solely with matters of basic justice while the latter is concerned with morality as a whole. He also distinguishes political constructivism from "Kantian moral constructivism" (*Political Liberalism*, pp. 99–101).

possibility of an overlapping consensus on its fundamental political values."[30] This suggests that, in Rawls' mind at least, the methodological and substantive issues are interrelated.

I shall not offer a complete analysis of the method of political constructivism here. That task is much too big for present concerns. But before we evaluate Rawls' arguments that citizens have moral reasons to show restraint, we need to say at least a few words about it. The reason for this should become clearer when we evaluate these arguments. We will find that the method of political constructivism often looms in the background.

Political constructivism purports to construct or constitute reasonable[31] principles of justice. Its basic features include: (a) the specification of a reasonable and rational procedure of construction, (b) a description of appropriate conceptions of society and person to go with the procedure and (c) an argument as to which principles would issue from the procedure if it were correctly followed. Each of these features calls for further comment.

The reasonable and rational procedure of construction is illustrated by Rawls' original position. This is an imaginary choice-situation in which the parties are to choose the principles of justice to regulate the basic structure of their society. The original position imposes reasonable conditions on the choice of principles. As is well known, in *A Theory of Justice* Rawls argues that reasonable conditions consist of the exclusion of morally arbitrary information from the choosing parties and the stipulation that the parties know only widely shared non-controversial information such as basic facts about human psychology and human societies. In his more recent work Rawls emphasizes that the original position is best understood as a device for representing or "modeling" certain fundamental ideas implicit in the public political culture of the society.

Understood as one possible model of a reasonable and rational procedure of construction,[32] the original position must be set out in conjunction with basic conceptions of society and person. These conceptions characterize the agents in the procedure of construction, both as to their fundamental nature and as to the problems they are to address. In Rawls' version the agents are to be understood as free and equal in virtue

---

[30] Ibid. p. 90.

[31] To avoid confusion I use the term "reasonable" to refer to principles of justice that are selected by the constructivist procedure. Thus defined, "reasonable" principles are not necessarily sound. I reserve the term "correct" for principles that are sound.

[32] The original position is not essential to political constructivism. Rawls now concedes that political constructivism could proceed without it. However, this would require the specification of an alternative procedure (ibid. pp. 226–27).

of their possessing two moral powers, the power to form, to revise and rationally to pursue a conception of the good and the power to understand, to apply and to act from a sense of justice; and they are to conceive of political society as a system of fair cooperation regulated by public principles that all could reasonably be expected to endorse. Thus, the conceptions of society and person complete and add substance to the specification of the reasonable and rational procedure of construction.

It is worth pointing out that both the procedure of construction and the conceptions of society and person that go with it are not themselves constructed. They are, in Rawls' words, simply "laid out"; and they are laid out in such a way as to model the fundamental ideas implicit in the public political culture. It is only the content of the political conception of justice that is constructed. This consists of the two types of values we discussed earlier, the values of political justice and the values of public reason. Political constructivism is completed with the presentation of an argument explaining why certain particular principles[33] would be chosen if the procedure were correctly followed. Rawls' justifications of the principle of equal liberty and the second principle (the principle of fair equality of opportunity and the difference principle) over other possible principles exemplify such an argument. The principles selected are the reasonable principles of justice. They are reasonable because they would arise from the procedure. In this way, political constructivism constructs or constitutes an appropriate conception of justice.

Now that I have described in broad outline the main features of political constructivism, I want to guard against a possible misunderstanding. It is tempting to think that if Rawls' political constructivism were correct, then citizens could have no moral reasons *not* to show restraint, for what counts as a moral reason would be determined by the procedure of construction; and if the principles selected by the procedure call for restraint, as Rawls argues, then citizens could have no moral reasons for objecting. However, this conclusion would be too hasty. It would be too hasty because it ignores the fact that political constructivism is limited in scope. It does not purport to construct all moral values, but only political values.[34] It also would be too hasty because it ignores the fact that the principles selected by the procedure are held to be reasonable, not necessarily correct. They are, Rawls claims, the most

---

[33] For convenience I refer to principles only. However, Rawls does argue that the parties in the original position are also to select values to govern the public discussion and presentation of the principles.

[34] According to Rawls, political values constitute "a subdomain of the realm of all values" (ibid. p. 139).

"reasonable" or "the most appropriate."[35] They do not, however, lay a claim to truth. Thus, political constructivism leaves open the possibility that other principles, not selected, could be the correct ones.[36]

This is sufficient for the challenge posed by the model citizen to get its grip. It cannot be said in advance that the model citizen could have no moral reasons not to show restraint. It is possible that she not only is seeking to advance correct principles of political morality, but also that she has good reasons for believing that she is advancing correct principles of political morality. Nevertheless, if Rawls' political constructivism is correct, she still acts "unreasonably."

We have yet to identify the grounds of this judgment. We still need to know what the basis is for the charge of unreasonableness. Consider now the following passage:

> Once we accept the fact that reasonable pluralism is a permanent condition of public culture under free institutions, the idea of the reasonable is more suitable as part of the basis of public justification for a constitutional regime than the idea of moral truth.[37]

These remarks suggest that the acceptance of the fact of reasonable pluralism should lead us to see that the idea of the reasonable is a more "suitable" basis of public justification than the idea of moral truth. This, in turn, accords with the method of political constructivism, "for it is only by affirming a constructivist conception – one which is political and not metaphysical – that citizens generally can expect to find principles that all can accept."[38] Therefore, the model citizen who bases her political action on moral truth (or her perception of moral truth) is making a mistake.[39] She is failing to grasp the full implications of the fact of reasonable pluralism.

But what type of mistake might this be? The fact of reasonable pluralism is just a fact about our social conditions. It is the fact that

---

[35] Ibid. pp. 95, 127.

[36] Rawls wishes to deny that political constructivism constructs moral truth. We might call this view *deep constructivism*. Deep constructivism is at odds with many philosophical views about the nature of moral truth. Hence, it violates the spirit of political liberalism. See Rawls' comments on Kant's constructivism in *Political Liberalism*, pp. 99–101. Also see D. Brink's comments on Rawls' constructivism and its relation to moral realism in *Moral Realism and the Foundations of Ethics*, pp. 303–21. It is worth noting that Rawls himself once endorsed deep constructivism. In "Kantian Constructivism in Moral Theory" he wrote: "An essential feature of a constructivist view, as illustrated by justice as fairness, is that its first principles single out what facts citizens in a well-ordered society are to count as reasons of justice. Apart from the procedure of constructing these principles, *there are no reasons of justice*." ("Kantian Constructivism in Moral Theory," p. 547, emphasis added). But in *Political Liberalism* Rawls no longer endorses this view.

[37] J. Rawls, *Political Liberalism*, p. 129.   [38] Ibid. p. 97.

[39] Assuming, that is, that his or her perception of moral truth conflicts with the principles selected by the constructivist procedure.

under reasonably free conditions citizens in modern western societies will tend to hold a multitude of incompatible, reasonable comprehensive doctrines. As Rawls notes, many of these comprehensive doctrines will have their own conceptions of moral truth. As a consequence, it is sensible to expect reasonable disagreement about moral truth. In the face of this reasonable disagreement, Rawls insists, it is unreasonable for citizens to put forward their own understanding of moral truth as a basis of public justification. But why, we must ask again, is this unreasonable?

Rawls' commitment to political constructivism suggests an answer. It is unreasonable because it misunderstands the nature of political justification. Capturing the spirit of the bracketing strategy, Rawls writes that "justification is addressed to others" and, therefore, should proceed "from what is, or can be, held in common."[40] This is accomplished by the method of political constructivism. As we have seen, it sets out a procedure of construction and conceptions of society and person that are worked up from the shared ideas of the public political culture. As such, it proceeds "from what is, or can be, held in common."[41] In contrast, the model citizen makes political arguments and supports political positions that do not necessarily proceed from shared beliefs. Therefore, the argument runs, she cannot justify her political action. Let us call this the *argument from political justification.*

As it stands, this argument begs the question. The model citizen believes that political justification should proceed from premises that are sound. Sound premises are not always uncontroversial. Sometimes they conflict with shared or generally accepted assumptions and judgments. Whether the model citizen is right or whether political justification should always proceed from premises that are held in common is precisely what is in dispute. It is a dispute about what method is the correct one for political justification.[42] Moreover, the dispute is not just a methodological one. It is a substantive one as well. It cannot be resolved solely by appealing to the nature of political justification.

This is an important point; and I want to suggest a second reason for

---

[40] Ibid. p. 100.

[41] The phrase "can be held in common" is ambiguous. Broadly interpreted, it means that all people who are minimally reasonable, i.e. have consistent views and do not make obvious logical mistakes, can accept it. As far as I can tell, Rawls uses the phrase in this broad sense. But Rawls' understanding of the idea of reasonableness is a tricky subject. I shall have more to say about it in chapter 4.

[42] Some writers simply announce that political justification is about getting others to accept one's view. For instance, J. P. Dobel in "The End of Ethics: The Beginning of Politics" writes that political justification "makes no sense unless our reasons are accepted" and that "the people who accept . . . determine what constitutes a good reason." This erases the distinction between what people should accept and what people can be made to accept. There are surely reasons for holding on to this distinction.

believing that it is correct. Many people today are attracted to Rawls'
idea of political constructivism. They believe that we live in "a post-
metaphysical age" and that we must give up the notion that there exists
an independent order of moral facts. Given that there are no moral facts
out there to be discovered, they reason, we must create or construct them
and the Rawlsian method of constructivism seems just the way to do it.
In my view this turning away from metaphysics is premature, but I do
not want to argue this point here. Instead, I want to show that even if we
ought to accept constructivism, this does not provide support for the
bracketing strategy. The first step in making good on this claim is to
distinguish two types of constructivist procedures. One type we can,
following Rawls, call *political constructivism*. This was described above.
The second type we can call *first-person constructivism*. The main
difference between these two types of constructivist procedures concerns
the ways in which the procedure of construction and the conceptions of
society and person that go with it are "laid out." As we have seen, with
political constructivism these elements are laid out in such a way as to
model the fundamental ideas implicit in the public political culture of the
society in question. But with first-person constructivism there is no such
requirement. According to first-person constructivism, the procedure of
construction and the conceptions of society and person are based on
sound reasons and trustworthy evidence from the standpoint of the
person engaging in the process of construction.[43]

With this distinction in hand, we can now see why the truth of
constructivism does not lend support to the bracketing strategy. Even if
we come to believe that there is no independent order of moral facts and
that we must opt for a constructivist procedure, it does not follow that
we would have to accept political constructivism. We might well believe
that we ought to accept the best constructivist procedure and that the
best constructivist procedure is a first-person one. In other words, we
might have good reason to think that our understanding of an appropriate procedure of construction and the concomitant conceptions of
person and society were better than those of political constructivism. For
instance, we might think that many ideas deeply embedded in the public

---

[43] The contrast I am drawing here between political constructivism and first-person
constructivism has obvious affinities with the contrast between the method of reflective
equilibrium understood as a first-person enterprise and reflective equilibrium understood
as a joint enterprise. In the former, the considered judgments that provide the starting
points for reflection are those of the person engaging in the method of reflective
equilibrium. In the latter, the considered judgments are understood as a kind of
sociological fact, i.e. what people in one's society deeply believe. It should be clear that
there is no guarantee that the first-person and joint approaches will yield the same
results.

culture of our society were misguided or unattractive in some other way; and then we would have no good reason to prefer political constructivism to first-person constructivism. And if we adopt first-person constructivism instead of political constructivism, there is no guarantee that the conclusions we draw from the procedure will not be subject to reasonable disagreement. Thus, even if Rawls is right about constructivism, this methodological truth would not provide a reason for accepting the bracketing strategy.

Against this, it might be said that political justification is essentially intersubjective. It is this feature of political justification that recommends a procedure of construction like the one Rawls advances.[44] This objection could be buttressed by a skeptical argument about moral truth. Rejecting the possibility of an independent order of moral facts, the skeptic could insist that we must aim for intersubjective agreement because there is nothing else to aim for. But this line of argument is of no help to Rawls. As he acknowledges, skepticism about moral truth is a controversial philosophical position. Endorsing it would endanger his commitment to a political conception of justice.[45]

We need, then, an alternative rationale for why political justification is essentially intersubjective. Before trying to identify what that rationale might be, it will be helpful to clarify the idea behind intersubjectivity. To say that political justification is essentially intersubjective is to say that any successful political justification must be accepted by some specified group. The basic idea is expressed by the following methodological principle:

A successful political justification of some set of principles, P, is one such that all members of some group, S, accept or would accept it.

This formulation underscores two important points. First, the fact of acceptance of P by S is taken to be a necessary condition for the successful political justification of P. Second, intersubjective justification requires the specification of the relevant reference group S. The first point can be understood to mean either that acceptance of P by group S *constitutes* its successful political justification or, more weakly, that it is

---

[44] I consider this argument because some who are sympathetic to Rawls might press it. However, it is not clear that Rawls himself believes that political justification is essentially intersubjective. Perhaps the most prominent exponent of this view is J. Habermas. See his *Moral Consciousness and Communicative Action* and *Justification and Application*.

[45] This is not a fully satisfactory response for even if Rawls, given his other commitments, cannot advance a skeptical argument, it does not follow that the bracketing strategy could not be supported by such an argument. Perhaps someone else, unburdened by Rawls' commitments, could make the argument work. I return to the issue of skepticism in chapter 4 and I try to give a more complete response to it there.

the *mark* of its successful political justification. The second point calls attention to the fact that before we talk about acceptance we must have in mind an answer to the question, accepted by whom?

Both points bring to light some of the ambiguities in the claim that political justification is essentially intersubjective. For instance, the requirement that we specify a reference group gives rise to the following problem. If it is said that the relevant reference group is simply all adult citizens in the political community, then we have a clear descriptive criterion for identifying the reference group; but in this case it is highly unlikely that any principles would be accepted by all the members of the group. On the other hand, if we restrict the reference group to all "reasonable" people, then not only must we identify a criterion of reasonableness to delimit the reasonable from the unreasonable, but also we must explain why further restriction is not justified. For if we exclude the unreasonable from the reference group, why should we not also exclude the reasonable who do not have full information? And if we should exclude them, then why should we not also exclude the reasonable who are not responsive to all relevant considerations? Once we start placing epistemic restrictions on the reference group, there is pressure to go all the way and identify the relevant reference group with those who have sound views. Taken to the limit, these restrictions vitiate the idea of intersubjectivity.

Perhaps there is some principled way to admit certain restrictions on the reference group without going all the way to the limit. I shall consider this response shortly. For now consider a second problem with intersubjectivity. This problem bears more directly on Rawls' own argument. According to the above formulation, acceptance by the members of the reference group S either constitutes or is a mark of reasonable principles of justice. But this is in tension with Rawls' idea of an overlapping consensus. As we have seen, an overlapping consensus does not require that all its adherents support the principles of justice for the same reasons. Rawls' metaphor of a module is intended to make it plain that each citizen can accept the principles from within his or her own comprehensive conception. Thus, it is not unreasonable to think that many citizens will believe that the principles are sound in the light of their own comprehensive views. But if this is true, then these citizens will not accept the principles because they are principles that can be accepted by other members of the reference group S. They will accept them because they believe them to be sound on other grounds. This entails that these citizens would reject the idea that acceptance by group S constitutes or is a mark of successful political justification.

Rawls could respond by insisting that citizens not only accept the principles of justice that make an overlapping consensus possible, but also accept them *for this reason*. But this brings its own problems. The more that citizens are required to accept the harder it will be to establish a consensus.[46] If adherents of an overlapping consensus must not only accept certain principles, but also accept them for the same reasons, then Rawls risks abandoning the important insight expressed by the module metaphor. The plausibility of an overlapping consensus hinges crucially on the claim that citizens can accept the same principles of justice for different reasons. If that claim is rejected, an overlapping consensus starts to look utopian.

So it appears that if an overlapping consensus is at all plausible, many of its adherents will not accept (and should not be expected to accept) the claim that acceptance of principles of justice by the reference group constitutes or marks their reasonableness. In other words, adherents of the overlapping consensus need not accept the methodological principle of intersubjectivity. And if this is the case, then Rawls will not be able to claim that political justification is essentially intersubjective. That claim now is seen to be a partisan claim. Theorists of a political conception of justice must not commit themselves to it.[47]

This should be enough to turn back the claim that political constructivism is the correct method of political justification because political justification is essentially intersubjective. But let us return to the problem of placing restrictions on the relevant reference group. These restrictions are often characterized in epistemic terms. In order to secure the possibility of acceptance, the theorist of intersubjective political justification defines the reference group so as to exclude the unreasonable and the irrational. But if it is permissible to exclude people from the reference group because of epistemic defects, it is not clear why one should not go further and exclude all but the most epistemically competent, i.e. those with sound views. As we have seen, this vitiates the idea of intersubjectivity. The claim that a successful political justification is one that the wise would accept has next to nothing to do with intersubjective agreement.

However, it may be objected that the restrictions on the reference

---

[46] In different ways, this point has been made by others. See S. Scheffler "The Appeal of Political Liberalism" and L. Wenar "Political Liberalism: An Internal Critique."

[47] In his reply to Habermas, Rawls objects to Habermas' characterization of him as a natural law theorist. He then makes the following statements. "[J]ustice as fairness is a political conception of justice, and while of course a moral conception, it is not an instance of a natural law doctrine. It neither denies nor asserts any such view" ("Reply to Habermas," p. 159). Note that if justice as fairness "neither denies nor asserts" a natural law doctrine it cannot endorse the methodological principle of intersubjectivity, for endorsing that principle would amount to a denial of natural law doctrines.

group are not epistemological, but moral. This is suggested by Rawls'
contractualist account of the notion of reasonableness. The reasonable
person, he says, is one who has "a basic desire to be able to justify [his
actions] to others on grounds they could not reasonably reject – reasonably, that is, given the desire to find principles that others similarly
motivated could not reasonably reject."[48] With this account of the
reasonable, one might then define the reference group as all reasonable
people in the political community. This restriction, since it is not
epistemological, does not run into the problem discussed above. But it
does raise the question why citizens *should* have this basic desire. If the
notion of reasonableness is cast in moral terms, we need moral arguments
to support it. This brings us back to the idea that disputes over what is
the correct method of political justification are in part substantive moral
disputes.

We should conclude that Rawls' view of political justification cannot
vindicate the bracketing strategy; for its plausibility depends – in part, at
least – on the truth of the conclusion that the bracketing strategy seeks to
esstablish.

Conclusion

This completes my discussion of the prefatory arguments in support of
the bracketing strategy. Standing on their own, neither the pragmatic
argument nor the argument from political justification has force. But
Rawls of course does not leave them standing on their own. He puts
forward two important further arguments to show that we ought to
accept the bracketing strategy. These arguments can be called the
argument from democratic toleration and the *transparency argument*. The
objective of the next two chapters is to consider them in detail.

---

[48] J. Rawls, *Political Liberalism*, p. 49. See also the discussion of the contractualist
understanding of reasonable rejectability in chapter 2 above.

4   Toleration, reasonable rejectability and restraint

In chapter 3 I considered and rejected two arguments for restraint: the pragmatic argument and the argument from political justification. I tried to show that neither argument provides moral reasons for the model citizen to exercise restraint. I turn now to a third argument. This argument invokes the value of toleration. Since toleration has moral value, it is the right type of argument.

This chapter divides into seven sections. The first analyzes the concept of toleration. The second discusses two justifications of toleration that the model citizen can endorse. The third contrasts these justifications of toleration with Rawls' "democratic idea" of toleration. Then in the next three sections the case against the democratic idea of toleration is presented and developed. The final section concludes the chapter with some reflections on political justification and moral luck.

The concept of toleration

Let us begin with a few words about the concept of toleration.[1] I will not put forward a complete analysis of the concept. Instead, I will simply identify some of its main features as it is used in contemporary political theory. This should suffice for present purposes.

Tolerance is not the same as nonchalance. The person without a concern or care has no disposition to repress, harm or offend others. Effortlessly, he welcomes diversity; and when confronted with disagreeable things such as prostitution or cruelty to animals he feels no disgust or moral outrage. Whatever else may be said in his favor, the nonchalant person is not tolerant. Lacking convictions, he is disabled from displaying it.

Another character it is useful to distinguish from the tolerant person is (as I shall call him) the efficient persecutor. The efficient persecutor has a

---

[1] Throughout this chapter I use the terms "toleration" and "tolerance" interchangeably.

disposition to repress[2] other people because they are engaging in conduct he deems wrong, but he restrains this disposition because he has been persuaded that in the present circumstances repression would be either ineffective or counterproductive. In his *A Letter Concerning Toleration* Locke famously seeks to demonstrate that religious persecution is irrational. Its means, external force, are inappropriate to its end, religious conversion. Those who accept this Lockean argument and for that reason alone curb their inclination to repress conduct do not, however, tolerate that conduct. True, they acknowledge the futility of repression, but this acknowledgment falls short of toleration.[3] In contrast, tolerant people refrain from repression even when they know, or at least have reason to think, that repression would be effective.

The tolerant person, then, lies in between the nonchalant person and the efficient persecutor. Like the efficient persecutor he has sincere convictions. Like the nonchalant person he does not repress others even when he knows there are effective methods at his disposal for doing so. From these contrasts we can piece together the following summary account of toleration: A person is tolerant if, and only if, he (a) disapproves of certain types of conduct, behavior, social practices, etc.; (b) has a disposition to repress that which he disapproves of; (c) has at his disposal – and is aware that he has at his disposal – some effective means for repressing what he disapproves of; but (d) restrains his disposition to repress and (e) does so for the right type of reason.

Two ambiguities in this account need to be cleared up. The first one concerns the word "disapprove." It can be understood in a moralized sense or in a broader sense which includes moral disapproval, but is not limited to it. I will come back to this point in a moment. The second ambiguity is more prominent. The account stipulates that the tolerant person must act for the right type of reason. But what type of reason must this be? I have suggested that the tolerant person not only restrains his disposition to repress, but is morally motivated to do so. This explains why the efficient persecutor does not display tolerance.

But it is not easy to give a precise characterization of the moral motivation that must be present. At an abstract level, it involves the recognition that others are entitled to respect. But this is much too vague. We need something more definite. As a first approximation, let us say that the tolerant person is one who believes that if another person

---

[2] Unless specified otherwise, in this chapter I use the term "repress" very broadly to stand for repress, persecute, harm, offend, insult, etc.

[3] In defense of Locke it should be pointed out that in *A Letter Concerning Toleration* he does not advance only the argument that the efficient persecutor accepts, but others as well. For discussion, see R. Kraynak, "John Locke: From Absolutism to Toleration."

thinks that it is permissible for him or her to engage in some type of conduct[4], then this provides a reason, albeit a defeasible one, for the tolerant person to let him or her do it. Thus the tolerant person accepts that there is always a reason – however weak or defeasible it may be – for letting people do what they think they are entitled to do; and when he restrains his disposition to repress the conduct of another it is this belief which motivates this restraint.[5] Later I will have more to say about this idea. We will see that it helps explain the attraction of some of Rawls' claims about toleration.

Return now to the ambiguity concerning disapproval. Some writers insist that toleration applies only to conduct, behavior, social practices, etc. that are morally wrong or deemed to be morally wrong. Mere dislikes or prejudices, they contend, do not fall within its ambit.[6] This view is contested by others who construe toleration as applying to non-moral as well as moral objects of disapproval. On this issue consider the following remarks by Raz:

> A person can tolerate another's very deliberate manner of speech, or his slow and methodical way of considering every issue, and so on. In all such cases what is tolerated is neither wrong nor necessarily bad. It is the absence of a certain accomplishment . . . When we tolerate the limitations of others we may be aware that these are but the other side of their virtues and personal strengths.[7]

As these remarks indicate, it seems clear that in ordinary usage the term toleration is used to cover the non-moral as well as the moral. All that is necessary is that what is tolerated be deemed to be deficient in some respect. However, it still can be maintained that one cannot tolerate conduct that one merely dislikes. One needs a reason for believing that the conduct that is disliked is deficient in some respect. In Raz's example when I tolerate someone's deliberate manner of speech I must believe his manner of speech is a real defect or "the absence of a certain accomplishment." This is, I must further believe, a fact about the person, not a fact about my own psychological dispositions.

It might be objected here that this fails to take account of the idea that people can be asked to tolerate that which they dislike irrationally and

---

[4] In this chapter I will usually speak of toleration as applying to conduct or behavior. However, I do not mean to suggest that only conduct or behavior could be objects of toleration.

[5] This is not meant to imply that this belief must enter overtly into the deliberations of the tolerant person. In general there are many ways in which moral considerations can impinge on the deliberations of a person who acts appropriately from the standpoint of morality. I pass over the numerous complications raised by this, but the reader should consult S. Scheffler's *Human Morality*, pp. 29–51.

[6] See P. Nicholson, "Toleration as a Moral Ideal." Also see the discussion in S. Mendus, *Toleration and the Limits of Liberalism*, pp. 9–18.

[7] J. Raz, "Autonomy, Toleration and the Harm Principle," p. 320.

ungroundedly. Even if someone has no reason at all, not even a bad one, for thinking that some object is deficient in some respect, can we still not ask him or her to tolerate it?[8] Ordinary usage does indeed sometimes incline us in this direction. We speak of racial tolerance in contexts where it is plain that people do not have reasons, not even bad ones, for repression. They simply do not like the people they are being asked to associate with.

But there is a good reason for resisting this extension of the scope of toleration. By broadening it to include objects that are merely disliked as well as objects that are deemed to be deficient in some respect, we obscure the philosophically interesting feature of toleration. If someone engages in repression for no reason at all, the repression is wrong and irrational. It is like the repression of a gunman who picks someone at random and shoots him. Seeing that this is wrong raises no puzzle. But toleration is often thought to be an elusive virtue because it asks us to refrain from repressing that which we believe ought to be repressed. It demands that we respect that which, according to our lights, does not warrant respect, even when we are correct in thinking that it does not warrant respect. It is precisely this feature, I believe, that makes intolerance distinct from other types of repression and ties it to judgments of disapproval or deficiency.

If this is right, the relevant distinction is not one between the moral and the non-moral, but one between judgments broadly construed and mere dislikes or feelings. We tolerate that which we judge to be deficient in some respect. We do not tolerate that which we merely dislike or have a negative sentiment toward, but which we do not judge to be deficient in any respect. For example, suppose someone has a strong negative emotional response at the sight of a painting by Magritte. It fills her with anger. If she does not believe that there is anything defective about Magritte's paintings, then we should not say that she tolerates them when she checks the urge to destroy them.[9] We should say, rather, that she restrains her idiosyncratic emotional reactions. However, if she were to inform us that not only do the paintings fill her with anger, but also that she sincerely believes that they fail terribly as art and that this belief

---

[8] In conversation Raymond Geuss pressed this objection. He suggested that toleration is better understood relative to the notion of deviation. We tolerate that which we are unfamiliar with, not necessarily that which we disapprove of or judge to be deficient.

[9] It might be wondered how a painting could fill a person with anger if the person did not also judge the painting to be an aesthetic failure. But the painting might remind the person of some terrible childhood experience and she might be aware of this. If so, she could say with no inconsistency that the painting fills her with anger and that it is a fine piece of art.

accounts for why they fill her with anger, then we could more appropriately describe her behavior as tolerant.

One final point deserves mention. Tolerance is not the same as evenhandedness. Tolerant people do not need to promote or encourage that which they tolerate. They are tolerant if they do not repress what they disapprove of. But there is no further requirement that they treat the disfavored conduct with the same respect as other types of conduct. If one tolerates the sport of bull fighting, one does not have to act as if the sport is as good as cricket. This point is obscured by writers who identify toleration with neutrality, but the impulse to make this identification should be resisted. This is not to say that neutrality, understood as evenhanded treatment, is never a good thing. In some contexts it clearly is, but we should keep the concepts of toleration and neutrality distinct. We should keep them distinct because the latter demands more than the former.

Justifying toleration

Tolerance is not always a virtue. Sometimes it is morally inappropriate to tolerate conduct that one disapproves of. Examples are not hard to come by. If your neighbor beats his wife, you act wrongly if you tolerate his conduct and do nothing to stop him. If your friend takes a self-destructive drug, you act wrongly if you do nothing to dissuade him or her from doing so. This demonstrates that a satisfactory account of toleration must tell us when tolerance is morally appropriate and when it is not. And to discern the limits of toleration we must examine the considerations that justify it.

In this section I will briefly discuss two justifications of toleration. It is worth pausing to consider these justifications because they are ones that the model citizen can accept. As we shall see, understanding them helps us to identify more precisely the distinctive character of Rawls' argument for toleration.

What, then, makes tolerance a virtue? One answer stands out. In open pluralistic societies the presence of diverse social groups generates tension. In realms of thought, sentiment and action, groups come into conflict. There is pressure for them to develop norms that facilitate cooperation. Toleration is just such a norm. It paves the road to social peace.

This goes some distance toward explaining why tolerance is regarded as a virtue in these societies. But it does not fully justify toleration. If our account of toleration is correct, then people have reason not to repress others even when they could do so without undermining social cooperation. Toleration is directed toward conduct that is deemed morally wrong or deficient in some other respect. And, assuming that repression would not undermine social cooperation, it may be wondered how anyone could have good reason to curb his or her disposition to repress such conduct.

It is true that we often urge others to tolerate conduct that *they* disapprove of, but with which we see nothing wrong. We tell them to tolerate interracial marriage when we think there is nothing wrong with it. Perhaps we do this because we think we have a better chance of persuading them to tolerate the conduct than we do of persuading them that they are wrong to think that it is wrong. But, at any rate, this fact about us does nothing to justify toleration.

So we still lack an adequate justification. It is easier to justify toleration when the conduct in question is not judged to be morally wrong. To take a mundane example, suppose you have dinner with someone who has poor table manners. You might be offended. You might think that this reveals a defect in his or her character or upbringing. But you know that not much is at stake. Curbing your impulse to upbraid the person is not related to any significant costs or harms. Knowing this, you conclude that it is worth biting your tongue for the sake of a more cordial evening. But when someone is doing something that is morally wrong, tolerating it seems to countenance grave costs. How could this ever be a virtue?

One answer is suggested by the above remarks from Raz. We might have good reason to tolerate conduct that is morally wrong, but which is an integral part of a larger way of life which itself is valuable. In such a case we tolerate the wrongful conduct because we wish to sustain the valuable way of life of which it is an integral part. The moral wrong, we tell ourselves, is the reverse side of what is valuable.

This makes perfect sense, but it is a difficult judgment to sustain. Surely, if we think that the conduct is morally wrong and we also think that the conduct is integral to the way of life, we will think that this counts against the way of life. A whole way of life might grow up around the practice of slavery, and much of this way of life might be valuable; but if the whole way of life can only be preserved by maintaining slavery, we ought to conclude that the way of life must go. It does not warrant toleration.

Of course not all moral wrongs are as severe as slavery. There will be cases where we correctly judge that the wrongful conduct does not negate the value of the way of life of which it is an integral part. To this extent, we have a good justification for toleration. But this justification is limited in a second respect. For it to stand up it must be true that the tolerated conduct is indeed an integral part of the way of life that is deemed to be valuable. People often claim that any reform of their way of life would utterly destroy it. But these claims are often false or exaggerated. If we have good reason to believe that the wrongful conduct could be eliminated or reformed without destroying the way of life of which it is a part, then we lose our reason to tolerate it. Still, despite these limitations, this justification of toleration is sound. Let us call it the *pluralist justification* of toleration.

The pluralist justification does not exhaust the considerations in favor of toleration. Another justification is available. Earlier I claimed that tolerant people accept that the fact that someone believes that he or she is entitled to do something gives them a reason to let him or her do it. Building on this thought, it now can be said that repression always imposes costs. The costs can be represented as a function of the expected frustration or pain or humiliation that would be generated by repression. Call these *repression costs*. Opposed to repression costs are the expected costs that would be generated by permitting people to engage in the wrongful conduct. Call these *toleration costs*. There is no reason to think that the costs of repression, no matter what the circumstances, could never outweigh the costs of toleration. In cases where they did, it would be wrong to repress the conduct. Toleration would be justified.

This gives us a second, considerably broader, justification. Let us call it the *cost-based justification* for toleration. Yet while there is truth in this justification, the metaphor of weighing is not particularly apt. Injunctions to weigh costs call to mind a scale on which different interests could be measured. But no such scale exists. Our judgments on these matters must be rough and impressionistic.[10] More fundamentally, it matters what type of costs are involved. The costs of toleration consist of different types of costs; and some of these are more pressing than others. For example, tolerated conduct can result in physical harm to the person engaging in it or in moral harm to the person engaging in it or it can result in physical harm to people not engaging in it or moral harm to people not engaging in it. Of course, not infrequently, conduct generates several types of costs at once; but it is possible, nonetheless, to distinguish between the different types. For the cost-based justification of toleration to yield determinate answers about what ought to be tolerated, we need to decide which types of costs are more important than others.

For the same reason, the costs of repression need to be disaggregated. But perhaps I have said enough to establish the general point that I am seeking to establish – judgments about the justification of toleration must

---

[10] But see J. Feinberg *Harm to Others* for some thoughts on what types of considerations are relevant.

be embedded within a larger moral theory that identifies which interests and harms are significant. Such a moral theory would also identify the limits of toleration. It would tell us when toleration ceases to be a virtue and when it becomes a morally inappropriate response.

It should now be abundantly clear that both the pluralist justification and the cost-based justification of toleration are heavily moralized. To apply them we need to make judgments not only about particular types of conduct, but also about the value of whole ways of life. We also need to draw on a background understanding of what interests contribute to a sound and fulfilling life. These are tasks that the model citizen freely accepts. She will draw on her comprehensive philosophical, moral and religious views in order to determine the proper scope and limits of toleration.

Bearing all this in mind, we can now turn to the main subject of this chapter.

The democratic idea of toleration

This concerns Rawls' claim that the value of toleration provides citizens with moral reasons to accept the principles of restraint. If this claim is correct, then the model citizen may act wrongly if she tries to enforce her controversial views.

Most of my discussion will center on Rawls' more recent views on toleration, but let us begin by looking very briefly at his treatment of religious toleration in *A Theory of Justice*. In this work Rawls justifies toleration by reference to the principles of justice.[11] In particular, the first principle, the principle of equal liberty, guides his analysis. Thus, Rawls maintains that we should tolerate religious views, even when we think they are false, because this is a requirement of justice.

Now it might be objected that if we know that a particular religious view is false and we know that it impedes the well-being of those who participate in its way of life, then we have grounds for suppressing it. But Rawls seeks to block this judgment. His argument instructs us to consider the issue of toleration not in light of our knowledge about different religious doctrines; but rather from the standpoint of the original position where, by stipulation, we have no knowledge at all of religious doctrines and practices. From this standpoint, the merits of particular religious doctrines are irrelevant to judgments about the limits of toleration.[12]

[11] J. Rawls, *A Theory of Justice*, pp. 211–21.
[12] This does not do justice to Rawls' argument. He does not just stipulate that the original position is the appropriate standpoint for considering issues of toleration, he provides

It is possible to believe that some religious doctrines are false and pernicious and still accept Rawls' argument that these beliefs are not relevant to the issue of toleration. But to believe this one would not only have to accept Rawls' account of justice, but also agree that it is more important that justice be done than that false religions be suppressed. These beliefs are not necessarily inconsistent and there may well be people who actually hold them. But there is something odd about them, nonetheless. The oddity is that for those who have religious views these views will in all likelihood influence or inform their views about morality in general and justice in particular. And if this is the case, then it is hard to see how, even if they agree with Rawls that it is more important that justice be done than that false religions be suppressed, they could further believe that the appropriate standpoint for thinking about justice (and derivatively toleration) is a standpoint in which they know nothing about religious doctrines and practices.

There is no reason why this must occasion worry for Rawls. It is open to him to say that his principles of justice are the correct ones. They bind everyone, even those who refuse to acknowledge their authority. He then would have a response to all who reject the original position as the proper standpoint for thinking about toleration. Such people, he could say, are not inclined to act justly. Their religious views distort their sense of justice. If these people protest that their understanding of religious truth compels them to reject the principles of justice, Rawls could firmly reply, that, if so, "their nature is their misfortune."[13]

There is evidence that this is the type of response Rawls would have made when he wrote *A Theory of Justice*.[14] But I am not interested in arguing the interpretive point here. Instead, I want to contrast this view with the view that Rawls now puts forward. The new view is presented as "the democratic idea of toleration."[15] According to Rawls, this idea is a refinement or an extension of the ideal of toleration that arose in response to post-Reformation religious struggles. This ideal, he tells us, was subsequently extended to other areas of life; now it can and should be extended still further to apply to philosophy itself.[16] This further extension is the hallmark of the democratic idea of toleration.

We need to know, then, what it means to apply toleration to

arguments for why this is so. See *ibid.* pp. 195–258, 440–46. But it is not necessary for us to discuss these arguments here.

[13] Ibid., p. 576.

[14] See pp. 255–56. Also see J. Hampton "Should Political Philosophy Be Done Without Metaphysics?" for a similar interpretation.

[15] J. Rawls, *Political Liberalism*, p. 58.

[16] Ibid. p. 154. Note that in this context philosophy is understood broadly to include religious and moral views.

philosophy itself. Correctly interpreted, the democratic idea of toleration is a guide for formulating principles of political morality. In formulating a conception of justice it instructs us not to appeal to controversial philosophical ideas. If we do so, then the resulting conception of justice will not "tolerate" those who hold opposing philosophical views. It will be objectionably sectarian. So understood, the democratic idea of toleration is the reverse side of the principles of restraint. To the extent that citizens contravene the principles of restraint, they fail to tolerate those who disagree with them. Since toleration has (or can have) moral value, citizens have moral reasons to comply with the principles of restraint.

This is Rawls' most important argument in defense of restraint. We can call it the *argument from democratic toleration*. Before looking at it in more detail, it may help to contrast the democratic idea of toleration with Rawls' view of toleration in *A Theory of Justice*, as I interpreted it above. That view, to recall, justified toleration by reference to the principles of justice. The idea was first to formulate principles of justice and then to use them to distinguish morally appropriate from morally inappropriate instances of toleration. The new view does not allow for the same progression of thought. If we accept the democratic idea of toleration, we cannot formulate principles of justice independently of our concern for toleration. Our concern for toleration must guide us in determining those very principles of justice. But this means that we cannot refer to principles of justice to identify the limits of toleration. And this gives rise to the following worry. We know that toleration is not always morally appropriate. As we saw in the last section, we need a moral theory to identify its limits. But if toleration guides us in formulating principles of justice, how are we to distinguish morally appropriate from morally inappropriate instances of it?

This is a worry that the model citizen could try to exploit in arguing against the principles of restraint. But Rawls has something of an answer to the problem that gives rise to it. His account of toleration is linked to a norm of reasonableness. The link occurs at two points. Tolerant people are reasonable themselves and they tolerate other reasonable people. It follows that reasonable people need not tolerate unreasonable people. Thus the norm of reasonableness provides a standard for distinguishing morally appropriate from inappropriate toleration. As Rawls has put it in a recent essay, "whenever the scope of toleration is extended: the criteria of reasonableness are relaxed."[17]

This is all very abstract. A great deal turns on how the norm of reasonableness is spelled out. As Rawls acknowledges, the norm of

---

[17] J. Rawls, "The Law of Peoples," p. 78.

reasonableness that he relies on is based on Scanlon's contractualist account of moral motivation. Scanlon identifies moral motivation with the "desire to be able to justify one's actions to others on grounds they could not reasonably reject."[18] As we saw in the last chapter, the term reasonable is used both as an epistemological and as a moral idea. The trick to understanding the contractualist norm of reasonableness is to figure out how the epistemological and moral ideas fit together in its formulation.

Unfortunately, Rawls is not very clear on this crucial matter. Consider these passages from *Political Liberalism*.

[The reasonable person has a moral psychology that includes the] readiness to propose fair terms of cooperation it is reasonable to expect others to endorse, as well as their willingness to abide by these terms provided others can be relied on to do likewise.[19]

Observe that here being reasonable is not an epistemological idea (though it has epistemological elements). Rather, it is part of a political idea of democratic citizenship that includes the idea of public reason. The content of this ideal includes what free and equal citizens as reasonable can require of each other with respect to their reasonable comprehensive views.[20]

These passages are representative of many other descriptions of the norm of reasonableness in *Political Liberalism*.[21] They are suggestive, but they require clarification. The central element in the norm of reasonableness is the desire to find principles that others could accept, given that they too have this same desire. Let us call this the *agreement disposition*. This is not an epistemological idea, but a moral motivation. Still, one might have the agreement disposition and insist, nonetheless, that one's controversial views are correct and, hence, ought to be agreed to by everyone else. It is here that "the epistemological elements" come into play. People who maintain that their controversial views are correct and that others should accept them because they are correct are being unreasonable in an epistemological sense. They are denying what Rawls terms "the burdens of judgment."[22] Let us call a person who accepts the burdens of judgment *epistemically charitable*. The epistemically charitable person believes that others can reasonably disagree with him, even when he is correct. These

[18] T. Scanlon, "Contractualism and Utilitarianism," p. 116.
[19] J. Rawls, *Political Liberalism*, p. 81.   [20] Ibid. p. 62.
[21] Ibid. pp. xx, 48, 49, 54, 61–63, 94, 116, 127–29.
[22] Rawls characterizes the burdens of judgment as sources of reasonable disagreement. I will discuss the burdens of judgment in more detail on pp. 91–94. For now, it is important to note that the burdens of judgment do not entail skepticism. See *Political Liberalism*, pp. 54–58.

distinctions show that for Rawls the fully reasonable person is the person who has both the agreement disposition *and* is epistemically charitable.

Notice that these two ideas – the agreement disposition and epistemic charity – complement each other. If one is not epistemically charitable, one will likely reject the agreement disposition; and if one accepts the agreement disposition, one will likely be epistemically charitable. Still, there is no necessary connection between the two. It is possible to accept epistemic charity and reject the agreement disposition. In such a case one would acknowledge that others reasonably can disagree with one's views, but one would not believe that this epistemological fact gives one any moral reason to value agreement over correctness (as one perceives it).

This clarification of the norm of reasonableness allows us to see more clearly how Rawls can provide a standard for distinguishing morally appropriate from inappropriate toleration. Two classes of people can be identified as unreasonable: those who reject the agreement disposition and those who are not epistemically charitable.[23] Of these two classes only those in the former pose a clear problem for Rawls' political conception of justice. Those who are not epistemically charitable, but accept the agreement disposition, do not threaten the project of securing a stable overlapping consensus. But those who reject the agreement disposition – for whatever reason – cannot be accommodated within Rawls' framework. They will need to be portrayed as "unreasonable"; and "like war and disease" they will need to be contained "so that they do not overturn political justice."[24]

Bringing these points together, a reasonably clear picture of the democratic idea of toleration comes into view. This understanding of toleration commits one to a norm of reasonableness which, in turn, commits one to a political conception of justice. Those who reject the political conception of justice contradict the norm of reasonableness and need not be tolerated.[25]

In this way, the democratic idea of toleration poses a double threat to the model citizen. First, it shows that she has moral reasons not to promote her controversial views; namely, she has moral reasons to accept the principles of restraint. Second, it shows that she is a member of the

---

[23] Sometimes Rawls identifies the unreasonable with those whose views require the rejection of democratic freedoms. (See ibid. pp. 64–65). However, according to the above criteria, this would constitute only a subclass of the larger class of unreasonable views. So it can be put to one side.

[24] Ibid. p. 64.

[25] This sounds stronger than it is. To say that the "unreasonable" need not be tolerated is not to say that they should be persecuted. Rawls does not tell us how he would "contain" the unreasonable. Presumably, this is a question for non-ideal theory.

class of persons whose views do not warrant respect. To the extent that she does not accept the principles of restraint, she is unreasonable.

It is now time to assess whether either threat carries force.

The case against democratic toleration

Over the next three sections I will argue that the argument from democratic toleration does not give the model citizen reason to show restraint because it rests on a flawed account of toleration. It should be borne in mind that this does not imply that the model citizen could not value toleration. As we have seen, she could accept the two justifications sketched above (see p. 69).

In developing the argument against Rawls' understanding of toleration, the first task is to pinpoint more precisely what is distinctive about it. We need to isolate cases where it would be morally inappropriate to tolerate conduct according to the pluralist and cost-based justifications of toleration, but morally appropriate according to the democratic idea of toleration. In this way, we can identify the distinctive moral claim behind the democratic idea of toleration.

I start, then, by distinguishing some cases.

(1) A society uses political power to impose ideals derived from, or constitutive of, a controversial philosophical doctrine. The forcible imposition of these ideals prevents some citizens from realizing the ideals derived from, or constitutive of, their philosophical doctrines.[26]

(2) A society uses political power to support or promote ideals derived from, or constitutive of, a controversial philosophical doctrine. But this political action does not prevent anyone, although it may advantage some and disadvantage others, from realizing the ideals derived from, or constitutive of, his or her philosophical doctrine.[27]

(3) A society uses political power to prevent citizens from performing certain actions (or from refraining from performing them) and it justifies this with a controversial philosophical conception of justice.[28]

Distinguishing these cases serves two purposes. First, it allows us to

---

[26] Examples include the legal persecution of religious sects, the legal repression of homosexuality and (perhaps) the criminalization of recreational drugs.

[27] Examples include the public establishment of a national church and legal disqualifications for benefits of those who hold disfavored doctrines (e.g. Catholics not being permitted to run for public office).

[28] Examples include legislation that makes vegetarianism mandatory, a constitutional amendment against abortion and a legal rule that imposes criminal sanctions on anyone who is caught helping others to commit suicide.

contrast political morality in general with justice in particular. Cases (1) and (2) refer to exercises of political power that are not necessarily motivated by considerations of justice. The imposition of ideals derived from a controversial philosophical doctrine may be consistent with justice, but not required by it.[29] Second, it allows us to focus our analysis more precisely. As we shall see, the model citizen can agree with Rawls about issues that fall under cases (1) and (2). It is case (3) where she must take a stand.

Rawls does not distinguish these three cases. But his rhetoric leads one to believe that when he is discussing toleration he has cases like case (1) foremost in mind. He writes that "it is unreasonable for us to use political power, should we possess it, or share it with others, to repress comprehensive views that are not unreasonable."[30] And, again, he states "it is unreasonable or worse to want to use the sanctions of state power to correct, or to punish, those who disagree with us."[31] Talk of repression and punishment strongly suggests case (1) political action.

But in cases like these there are many arguments, other than ones that rely on Rawls' democratic idea of toleration, that show that it would be wrong to use political power to impose the ideals of one philosophical doctrine. To take just one: If value pluralism is true, there are many sound ideals and values. This implies that citizens can lead good lives in many different ways. When political power is used to prevent them from doing so, it invades their autonomy.

There is no reason to think that (what I am calling) the model citizen could not recognize the value of allowing people to lead sound autonomous lives. Nor is there any reason to depict her as a value monist or as one who believes there is only one reasonable conception of the good life. She, like Rawls, could reject the type of repression illustrated by case (1).[32]

However, such a citizen might believe that some ways of life are

---

[29] This is true if we make the not uncommon assumption that justice is a subdomain of the larger domain of political morality.

[30] J. Rawls, *Political Liberalism*, p. 61.   [31] Ibid. p. 138.

[32] Rawls has a tendency to overlook the possibility that one can be both a proponent of a comprehensive political morality and a value pluralist. For instance, he writes that one of the "deepest distinctions between conceptions of justice is between those that allow for a plurality of reasonable though opposing comprehensive doctrines each with its own conception of the good, and those that hold that there is but one such conception to be recognized by all citizens who are fully reasonable and rational." He then associates the latter view with the dominant tradition of political philosophy, which, he claims, extends from Plato and Aristotle through the classical utilitarians to the recent forms of ethical liberalism expressed by Joseph Raz and Ronald Dworkin (ibid. pp. 134–35, 135 n1). Whatever might be said about Plato and Aristotle or the classical utilitarians, it is surely incorrect to suggest that Raz and Dworkin believe that there is but one conception of the good life to be recognized by all fully reasonable people.

degrading. After all, acceptance of value pluralism does not entail an "anything goes" attitude. Think, for instance, of prostitution. Here the model citizen might consider using political power to repress a way of life. But he or she will also take into account the costs of such repression. As we saw in our discussion of the cost-based justification of toleration, it does not follow that if some way of life is objectively degrading, it is correct or permissible to use political force to repress it. The model citizen may conclude that repression would cause more harm than good in all such cases.[33] So even if we are dealing with cases in which a way of life is degrading or unsound, there may be no difference between Rawls' view and the view of the model citizen.[34]

This still leaves case (2) and case (3). In case (2) political power is used to support or promote ideals. But by stipulation no one is prevented from pursuing ideals derivative from, or constitutive of, his or her philosophical views. Still, it can be argued that any such political action would insult some citizens. They would experience it as an imposition, even if it did not prevent them from pursuing and realizing their own ideals. It can be further argued that insulting others in this way constitutes a form of intolerance.

In the abstract this argument is difficult to evaluate. It surely has some force in some contexts. But to know how much force it has we need to know the details of the particular case at hand. If political power is used to promote ideals that are sound, but widely disputed, such action might do more harm than good. Citizens might think that the political action is not simply an endorsement of certain ideals, but also an indirect condemnation of others. This perception, whether accurate or not, might cause harm to those citizens by injuring their self-respect. But, even if this is granted and even if we assign a high value to self-respect, there is no reason to think that all instances of case (2) would have these consequences. It may be perfectly understood by all citizens that when political power is used to promote some ideals it is not condemning others. Consider, for example, the political support for opera. To be sure, citizens often think that this is not the best way to spend public money. But hardly anyone thinks that such action, in and of itself, signals a condemnation of other pursuits.

It is important to see that Rawls need not disagree. The public funding

---

[33] For the model citizen the question of when it is correct or permissible to repress a degrading way of life is obviously an important one. For relevant discussion, see J. Raz, *The Morality of Freedom*, pp. 412–20, and R. George, *Making Men Moral*, pp. 161–88.

[34] Perhaps the model citizen should disagree with Rawls on some of these cases. But there is no reason why he *must*; and here our task is to find a case where the model citizen and Rawls must part ways over the value of toleration.

of opera, he could maintain, is not a constitutional essential or a basic question of justice. Therefore, the principles of restraint do not apply to it. As I noted earlier, this response is not entirely satisfactory since Rawls gives no developed account of how one draws the distinction between matters of basic justice and other non-basic political matters. But, assuming the distinction can be drawn, the response is coherent enough. It is not easy, then, to think of examples that fall under case (1) or case (2) that unambiguously distinguish Rawls' view from that of the model citizen. So we do well to turn to case (3), where the contrast is more apparent. Here, by stipulation, we are dealing with matters of justice. For example, let us imagine a society that prohibits its citizens from performing some action[35] and justifies this prohibition by reference to a controversial conception of justice. Roughly, we can divide the citizens in this society into three groups: those who accept the conception of justice and therefore accept the prohibition; those who do not accept the conception of justice, but do not reject the prohibition either because their own conception of justice does not contradict it or has nothing to say about it; and those who reject the conception of justice and reject the prohibition.

Clearly, the first group is not treated intolerantly or shown disrespect by the political enforcement of this prohibition. It is their favored conception of justice that is being enforced. Nor does the second group have a complaint. They do not regard the prohibition as an unreasonable imposition. Its enforcement is consistent with their views about justice. Only the third group, those who reject the prohibition and the conception of justice that it is based on, could plausibly be said to have a legitimate grievance.

The grievance is that others have imposed a prohibition on them that they can reasonably reject. Rawls is committed to giving this grievance a great deal of weight. It is this commitment that lies at the heart of the democratic idea of toleration. If we can show that it is misguided, we can show that the democratic idea of toleration is flawed. To assess the democratic idea of toleration, then, we need to put the focus on case (3) examples.

Does the third group, then, have a genuine grievance? Recall that they are the ones who reject the prohibition and the conception of justice that it is based on. Let us simplify matters even further. Consider a case of interaction between two groups of people, the Reds and the Greens. Suppose the Reds compel the Greens to act in accordance with principles

---

[35] Here one should substitute a favorite example for the action that is prohibited – abortion, euthanasia, the slaughter of animals, etc.

of justice that the Greens can reasonably reject. In principle there are many possible states of affairs that could fit this description.

(1) The Reds' principles are sound and the Reds have good reasons for believing they are sound.
(2) The Reds' principles are sound, but the Reds are not justified in believing they are sound.
(3) The Reds' principles are not sound, but the Reds are justified in believing they are sound.
(4) The Reds' principles are not sound and the Reds are not justified in believing they are sound.
(5) The Reds' principles are no more sound than the Greens' principles.

The democratic idea of toleration maintains that it is wrong to compel people to comply with principles of justice that they could reasonably reject. To show that this understanding of toleration is flawed we need only show that in *one* of these states of affairs the Greens are not treated wrongly. I shall argue that in (1), and possibly in (5) as well, this is the case.

But before advancing this argument, it is necessary to confront an initial objection. It might be said that the way that I have set up this example cooks the case against the democratic idea of toleration, for Rawls might insist that the value of toleration has so much moral weight that it is impossible for sound principles of justice to diverge from the principles of justice that all persons could reasonably accept.[36] If this were so, states of affairs (1) and (2) would not be real possibilities.

For this to be true, toleration must be construed to be lexically prior to all other values in the political domain. To bring this out more clearly, it will be helpful to distinguish two types of considerations relevant to the determination of sound principles of justice. The first type concerns substantive answers to political problems: Should abortion be legally protected? Is the best distribution of wealth the one specified by the difference principle? Should capital punishment be abolished? etc. Here we assume that there are correct answers to these questions (or at least a range of answers that are equally correct); and we further assume that if the correct answers to these questions are not accepted by all people, or all reasonable people, this fact does not impugn their correctness. Call these *content considerations*. The second type of consideration concerns the civic bonds that obtain between citizens. A number of different considerations might be brought under this rubric; but, for now, let us

---

[36] I use the phrases "could reasonably accept" and "could not reasonably reject" interchangeably. There are subtle differences between them. For discussion, see T. Nagel, *Equality and Partiality*, pp. 33–40. But nothing in this chapter turns on these differences.

focus on just one; namely, the civic bond that obtains when the political order is regulated by principles that all citizens reasonably accept. Call this the *civility consideration*.

This distinction allows us to clarify the objection in question. For states of affairs (1) and (2) to be illusory it must be true that the civility consideration always takes precedence over content considerations. In other words, if the civility consideration has priority over all other considerations, then it is not possible for us to ask the question we want to ask; namely: Is it permissible for the Reds to impose sound principles on the Greens even though the Greens could reasonably reject them? It would not be possible to ask this question because if the Greens could reasonably reject the principles, by stipulation, they would not be sound. But notice that this is just another way of saying that the correct principles of justice simply are the principles that no one could reasonably reject; and it is precisely this claim that we are seeking to evaluate. Seen in this light, the objection begs the crucial question.

Still, we should not beg the question in the opposite direction. Let us say, then, that in state of affairs (1)–(5) when it is claimed that the principles of justice are sound this refers only to content considerations.[37] Thus, states of affairs (1) and (2) are real possibilities; but whether or not they remain real possibilities once the civility consideration is brought into the picture is left an open matter. Our discussion, then, can be understood as an inquiry into the question of whether Rawls' democratic idea of toleration provides reasons for thinking that the civility consideration always takes precedence over content considerations in the determination of sound principles of justice.

With this clarification in place, return now to the five states of affairs. Let us start with the easiest one. In (4) there is no trouble explaining why the Greens have a genuine complaint. The principles they are being forced to comply with are unsound principles. Moreover, the Reds do not even have good grounds for imposing them. The Greens clearly are treated wrongly.

In (3) the Greens also have a genuine complaint. They are being forced to comply with unsound principles. The fact that the Reds are justified in believing they are sound does not change the fact that the Reds are making the Greens comply with unsound principles. We should, of course, temper our judgment of the Reds. They act wrongly; but their wrongdoing is blameless, for they have good reasons for thinking their principles are sound.

---

[37] In other words, the principles would be sound if content considerations were the only relevant considerations.

In (2) matters are more tricky. You might think the Greens have no complaint because the principles being enforced are sound and that is all that matters. But this judgment is too quick. A strong case can be made that the Reds act wrongly because it is wrong to enforce principles of justice on others if one does not have good grounds for believing the principles are sound. In this situation the Reds' principles are sound, but they are sound by sheer good fortune. And it is wrong to rely on good fortune when enforcing principles of justice on others.[38] And if the Reds act wrongly, we can infer that the Greens have a genuine complaint.

This brings us to (5). Here we drop the assumption that there is a uniquely correct set of principles of justice. Instead, we assume there is a plurality of such sets among which reason cannot adjudicate. Thus, it makes sense to say that from the standpoint of reason the Reds' principles are as sound as the Greens'. Do the Greens, then, have a valid complaint against the Reds? The short answer is "no." So long as the principles being enforced fall within the range of principles that are sound (or not unsound) no one is treated unjustly or unfairly. It might be objected that principles that are equally sound would, nonetheless, have differential effects on people's lives and that people could come to know this. This, in turn, might give rise to a political conflict over justice in which both sides to the conflict act in accord with reason (or at least not against reason).

Does this possibility threaten the claim that if either one of these principles is enforced no one has a complaint? The short answer is still "no." Given the assumptions we have made, no injustice would be done if either side imposed their principles on the other side. This conflict over justice would resemble other political conflicts where justice is not at stake and where reason has nothing to say, e.g. whether a political society should build a public park or a football stadium with public money. In these cases what is important from the standpoint of political morality is not what is decided, but how it is decided. Thus, the complete answer to the question of whether the Greens have a complaint in (5)

---

[38] You might object: "If we believe that it is wrong to rely on good fortune when imposing principles of justice, then it is not enough for the Reds to have good reasons for imposing their sound principles of justice. To act rightly, they would need to *know* that their principles were sound. This is true because we could imagine a Gettier case example where the Reds impose sound views and have good reasons for believing their views are sound; but, as it turns out, their good reasons have nothing to do with the soundness of their views. In such a case the Reds would be right by good fortune." My reply is: "Even if the Reds' principles were right by good fortune, it would not follow that the Reds were relying on good fortune to be right. On my view, people do not act wrongly if they rely on good reasons in enforcing principles on others, but are right by good fortune." This raises some perplexing questions. I say something about them in the final section of this chapter.

would require us to consider the further issue of how it is that the Reds got into a position to impose authoritatively their principles on the Greens. This issue raises a host of further questions that need not detain us here.[39] The important point is that there is no reason to think that in (5) the Reds necessarily act wrongly in enforcing their principles. However, we do not need to pursue this point, since we need only one case to refute the democratic idea of toleration; and in (1) matters are even clearer than in (5).

Turn, then, to state of affairs (1). If the Reds' principles are correct and if the Reds are justified in believing they are correct, then it is hard to see how the Greens could have a legitimate grievance. The Greens might be reasonable people. They might have reasons for rejecting the principles. But it is hard to see how they could have a legitimate grievance. If they came to know that they were mistaken, they would cease to believe that they had a grievance. Their belief that they have a grievance is based on a false belief. Normally, this is enough to show that a person does not have a grievance.[40] Virtually no one claims that it is right to commit injustice if one reasonably thinks that what one is doing is just, even though, in fact, it is not. But this is the gravamen of the claim the Greens must establish in (1) if we are to conclude they have a genuine grievance.

This shifts the burden of proof on to the defender of the democratic idea of toleration. We need a reason for believing that the Greens have a real grievance in (1). If no compelling reason can be given, then the claim that people are treated wrongly or inappropriately if they are forced to comply with principles of justice that they could reasonably reject, is refuted. Rawls does not advance an argument that could rebut the presumption that the Greens do not have a grievance in states of affairs like (1).[41] I will consider, then, some further arguments that he does not make, but which, it might be thought, are available to him.

---

[39] The question of how it is that the Reds got into a position to impose authoritatively their principles on the Greens is one that also has relevance for assessments of states of affairs (1)–(4). Some suggestions as to what we should do when reason provides no guidance are discussed (in a more general context) by J. Elster in *Solomonic Judgments*, pp. 36–122.

[40] Normally, but not always. It is possible for someone to (a) believe he has a legitimate grievance, (b) believe this because he has a false belief about justice, but (c) still have a legitimate grievance. This is possible because someone might have a legitimate grievance for reasons he is unaware of. In such a case the person would correctly believe he has a legitimate grievance even though his reasons for thinking this were bad ones. In the case that we are considering, however, this possibility can be put to one side.

[41] In a sense this is not entirely fair to Rawls. He does have an argument which appeals to the values of public reason. But since I discuss this argument in detail in the next chapter, I do not discuss it here.

Supplementary arguments

Some who are sympathetic to the democratic idea of toleration have suggested that it is wrong to force people to comply with principles of justice that they could reasonably reject because to do so is to violate a norm of respect. It is to treat the people in question as mere means and not as ends in themselves. Along these lines, Thomas Nagel explicitly invokes the Kantian maxim as a justification for the view that "if you force someone to serve an end that he cannot be given adequate reason to share, you are treating him as a mere means – even if the end is his own good, as you see it but he doesn't."[42] Assuming that not being able to give the person "an adequate reason" just amounts to treating him or her in a way that he or she could reasonably reject, it would follow that in a state of affairs like (1), if the Reds force the Greens to adhere to sound principles of justice, the Reds would disregard the Greens' reasonable opposition to those principles. In so doing, they would treat the Greens as mere means and not as ends in themselves.

Let it be granted that it is wrong to treat others as mere means. Does Nagel give us any reason to interpret the Kantian maxim in this way? His argument draws inspiration from Kant's second formulation of the categorical imperative, but it rests on a peculiar reading of that formulation. Kant holds that the correct principles of justice specify the conditions under which "the freedom of the will of each can coexist with the freedom of everyone in accordance with a universal law."[43] For our purposes, the substance of this claim is less important than Kant's belief that these principles are objective and determinate. For Kant, the correct distribution of freedom does not depend on the will or the beliefs of people. It is a matter of objective practical reason. Thus, whether the Reds treat the Greens as mere means cannot, on Kant's view, depend on the beliefs, reasonable or not, of the Reds and the Greens. It must depend on the correctness of the principles that are being enforced.[44] Since in (1), by stipulation, the Reds enforce sound principles of justice, it follows that the Reds do not treat the Greens as mere means.

Of course this does not show that Nagel's argument is wrong. It just suggests that his appeal to Kant does no work. However, it does arouse the suspicion that Nagel has not given us an argument at all. The appeal to Kantian respect is a place holder for an argument that remains to be made. One could, after all, assume that the correct principles of justice are just those principles that all persons could reasonably accept (e.g. one

---

[42] See T. Nagel, *Equality and Partiality*, p. 159.
[43] I. Kant, *The Metaphysical Elements of Justice*, p. 35.
[44] See M. Gregor, *Laws of Freedom*.

could assume that the civility consideration always takes precedence over content considerations) and then one could interpret the Kantian norm of equal respect in a way that would show that the Reds treat the Greens wrongly. But this would just beg the question. The Kantian norm of equal respect would provide no independent support for the conclusion. What this suggests is that we need a moral argument to give content to the Kantian norm. Without such an argument, the Kantian norm of equal respect is an empty vessel.[45]

Nagel's treatment of Kantian respect is too brief.[46] But others who share his sympathy for the democratic idea of toleration have provided more thorough analyses. To give this argument a fair hearing we need to examine a more finished account of equal respect. Let us consider, then, the one propounded by Charles Larmore in his book *Patterns of Moral Complexity*.[47] Larmore says a number of interesting things about the moral importance of equal respect. If what he says is right, it may provide Rawls with the argument he needs to rebut the presumption against the democratic idea of toleration established in the last section.

Larmore depicts equal respect as a substantive moral commitment; but it is, he stresses, a "minimalist" moral commitment. This is important, for Larmore is eager to establish that it could be accepted by people with a wide range of comprehensive moral views. Equal respect, understood in this minimalist sense, draws on two thoughts. First, "however much we may disagree with others and repudiate what they stand for, we cannot treat them merely as objects of our will" and second that we owe others "an explanation for those actions of ours that affect them."[48] Taken on their own, these thoughts are hardly compelling. The first thought resembles Nagel's appeal to the Kantian maxim. At best, it is a place holder for an argument that remains to be made. The second thought does not do much work either. Even if we accept that we owe others an

---

[45] This basic point has been well put by W. Frankena in his discussion of the principle of respect for persons: "The principle that we are to respect persons . . . says only that there are morally right and wrong, good and bad, ways of treating or relating to persons, as such for their own sakes. *It does not tell us which ways of treating or relating to them are right or wrong, good or bad.*" "The Ethics of Respect for Persons," p. 157 (emphasis added).

[46] Nagel advanced a different line of argument in his article "Moral Conflict and Political Legitimacy." I do not discuss the argument of this article here because it has been forcefully criticized by others and Nagel himself has conceded that it does not work. For the concession see *Equality and Partiality*, p. 163. For criticism see J. Raz, "Facing Diversity: The Case of Epistemic Abstinence."

[47] See also Larmore's subsequent article "Political Liberalism." Larmore writes that he is "convinced that the norm of equal respect lies at the basis of Rawls's own theory of justice." (p. 354) This is in line with my view that Rawls needs an argument to rebut the presumption against the democratic idea of toleration.

[48] C. Larmore, *Patterns of Moral Complexity*, p. 62.

explanation (i.e. a justification) for our conduct that affects them in some significant way, this does not give us a reason to accept the democratic idea of toleration.

Larmore, however, has more to say on the matter. He presents an interpretation of these two thoughts that gives them significantly more critical force. The crux of his interpretation rests on a distinction between respecting the beliefs of people and respecting people as such. Larmore argues that when we respect the beliefs of other people we recognize that their beliefs are justified given their epistemic situation. This recognition does not require us to think that their beliefs are true. We may know that they are false. But if we respect their beliefs, we believe that we would believe them if we were in the other people's shoes. Now it is true that we do respect the beliefs (in Larmore's sense) of some people with whom we disagree. We maintain that they are making a mistake, but that it is a mistake that they are justified in making. They are, we say, epistemically blameless. Others with whom we disagree we hold to be epistemically blameworthy. We think that they are not only mistaken, but unjustifiably mistaken.

This is all true, but it is not clear why it is morally significant. When deciding how we should treat others, why should it matter whether we respect their beliefs or not? Larmore is fully aware that this question needs an answer. He makes his case not by appealing to respect for beliefs, but respect for people as such. Nevertheless, he maintains that there is an important connection between respecting people and respecting their beliefs.

The connection is established by the recognition that others have "the capacity" for "coherently developing beliefs from within their own perspective."[49] That is, we can recognize that others have the capacity to hold beliefs that we could respect. And Larmore contends that the possession of this capacity is of great moral significance. The fact that others have it grounds an obligation on our part "to treat [them] in a certain way."[50] We must, Larmore tells us, treat others "acceptingly," which means that we must not force them to comply with controversial ideals and values. When we do not treat them "acceptingly," we run roughshod over their capacity for working out their own view of the world and their own conception of a rewarding life. So equal respect amounts to respect for the capacity of people to form beliefs that we could respect, even if we do not, in fact, think their beliefs are true.

Let us look more carefully at this more nuanced characterization of equal respect to see if it can provide support for Rawls' democratic idea

---

[49] Ibid. p. 64.   [50] Ibid.

of toleration. Larmore's argument brings to light an interesting distinction. When the Reds force the Greens to comply with sound principles of justice two different things might be occurring: the Greens in rejecting the principles may be acting in a manner that is epistemically justified or they may be acting in a manner that is *not* epistemically justified. It might seem that Larmore's argument that equal respect gives us reason not to impose controversial views on others has considerably more force in the latter case than in the former. For when people are not only wrong, but also capable of understanding that they are wrong from within their own epistemic situation, then it is hard to see how they are not treated with respect when they are made to comply with requirements that they themselves could and ought to accept.

However, the distinction calls for more explanation. How, it may be asked, is it possible for the Greens to be epistemically justified in rejecting principles that are sound and known to be sound by the Reds? The answer is that the Greens, like everyone else, base their beliefs about political morality (as well as on other matters) on the reasons and evidence available to them. But this stock of evidence and reasons is never complete. Moreover, it is not reasonable to expect the Greens or anyone else to consider all the relevant evidence and all the relevant reasons that bear on an issue before making a reasoned judgment. People's time is limited. They can gather only so much evidence and deliberate only for so long. Given this, it is possible for them to be epistemically justified in believing false things that others know to be false or in believing things to be false that others know to be true.[51]

Does this possibility matter when one is considering the justification of enforcing controversial principles of justice? The first thing to say is that it should not be exaggerated. We often disagree with others about a moral issue and when we do we do not usually think "Well, they are justified in believing what they believe from their perspective." In many cases we believe our disputants are not only mistaken, but epistemically blameworthy. This suggests that Larmore's argument has a limited reach. Still, we should concede the possibility that at least in some cases those who disagree with us are epistemically blameless. And this raises a tough question, what should be done in such cases?

The key to answering the question correctly is to see all the sides to the problem. Those, like Larmore, who put great stress on the value of equal respect fail to give due weight to the other relevant considerations. It needs to be kept in mind that in the example that we are considering the Reds have sound views. If they do not enforce these views, injustice will

---

[51] See N. Rescher, *Pluralism*, pp. 64–126.

result. To help focus one's judgments it is helpful to consider some concrete moral issue. Suppose abortion in the standard case is morally impermissible. The Reds know this; but they cannot convince the Greens.[52] Moreover, the Greens, given their epistemic situation, are justified in rejecting this view. The Reds now have a choice. They can either enforce their view and thus fail to treat the Greens with equal respect (in Larmore's sense) or they can step back from their view and thus countenance morally impermissible actions. Put in these terms, it is clear that either choice brings moral costs. For the Reds to make a sound judgment they must decide which costs are more grave.

This fits nicely with the cost-based justification for toleration discussed above (see p. 69). In some cases it may turn out that the correct thing for one to do is to step back from one's considered views in order to treat others with equal respect (in Larmore's sense). But it is difficult to believe that this will always be the case, no matter what issues are on the table; and this is what we must believe if we are to conclude that the Reds necessarily act wrongly in (1). If this is right, the appeal to equal respect does not rescue Rawls' democratic idea of toleration. That conception of toleration still looks like a flawed one.

Consider a second argument that might be brought forward to help Rawls. Some have suggested that if a person sincerely believes that he has a grievance, then he does, in fact, have a grievance.[53] On this view, the mere 'experience' of being treated unjustly itself constitutes actually being treated unjustly. Put this crudely, the argument is surely not plausible. It has the strongly counter-intuitive consequence that the slave owner is treated unjustly by the abolition of slavery if he sincerely believes that he is wronged by such action. But the argument can be made to look more credible if it is said that not just any perceived grievance constitutes mistreatment, but only *reasonably perceived grievances*. Let us assume, then, that there is some principled way to delimit the class of reasonably perceived grievances from the more general class of perceived grievances.

Thus amended, the argument might have force; and it might be able to support the claim that the Greens have a legitimate grievance in (1). To see whether it really can do this, we need to be clearer about how it is that the experience of injustice could ever constitute a real injustice, for this claim looks paradoxical. Surely, we need to hold on to the distinction

---

[52] To make the example tighter, suppose that for the Reds to make their case they must appeal to a controversial moral doctrine that the Greens reject, but that the Greens can make their case without appeal to any controversial doctrine.

[53] Such a suggestion is implicit in J. Donald Moon's *Constructing Community*. Moon repeatedly asserts that liberalism must be sensitive to the "experience" of injustice.

between the perception of injustice and the reality of injustice. But how can we do this and, at the same time, maintain that when people reasonably believe they are being treated unjustly they, in fact, are being treated unjustly, even if their reasonable beliefs are false?

An answer to this puzzling question is suggested by Ronald Dworkin. In describing his conception of liberal political morality he writes that "government must treat people as equals in the following sense. It must impose no sacrifice or constraint on any citizen in virtue of an argument that the citizen could not accept without abandoning his sense of his equal worth."[54] What is noteworthy about this claim is that it does not refer to the soundness of the government action in question. Even if a government has good reason to impose a sacrifice or constraint on its citizens, if they could not accept this action without losing their sense of equal worth, then the government should not undertake the action. If it did undertake the action, then the citizens would be treated unjustly, not because the action was wrong, but because the citizens believed that it was wrong and the government action conjoined with this false belief would undermine their sense of equal worth. Thus, if Dworkin's claim is correct, this would show how it is possible for the experience of unjust treatment to be a sufficient constitutive condition of actual unjust treatment.

However, Dworkin's claim, while it contains a genuine insight, is much too strong. The genuine insight is that governments have an obligation to consider how their actions will affect the well-being of their subjects. Given that a sense of self-worth is an important element of psychological well-being, governments have an obligation to consider how their actions will affect the sense of self-worth of their subjects. But this insight is easily exaggerated; and Dworkin falls prey to the exaggeration. To see this we need to introduce a second claim that many have thought to be a very important one for liberal political morality. This is the claim that the fact that people are distressed or offended because they believe that some action of some person or group of persons is wrong is not itself a reason for prohibiting that action. Let us call this the *Millian claim*. It is expressed when Mill contends that if a society consisted of a majority of Muslims who wished to prohibit the eating of pork because they believed that eating pork was contrary to divine law, then the mere fact that they held this belief would not count as a reason for the prohibition.[55]

Without too much distortion, Mill's example can be modified. Suppose the Muslims claim that if people are permitted to eat pork in their society

[54] R. Dworkin, "Why Liberals Should Care about Equality," p. 205.
[55] J. S. Mill, *On Liberty*, p. 83.

this will undermine their sense of self-worth. They will interpret it as a public rebuke of their most cherished beliefs. And suppose that we know that the Muslims are sincere in claiming this. The Millian claim still tells us to discount this. We should not give weight to "harms" which are only harms because people hold false beliefs. It should now be clear that the Millian claim and Dworkin's claim can conflict. Dworkin believes that his claim provides support for "the traditional liberal principle that government should not enforce private morality;"[56] but it does no such thing. Probably he is led to believe this because he does not consider the possibility that government inaction, as well as action, can impose sacrifices on people in such a way that it wounds their sense of self-worth. This is exactly what occurs in the (modified) Millian example about the Muslims and the restriction on eating pork.

The crucial difference, then, between the Millian claim and Dworkin's claim is that the former, but not the latter, denies that harms caused (or partly caused) by the false beliefs of those who suffer them should matter from the standpoint of political morality. Mill believed that in order for A to harm B in a morally relevant sense, A must not only set back B's interests; but do so wrongfully.[57] In contrast, Dworkin puts the emphasis on what B could or could not accept, given B's need to have a sense of self-worth; and, for all we know, B might have a number of false beliefs that are bound up with his sense of self-worth.

Thus the question that Dworkin's claim raises is how important it is to respect a person's sense of self-worth, if this sense of self-worth is based on false beliefs *and* if respecting it would require us to countenance injustice. To get a better handle on this question I will introduce some more terminology. Let us distinguish a *tangible harm* from a *symbolic harm*. A tangible harm occurs when a person's interests are set back – without injury to his sense of self-worth – by the actions of others that are objectively wrong. A symbolic harm occurs when a person's sense of self-worth is wounded by the actions of others because he holds a set of beliefs that confer meaning on these actions. And let us call this set of beliefs *symbolizing beliefs*.

Working with these distinctions, we can further distinguish *genuine symbolic harms* from *suspect symbolic harms*. A genuine symbolic harm is a symbolic harm that results when a person's symbolizing beliefs are true or apt and a suspect symbolic harm is one that results when a person's symbolizing beliefs are false or inapt. One final distinction is helpful. We can distinguish *irresistible* from *resistible* symbolic beliefs. Irresistible

---

[56] R. Dworkin, "Why Liberals Should Care about Equality," p. 206.
[57] For detailed discussion, see J. Feinberg, *Harm to Self*, pp. 105–25.

symbolic beliefs are symbolic beliefs that a person cannot abandon without giving up his deep and settled convictions about what is important to him, whereas resistible symbolic beliefs can be revised or abandoned without great cost. This last distinction is not particularly sharp. The resistibility of beliefs is a matter of degree.

Now return to the question Dworkin's claim raises. In deciding how important it is to respect people's sense of self-worth it ought to be clear that it matters both what type of harms are at stake in particular cases and how resistible people's symbolic beliefs are with respect to the issues in these cases. A full discussion of these matters would require at least a separate chapter. Rather than take this detour, I will simply, and somewhat dogmatically, propose two guidelines for making judgments in cases of political action that bear on people's sense of self-worth:

(a) Tangible harms should be given more weight than suspect symbolic harms; and
(b) The more irresistible a person's symbolic beliefs are, the more weight should be given to symbolic harms tied to or associated with them.

I believe that these guidelines are correct, but I will not defend them here. The relevant point is that Dworkin does not address these issues; and these issues must be addressed if one is to arrive at sound judgments about political action that affects people's sense of self-worth.[58]

So, as it stands, Dworkin's claim cannot be called on to provide support for Rawls' democratic idea of toleration. It fails to show that reasonably perceived grievances are *ipso facto* genuine grievances. More fundamentally, once all the issues are seen clearly, we have good reason to doubt that the claim could be developed in such a way as to provide that support. For, as I have stressed, the democratic idea of toleration maintains that it is wrong to enforce a conception of justice that could be reasonably rejected by some who are subject to it. This implies that the Reds always act wrongly in enforcing principles that the Greens could reasonably reject. Even if we concede, contra Mill, that the mere fact that the Greens "experience" an injustice constitutes a harm (because it is a symbolic harm), we cannot conclude that the Reds act wrongly in enforcing their conception of justice because to draw that conclusion we would need to consider the harms that result from the Reds' failure to enforce their conception of justice. And it is simply not plausible to maintain that symbolic harms, whether genuine or suspect and whether tied to irresistible or resistible symbolic beliefs, always outweigh all other considerations.

[58] For that matter, Mill does not address these issues either. So the correct position may lie somewhere in between the Millian claim and Dworkin's claim. But, again, these issues require much more discussion.

Neither supplementary argument, then, is of much help to Rawls. Neither argument demonstrates that the civility consideration should always take precedence over content considerations. The upshot of my discussion is that in (1), and possibly in (5) as well, the Reds do not necessarily act wrongly in enforcing sound principles of justice. This refutes the democratic idea of toleration.

A fresh start: skepticism and the problem of self-trust

By now, some readers may be frustrated. They will object that by stipulating that the Reds have sound views I have made it too easy to refute the democratic idea of toleration. They will protest that we do not live in a world of self-evident certainties or unassailable moral truths and that Rawlsian toleration is a fitting response to our epistemological predicament. And they will complain: "We cannot simply assume that the Reds have sound views, for in the real world *that* is precisely what we do not know."

This objection is important. In responding to it we need to distinguish two issues. The first issue is whether the objection is one that Rawls himself can make. Given his other commitments, is it available to him? The second issue is more important. It concerns whether the objection is sound. Irrespective of whether Rawls can make it or not, is the objection a good one? And if it is a good one, could it prop up the democratic idea of toleration?

I start with the first, less important, issue. Up to this point I have said relatively little about Rawls' account of the burdens of judgment. We saw above (p. 73) that the burdens of judgment are the "epistemological elements" in his norm of reasonableness. But we have not considered whether, and to what extent, they are related to his argument for democratic toleration. It is clear that Rawls himself thinks that these burdens of judgment are important. They are, he tells us, "of first significance for a democratic idea of toleration."[59] What is less clear is why he thinks this.

We know that for Rawls the reasonable person accepts the burdens of judgment. He is, as I put it earlier, epistemically charitable. He acknowledges that others can and do reasonably disagree with him about philosophical, moral and religious matters. But it is not obvious how this is supposed to bear on the issue of toleration. Rawls suggests that the person who accepts the burdens of judgment recognizes that his own controversial doctrine "has, and can have, for people

---

[59] J. Rawls, *Political Liberalism*, p. 58.

generally, no special claims on them beyond their own view of its merits."[60] But what does this mean? What does it mean to believe that one's doctrine has a special claim on others? Suppose I reject Darwin's theory of natural selection and you tell me that I ought to accept it. When you tell me this, do you think that the theory has a special claim on me? You do, if you think the theory is true or well confirmed. Its special claim is its truth (or its probability of being true). The fact that I reject it and the fact that I have a different reasonable view should not lead you to say, "Oh, in that case, its truth does not make a claim on you."

Rawls says other puzzling things. For instance, he stresses that when we claim that our beliefs are true, "this is a claim that all equally could make; it is also a claim that cannot be made good by anyone to citizens generally."[61] The first clause in this phrase is unobjectionable. Of course all people can equally make a claim to truth. What matters is how well they substantiate their claims. The second clause is the puzzling one. It trades on an ambiguity about what it means to make good on one's claims. This might mean that one could persuade all reasonable people that one's view is correct or it might mean that one could demonstrate that one's view is correct, even if one could not persuade every reasonable person to accept it.[62] If it means the former, then by stipulation the person who accepts the burdens of judgment must agree that he or she cannot make good on his or her controversial claims, for this is just what an acknowledgment of the burdens of judgment amounts to. But if it means the latter, then one could accept the burdens of judgment and still maintain that one could make good on one's controversial claims. Suppose, however, that one comes to believe that one cannot make good on one's claims in this latter sense. In other words, suppose one comes to believe that one's controversial views cannot be demonstrated (even to oneself) to be correct. In this case it would seem that one should concede that there is no decisive reason why one should accept them rather than some competing view.[63] And once one accepts this, one has given up on

---

[60] Ibid. p. 60.   [61] Ibid. p. 61.

[62] This calls for further comment. Virtually everyone accepts that there is a distinction between good and bad evidence. But this distinction does not line up with the distinction between evidence that is publicly demonstrable and evidence that is not publicly demonstrable. Sometimes we have good evidence that is not publicly demonstrable. So one might be able to demonstrate to one's own satisfaction that one's view is correct even if one could not publicly demonstrate it. It is also worth noting that even if all the evidence for one's view were publicly demonstrable, one might not be able to persuade all reasonable people to accept it. Perhaps others would (wrongly in one's view) assign different weights to different strands of evidence. In this case one could hold that one's view was both publicly demonstrable and subject to reasonable disagreement.

[63] This slides over an interesting complication. I might have good reasons for believing that

the claim that one's views are true. As Hume's Philo put it, once we admit that one doctrine has no more weight than another, the "mind must remain in suspense between them; and it is that very suspense or balance that is the triumph of skepticism."[64] If it is said, moreover, that all controversial views are like this, we have arrived at full-blown skepticism.

This would make sense of Rawls' puzzling remarks, but for the fact of his repeated denial that he is committed to skepticism. His rejection of skepticism is pellucid. Skepticism "must be avoided if an overlapping consensus is to be possible," hence, the account of the burdens of judgment "must not proceed as a skeptical argument."[65] As we saw in the last chapter, Rawls invokes the metaphor of a module to explain the possibility of an overlapping consensus. A political conception of justice, he insists, must be capable of fitting into a wide range of comprehensive doctrines. If a political conception of justice were based on moral skepticism, then it could not perform this essential function. It could be rejected by adherents of many reasonable comprehensive doctrines.

There are, then, two opposing lines of thought in Rawls' work. On the one hand, he argues that the recognition of the burdens of judgment should make us epistemically charitable. We should acknowledge the permanent fact of reasonable disagreement and we should stop claiming any special authority for our views. On the other hand, he argues that an overlapping consensus is not based on skepticism. Those who reject skepticism and believe that their views are true can and should be included within the consensus. These two lines of thought make for a violent mix. Rawls' response to the violence is to insist that for political purposes we do not need the concept of truth. In its place, we can put the concept of reasonableness. This more modest concept can serve as the appropriate standard of correctness.

But this ingenious move does not eliminate the tension. As we have seen, in Rawls' hands the concept of the reasonable has two dimensions: one moral, one epistemological. Rawls smoothes over the tension in his position by shifting back and forth between the two dimensions. He invokes the moral dimension to show why it is wrong to impose

---

some view is true that have nothing to do with its truth. Perhaps believing the view makes my life more meaningful. If so, I might have reasons for believing my view to be true, even if I could not demonstrate that it was true. This raises issues that I cannot address here. It is worth pointing out, however, that once people realize that their reasons for believing a view have nothing to do with its truth, there is psychological pressure for them to stop believing it. For discussion of some of these issues, see Robert Nozick, *The Nature of Rationality*, pp. 64–106.

[64] D. Hume, *Dialogues Concerning Natural Religion*, Part 1, p. 8.
[65] J. Rawls, *Political Liberalism*, pp. 62–63.

controversial principles on others. But, as I argued in the previous two sections, if we assume that the controversial principles are sound and known to be sound, then this is not a plausible view. In response, he appeals to the epistemological dimension to undercut any claim that a person's controversial views are sound and known to be sound. But this appeal, when thought through, leads to skepticism; and skepticism is incompatible with the idea of an overlapping consensus which is at the heart of Rawls' political liberalism.

For these reasons, Rawls' position is fundamentally unstable. He needs skepticism to make his case for democratic toleration; but he cannot endorse skepticism while still holding on to the idea of an overlapping consensus. This does not show that the democratic idea of toleration cannot be defended by an appeal to skepticism. It just shows that Rawls himself is barred from making the defense.

Let me turn, then, to the more important issue of whether skepticism could provide support for the democratic idea of toleration. Putting Rawls to one side, could the skeptic make the case for his understanding of toleration? There is reason to harbor some initial doubt. It is well known that moral skepticism does not cut a clear path to liberal conclusions. When asked "Why should we be tolerant?", the skeptic notoriously has a tough time. Rejecting moral knowledge wholesale, he has nowhere to stand to make his case. This suggests that if the skeptic is to provide support for the democratic idea of toleration, he must not reject moral knowledge wholesale. His skepticism must be discriminating and circumscribed.

Our task is to investigate whether such a circumscribed skepticism is available; and, if it is, whether it could shore up the case for democratic toleration. This task is made easier by the fact that such an argument recently has been advanced by Brian Barry. Barry has considerable sympathy for Rawls' conception of toleration, but believes that it can be shown to be sound only by adopting a certain form of skepticism.[66] This is exactly the type of argument we need to consider. By examining it, we can expose the difficulties inherent in skeptical arguments for toleration.

Crucial to Barry's argument is the sharp distinction he draws between justice and conceptions of the good. As he presents it, justice stands over and above competing conceptions of the good life. Its function is to set constraints on the pursuit of these conceptions.[67] This distinction makes

---

[66] See B. Barry, *Justice as Impartiality*, esp. Part II. Barry does not endorse all the restrictions Rawls includes in the democratic idea of toleration. He does not accept what Rawls calls the limits of public reason. In my terminology, he accepts the second, but not the third, principle of restraint.

[67] Ibid. p. 57.

possible a circumscribed skepticism. By separating questions of justice from questions of the good life, it becomes possible to maintain that we can have knowledge of the former, but not of the latter. This is the view Barry defends. It appears to be a more promising view than global moral skepticism because it allows one to make a moral case for the democratic idea of toleration. If we can have knowledge about justice, then skepticism about the good need not undercut the moral case for toleration.

Nevertheless, the plausibility of the distinction between justice and conceptions of the good is open to challenge. Shortly, I will argue that the distinction does not stand up; and if the distinction does not stand up, then Barry's circumscribed skepticism is in trouble. But before addressing this issue, more needs to be said about the type of skepticism that Barry is selling. Skepticism about conceptions of the good implies that we cannot have knowledge about what makes for a good or fulfilling life. More precisely, it implies that when two people reasonably disagree about which conception of the good is more sound, neither can claim to have knowledge on the matter. To know how strong this claim is we must know what it means to have knowledge about conceptions of the good. Here Barry says a number of different things. He suggests that a person does not have knowledge about the good life if:

(1) his view is "not susceptible to rational proof or disproof" (p. 30)
(2) his view "cannot be resolved by rational argument" (p. 30)
(3) his view cannot be justifiably held "with a degree of certainty that warrants its imposition" (p. 169)
(4) his view is "inherently uncertain" (p. 178)

These criteria fix the scope of Barry's skepticism. But it is important to see that each criterion does not necessarily have the same extension. That is, it is possible for someone's views to fall short of knowledge according to criterion (3), but not according to criterion (1). This would occur if the person could rationally prove her view, but could not prove it with sufficient confidence to warrant imposing it on others. Likewise, it is possible for someone's view to fall short of knowledge according to criterion (4), but not according to criterion (3). This would occur if the person could have sufficient rational confidence in her view to impose it on others, but could not demonstrate that it was certain, i.e. not subject to doubt.

Barry does not recognize these possibilities. He moves back and forth between the different criteria as if they were different statements of the same idea. This allows him to argue that if a person does not know for certain that his views are correct, then he is not justified in imposing them on others. But this does not follow if it is true that justifying the imposition of one's views does not require that one know with certainty that the views are correct. The model citizen could concede that she does not know very much with certainty. If asked whether she knows that 12 + 17 equals 29, she could say no, if knowledge requires certainty.[68] But this would not show that she is never justified in imposing her controversial views on others. It would just show that she cannot claim to know that her views are correct.

Perhaps Barry really believes that if one has some doubt about the correctness of one's views, then one is never justified in imposing them on others. But this is a hard claim to substantiate. Suppose the Reds concede that they do not know that their views are infallible. They recognize that it is possible that they are mistaken. If they are told that they therefore should not impose them on the Greens, they will say that while they have some doubt about the wisdom of imposing their views, they have more doubt about the wisdom of not imposing them. The possibility of doubt, they will rightly point out, cuts both ways. Given this, the Reds would have every reason to base their political action on what they take to be the best supported, if not infallible, views. Thus Barry's emphasis on certainty is misplaced. Not only is it not clear that certainty is a condition of knowledge, but even if it were, it would not follow that one should never impose views on others that one does not know to be sound.[69]

As noted above, Barry has other criteria for skepticism. Criteria (1) and (2) refer respectively to whether a view is susceptible to rational proof and whether a view is rationally resolvable. These criteria call for interpretation; but Barry's discussion of them makes it plain that he believes that if we cannot convince all reasonable people that our views are correct, then we must concede that they are not susceptible to rational proof and that they are not rationally resolvable. Since all conceptions of the good fail to meet this demanding standard, Barry can conclude that "nobody should be able to claim a privileged position for any conception of the good on the basis of its correctness or its superiority to others."[70]

---

[68] Does knowledge require certainty? Most philosophers think not. For a good argument that knowledge does not require that one know for certain that one is right, see K. Lehrer, *A Theory of Knowledge*, pp. 176–85. For the opposing view, see P. Unger, "A Defense of Skepticism." Note, however, that even Unger "happily accepts the fact that there is much that many of us correctly and reasonably believe" (p. 198).

[69] It is true that the more uncertain one is that one's views are correct the less weight one ought to place on their enforcement. To invoke my earlier terminology, as uncertainty increases one ought to discount content considerations based on the uncertain views. This suggests that beyond some point of uncertainty one would have reason not to enforce one's controversial views because the content considerations based on them would no longer have sufficient weight to override the civility consideration. But acknowledging this does not defeat the point made in the text.

[70] B. Barry, *Justice as Impartiality*, p. 142.

What should we make of these claims? The best way to make sense of them is to see them as calling into question the normative competence of anyone who proposes to promote controversial views about the good. If a person's views are rejected by some reasonable people, then we can ask that person why he thinks that we should trust his judgment. We can put a number of questions to him: What is so special about him? How does he have privileged access to the truth? If others are reasonable, how come they do not see matters the same way? That person then might try to convince us that he indeed is in a privileged position to know the truth. Perhaps he is privy to some relevant information or perhaps he could convince us that he is wise. But if we were not convinced, then we might conclude that we have no reason to trust his judgment; and if we have no reason to do so, then *he* has no reason to trust his judgment. By a parallel chain of reasoning we could show that everyone who has controversial views should not be trusted. This would lead to the type of skepticism that Barry endorses. In effect, everyone would have to say "I think that I am right; but I have no basis for thinking this, so I will not insist on it."

We can call this the *problem of self-trust*. To justify the imposition of our views on others we not only need to believe that our views are sound, we need to believe that we can trust ourselves to make sound judgments. But in a world of reasonable disagreement, how can we justify this self-trust? There is not an easy answer to this question; and this is what gives Barry's argument whatever persuasive force it has. One response is to point out that if we take normative discussion seriously, then we must trust our judgments. Otherwise, there would be no point in thinking through matters for ourselves. So a certain measure of self-trust appears to be a presupposition of participation in normative inquiry.[71] But this does not take us very far because once we recognize this, we recognize that others are in the same boat. They too must trust themselves for the same reason. How, then, can we convince ourselves that we are better judges than they are?

We might try to convince ourselves that we have certain properties that make for good judgment. For instance, we are well informed, disinterested and reflective. We have skill in reasoning and we have made good judgments in the past. But it is doubtful that we will be so lucky that all people who possess these properties agree with us; and, if some of those who possess these properties do not agree with us, then the problem of self-trust resurfaces. Of course we could stipulate that one of

---

[71] A. Gibbard, *Wise Choices, Apt Feelings*, p. 178.

the properties relevant for good judgment is the property of arriving at sound views (as we understand them) and this would exclude all those who disagree with us.[72] But this gets around the problem of self-trust by assuming that we are the best normative judges and this is exactly what the problem is asking us to demonstrate.

Exasperated, we might try to show that those who disagree with us are influenced by factors irrelevant to good judgment. Perhaps they hold their views because of some personal experience that leads them to discount important considerations. In this way, we could debunk their judgments. But, once again, it is doubtful that we will be so lucky that we can tell a plausible debunking story for every reasonable person who disagrees with us. Most of the time we will be forced to conclude that even if we think our disputants are making a mistake in judgment, we do not know the cause or source of the mistake. And this means that the problem of self-trust will still be with us.

Rather than trying to justify our normative competence, we might try considering the alternatives. We might try to identify those people most likely to make correct judgments about political morality and then let their judgments override ours when they conflict. But even if we could identify a group of such people, the problem of self-trust would not disappear. We would still face the question of how we can know that the group we identify is the right group. Others might identify different groups as those most likely to make sound judgments and then we would need to justify our competence in selecting the right group. The problem of self-trust would bedevil us at this higher order level.

Barry seems to have in mind a different alternative. When reasonable people disagree, they should retreat to common principles that all parties could accept. But this also fails as a response to the problem of self-trust. Each person could ask why they should have confidence in the common principles. Is it more likely that common principles will be correct than the values and ideals of any particular person? And is not the whole point of critical thought to discriminate the commonly accepted views that are sound from those that are not? Without answers to these questions, we could have no more confidence in commonly accepted views than we could have in our own more controversial views.[73]

---

[72] Gibbard refers to such a property of judgment as "content-fixed" because it is doctored to specific substantive views. Ibid. p. 195.

[73] Here it is necessary to introduce a distinction. Some views are commonly accepted in the sense that everyone accepts them even though they are led to accept them for different reasons. We can call these views *commonly agreed upon views*. Other views are commonly accepted in the sense that all parties could accept them if they bracketed their controversial views. We can call these *commonly accepted views*. Note that commonly accepted views could be views that no one would accept, but for the need to reach

There are indications that Barry himself does not really believe that commonly accepted principles are on firmer epistemological ground than controversial principles. His argument seems to be that because no one can demonstrate that his or her controversial views are sound the only fair thing to do is to base justice on what everyone could accept.[74] This does not imply any judgment on the soundness of the commonly accepted principles. They should be adopted because this is the fair thing to do, not because they can be shown to be better principles on other grounds. In this way, Barry's circumscribed skepticism is invoked to defeat alternatives. Its purpose is to clear the field of all competitors. In so doing, it does seem to provide support for the democratic idea of toleration. If it is unfair to enforce controversial views, then the model citizen has moral reasons to step back from her considered views and endorse principles that all could reasonably accept.

But there is an obvious problem with this line of thought. The problem of self-trust comes back to haunt those who use it to discredit others. Barry believes that when people disagree about conceptions of the good, fairness demands that they search for commonly accepted principles. But how, it may be asked, does Barry know this? He concedes that his conception of fairness is not shared by everyone. So it would seem that he owes us an account of why we should think that he is a better judge on the matter. And if we have no reason to think that he is better placed to know the truth about fairness than the rest of us, then it would seem that he has no reason to trust his judgments. The problem of self-trust threatens to engulf his view as well.

It is hard to see how Barry could respond to this problem. He might insist that his conception of fairness is not subject to reasonable doubt. Unlike conceptions of the good, it can be known with certainty. But this runs counter to common experience. On any plausible reading, questions about fairness are subject to reasonable disagreement. Barry might respond that this is true because people keep bringing in ideas of the good when they discuss fairness. If we all just put aside our conceptions of the good, he might argue, then we could all rationally agree on what fairness requires. There is reason to doubt that this is true; but even if we grant it, it misses the point. When people argue about the demands of fairness, they are trying to figure out the correct understanding of

---

agreement with others; whereas commonly agreed upon views are accepted by everyone irrespective of the need to reach agreement with others. Commonly agreed upon views may well be on firmer epistemological ground than controversial views. The fact that they are supported by so many different lines of thought adds to their credibility. My claim is that there is no reason to think that commonly accepted, as opposed to commonly agreed upon, views are on firmer epistemological ground.

[74] B. Barry, *Justice as Impartiality*, p. 13.

fairness. It is an open question whether the correct understanding would result from a discussion in which all parties bracketed their controversial ideas about the good.

This reveals what is suspect about the distinction between justice and conceptions of the good. It may be doubted whether any such distinction can withstand rational scrutiny. Once matters are seen clearly, we may have to conclude that ideals of personal conduct and ideals of inter-personal morality are too interwoven to be separated.[75] But even if we could draw the distinction, the question would remain of why we would have good reason to do so. If we think that we could get better judgments about fairness and justice by relying on our considered views about the good, then why would we want to bracket them in thinking about these important matters? It might be said that if we do not bracket our controversial views, then it will be more difficult to reach a consensus on what justice requires; and reaching a consensus on what justice requires is what is most important. But this is just another way of saying the civility consideration should always take precedence over content con-siderations; and this is the view we have found no good reason to accept.

For the proponent of the democratic idea of toleration, then, circum-scribed skepticism is either a dangerous or an ineffective sword to take into battle. It is dangerous because it easily becomes global moral skepticism, thus impaling those who use it – unless it is stipulated that we know that justice is about finding principles that all reasonable people could accept. But, if this stipulation is made, the sword has a very dull blade, for the stipulation simply restates the motivating idea behind Rawls' conception of toleration. If that motivating idea is flawed, as I have argued at length that it is, then the appeal to circumscribed skepticism can provide no support for the democratic idea of toleration.

Justification, truth and luck

This completes the case against the democratic idea of toleration. I have tried to show that this understanding of toleration is flawed; and I have argued that it cannot be successfully rehabilitated by appealing to a principle of respect, the moral importance of self-worth or skepticism about conceptions of the good. This shows that the argument from democratic toleration does not give the model citizen compelling moral reasons to accept the principles of restraint. As I have stressed, this does not imply that the model citizen rejects the value of toleration *tout court*.

---

[75] A number of writers recently have questioned the plausibility of this distinction. See J. Raz, *The Morality of Freedom*, S. Hampshire, *Innocence and Experience*, and M. Walzer, *Thick and Thin*.

We have seen that two alternative justifications are available to her, the pluralist and the cost-based justifications. Both of these justifications, however, are moralized in the sense that one must appeal to comprehensive philosophical, moral or religious ideas to determine their application.

In this final section I want to address one potentially disturbing implication of the position defended here. I have claimed that if people have sound political views and if they have good reasons for believing they are sound, then they do not necessarily act wrongly if they impose them on others. The fact that some may reasonably reject their views does not by itself show that they should not enforce them. But in discussing Larmore's principle of respect I have also conceded that it is possible for two people, given their different epistemic situations, to be justified in holding contradictory views. This concession brings with it the possibility that there may be cases where one group of people is epistemically justified in believing they have sound political views and another group is epistemically justified in believing that these same views are not sound. This presents us with a quandary – in such a situation how could anyone ever know who was right?

The quandary is made worse by the problem of self-trust discussed in the last section. If either group could demonstrate that they were better judges of the matter than the other group, this would resolve the quandary. The judgments of the group with more competence would override the judgments of the group with less competence. But, as we saw, it is very difficult for people to demonstrate that they have normative authority over all those who disagree with them. In the absence of such a demonstration they cannot conclude that their views are correct in virtue of the fact that they are better normative judges. Given this, there seems to be no way out of the quandary.

Does this mean, then, that we should conclude that both groups are in the right? To address this question, it is helpful to consider a similar type of case that arises in the criminal law. This is the case of "putative self-defense."[76] In such a case one party mistakenly, but justifiably, believes that the other party is attacking him. He then attacks the mistakenly identified aggressor who, in turn, attacks him in self-defense. Since both parties are justified in believing that they have been wrongfully attacked, it would seem that both act rightly (or at least permissibly) in attacking the other. It is tempting to conclude that neither party acts wrongly and so both must be in the right. However, this analysis fails to take account of

[76] For discussion of this case, see G. Fletcher, "The Right and the Reasonable," pp. 971–74.

one important feature of the case. One party, but not the other, has made a mistake. By stipulation, the mistake is justifiable; but it is still a mistake.

To take proper account of this feature we need to introduce more distinctions. Let us distinguish *subjective justification* from *objective justification*. A person's action is subjectively justified if it is an action that is required or permissible, given what he or she knows;[77] and an action is objectively justified if it is in accordance with right reason. Let us also say that an action is fully justified, if and only if, it is both subjectively and objectively justified. Thus, in the case of putative self-defense, while the actions of both parties are subjectively justified, the actions of only one party are fully justified.

The same is true in the quandary we are now considering. Both groups have political views that are subjectively justified; but only one group has views that are in accord with right reason.[78] If both groups act on their views, they will be brought into political conflict. We can call such a conflict a *tragic conflict*. It should be clear that a tragic conflict is not a conflict between people who hold different equally correct views on a political issue on which there is no uniquely correct answer. Such a conflict might arise because incommensurable values are at stake. It should also be clear that a tragic conflict is not a conflict in which one or both parties is epistemically blameworthy and, hence, not subjectively justified. These points need stressing so that we are not led to exaggerate the prevalence of tragic conflicts. If such conflicts exist, they are not the stuff of everyday politics.

Still, however rare they may be, tragic conflicts may exist; and we need to come to an understanding of them. One reason why it is appropriate to call these conflicts "tragic" is that even though both sides are subjectively justified, one side will necessarily be acting wrongly. Despite their best efforts to do what is right, they will fail from the standpoint of objective justification. This is of great importance, for objective justification is (in a sense) prior to subjective justification. We care about subjective justification because we care about objective justification. If we make sure that our actions are subjectively justified, there is a better chance that we will act in accord with right reason; and this is what gives subjective justification its point. This helps account for why people feel remorse when they discover that their actions, while subjectively justified,

---

[77] More precisely, subjective justification requires that the person's beliefs are well supported, that he or she is not negligent in gathering relevant information and that he or she makes no errors in reasoning.

[78] It is possible that both groups could be justifiably mistaken and that neither could be in the right. But assume here, for the sake of the example, that the views of one group are objectively justified.

were objectively wrong. In the case of putative self-defense the person who makes the mistake will feel bad upon learning that he attacked an innocent man. He may not blame himself. After all, he was subjectively justified in making the mistake; but he will know that he was in the wrong.

It is my view that these responses are appropriate. People should care not just about acting blamelessly, but also about acting correctly. Whether or not they have acted in accord with right reason should matter to them in assessing their lives.[79] If this is right, then we can glimpse the potentially disturbing implication of the position that I have defended in this chapter. In a tragic conflict it seems to be a matter of luck which side is in the right. If both sides are subjectively justified, and if neither side can demonstrate normative competence over the other, then which side turns out to be correct from the standpoint of objective justification will be determined by factors outside the control of the parties involved. Both sides will have done everything they could do; but only one side will be fully justified and they will be fully justified not because they have been more conscientious, but because they have been lucky.

This is a consequence of the fact that the reasons and evidence that come our way are not entirely subject to our control. We can scrutinize our epistemic belief set. We can do our best to detect bias. We can reason carefully; but, in the end, it is possible for us to be justified in believing things that are false because of bad luck.

According to the view defended here, this bad luck is relevant to the moral assessment of people's lives. This view is disturbing because we want to believe that moral assessment applies only to what an agent is responsible for and we know that things beyond the agent's control are things he or she is not responsible for. But it may be that accepting this disturbing view is the only way to make sense of a large number of our actual moral judgments.[80]

---

[79] It might be said that if a person never discovers he acted wrongly from the standpoint of objective justification, then this could have no bearing on his life. There are reasons to doubt this, however. Consider Parfit's example of the person whose most important concern is that he be a good parent. He works hard to raise his children well; but, unknown to him, he fails miserably. The children all have bad lives in part because of how they were raised. The fact that the parent never finds this out does not negate the fact that one of his most important goals has been a complete failure. His life is worse because of this fact. I think the same can be said about the morally conscientious citizen who cares very much about acting correctly in politics; but acts wrongly from the standpoint of objective justification. Even if he never finds this out, his life is the worse for it. See D. Parfit, *Reasons and Persons*, pp. 494–95 (discussing the "Success Theory" of well-being).

[80] Some reasons for thinking this is the case are provided by Nagel in his paper on moral luck. He considers a range of cases in which luck is relevant to (or seems to be relevant to) the moral assessment of people's lives. See T. Nagel, "Moral Luck." Also see B. Williams' paper with the same title.

This should be kept in mind in evaluating the democratic idea of toleration. We know that it is not easy to arrive at sound judgments in political morality. Many considerations bear on the issues that must be decided; and we know that our judgments are vulnerable at many points. When reasonable people disagree with us, we may come to doubt our views. In this state of doubt the Rawlsian idea of toleration has strong appeal. It seems safer to go with what everyone can accept, rather than insist on one's own controversial, possibly mistaken, views. But, as I have argued, Rawlsian conclusions themselves are not free from doubt. They too can be mistaken. Once we recognize this, the democratic idea of toleration loses much of its appeal.

This chapter has argued that when citizens have sound political views and when they have good reasons for believing they are sound they do not necessarily act wrongly in enforcing them on others. But, of course, no one ever knows for certain that his views are sound. Citizens have a duty to make sure their views are subjectively justified. They should strive for objective justification; but sometimes they will not get it and sometimes when they do not get it, it will not be their fault. Recognizing this should not drive us to moral skepticism. Nor should it lead us to bracket our views for ones that everyone could endorse. But perhaps it should lead us to accept a somewhat less disturbing, but still disturbing, conclusion – in politics, as in other areas of life, the moral character of our lives is at the mercy of forces beyond our control.

5   Public justification and the
         transparency argument

So far the discussion has shown that the pragmatic argument, the argument from political justification and the argument from democratic toleration all fail to justify the bracketing strategy. For the most part, however, the arguments we have considered have centered on the second principle of restraint, the principle that states that citizens should refrain from acting with the intention to promote through political action controversial ideals and values or comprehensive conceptions of justice. But it is arguable that the third principle of restraint is the one that is really fundamental. The third principle of restraint, to recall, requires citizens to refrain from basing their political arguments on reasons or considerations that are controversial or not publicly accessible.

The reason for believing that the third principle is the more fundamental principle of restraint is that we often do not have access to the intentions of political actors. It is possible, as I have pointed out, for citizens to seek to advance controversial ideals without appealing to those ideals in political argument. In other words, it is possible for citizens to satisfy the third principle of restraint while violating the second. Moreover, citizens often have good strategic reasons for complying with the third principle. Effective political argument aims to persuade, and persuasive arguments often need to start from shared beliefs and values. But if all this is true, why should the proponent of restraint especially care whether or not citizens *intend* to advance controversial ideals and values? Is it not enough if they show restraint in their public political discussion?

More to the point, if the second principle of restraint were dropped, an interesting consequence would follow for Rawls' argument. It no longer would be necessary for him to insist on a sharp distinction between a political and a comprehensive conception of justice. Instead, he could shift the focus entirely on to the arguments that are used to present and defend different conceptions of justice. Thus, the same conception of justice could be both political and comprehensive. Its characterization would depend on how it was actually presented and defended.[1]

This suggests that the failure to provide an adequate defense of the second principle of restraint need not be fatal to Rawls' argument in particular or the bracketing strategy in general. The third principle may be the only one that is necessary. More importantly, Rawls has an argument for the third principle of restraint that some may think is more formidable than the other arguments we have so far considered.

The argument in question concerns Rawls' claim that in a well-ordered society "the publicity condition" must be fully satisfied. For reasons that will become apparent, I shall call this the *transparency argument*. It seeks to show that if we accept the publicity condition, then we have good reason to accept the third principle of restraint. Assuming we ought to accept the publicity condition, this would go some distance toward vindicating the bracketing strategy.

I will start by sketching an outline of the transparency argument:

(a) To be well ordered, a modern western society must be regulated by a conception of justice that fully satisfies the publicity condition.
(b) For the publicity condition to be fully satisfied in a modern western society, citizens must accept and act in accordance with the third principle of restraint.
(c) Citizens in a modern western society have moral reasons to try to make (or keep) their society well ordered.
(d) Therefore, in a modern western society citizens have moral reasons to acknowledge and act in accordance with the third principle of restraint.

There is plenty of evidence that Rawls has this argument in mind. He claims that the publicity condition is particularly appropriate for a political conception of justice; and, in describing how it might be fully satisfied, he explicitly invokes the values of public reason. Indeed, it is plausible to characterize Rawls' recent emphasis on the values of public reason as an outgrowth or consequence of his strong commitment to the publicity condition.[2]

My strategy in this chapter is as follows. I will argue that the publicity condition is subject to several different interpretations, some of which are more credible than others. I then will argue that Rawls' failure to

---

[1] This intriguing suggestion is offered by S. Scheffler. He argues that "it might be less confusing and more illuminating to use the adjective 'political' to describe arguments for conceptions of justice rather than the conceptions themselves." "The Appeal of Political Liberalism," p. 13.

[2] See J. Rawls, *Political Liberalism*, pp. 66–71, 212–54. In particular see the discussion of the "full publicity condition" on pp. 66, 67, 71.

distinguish these different interpretations gives the transparency argument whatever force it has. Finally, I will argue that once the publicity condition is better understood, the transparency argument collapses.

Rival interpretations of the publicity condition

In *A Theory of Justice* Rawls described the publicity condition as one of the "formal constraints of the concept of right."[3] As such, it was intended to rule out of court all conceptions of justice that are based on esoteric knowledge.[4] One of the clearest examples of such a conception, and the one that Rawls had foremost in mind when he introduced the publicity condition, is Sidgwick's utilitarianism. As Sidgwick explained:

[O]n Utilitarian principles, it may be right to do and privately recommend, under certain circumstances, what it would not be right to advocate openly; it may be right to teach openly to one set of persons what it would be wrong to teach to others; it may be conceivably right to do, if it can be done with comparative secrecy, what it would be wrong to do in the face of the world.[5]

Rawls denies the possibility of this type of conception of justice by invoking formal or conceptual considerations. But he does acknowledge that "the merit of any definition [of morality] depends on the soundness of the theory that results."[6] So Rawls, in effect, concedes that if we are to reject Sidgwick's provocative suggestion, we need substantive moral reasons for doing so.

Why, then, should we think that in a well-ordered society the publicity condition must be fully satisfied? This is what is stated by premise (a) in the transparency argument. But what reasons support the premise?

To bring this question into sharper focus, suppose that the true conception of justice could best be implemented by deception.[7] Given

---

[3] J. Rawls, *A Theory of Justice*, pp. 130, 138. Here it is clear that Rawls conceives of the publicity condition as a constraint on conceptions of justice. But in his later work he extends it to cover political justification in general. Thus, we can understand the publicity condition as either a constraint on a conception of justice (i.e. a constraint that applies to the political philosopher) or as a constraint on how those in positions of political power can justify their exercise of that power (i.e. a constraint that applies to political authorities or citizens generally). In what follows I understand the publicity condition to include *both* types of constraint.

[4] By a conception of justice based on esoteric knowledge I mean one that either requires its own suppression or one whose content is not accessible to all people.

[5] H. Sidgwick, *The Methods of Ethics*, p. 489.

[6] J. Rawls, *A Theory of Justice*, p. 130.

[7] Derek Parfit has suggested that the dispute between Rawls and the utilitarian on this matter may turn on the nature of moral reasoning. As he points out, if morality is understood along the lines of political constructivism, then it may be impossible for the true conception of justice to violate the publicity condition. (*Reasons and Persons*, p. 43). This would make sense of Rawls' claim that the publicity condition is one of "the formal

this supposition, it might be argued that the publicity condition ought to be abandoned. After all, it could be pointed out, acceptance of the publicity condition would mean in practice settling for a conception of justice that was less good. And why, it may be asked, should we do that?

One response to this line of thought would be to point out that it overlooks the possibility that one of the elements of a just society is the relation that obtains between those who administer political power and those who are subject to it. Deception is decidedly not a neutral technique for administering political power. It dissolves the reciprocity between the rulers and the ruled.[8] The same point could be extended to explain the need for a conception of justice to be publicly accessible and open to public criticism. Political decisions made behind closed doors or shrouded in mystery are destructive of public trust.

Suppose all this is right. This would show that the publicity condition expresses a substantive moral idea. Let us call it the *basic justification requirement*. This requirement states that all citizens are owed a sincere,[9] honest, publicly accessible justification for the use of political power in their society. To deny them this justification is to deny that they are capable of understanding the principles and ideals that regulate their political life. This is, in effect, to treat them as if they were children.

Stated in these terms, the basic justification requirement appears to be on firm moral ground. However, some objections can be brought against it. It might seem obvious that rulers should never lie to their subjects and that they should give them sincere, publicly accessible justifications for their actions. This seems all the more true when we are dealing with democratic societies, for in these societies the rulers speak in the name of those they rule. But if we turn from abstract statements to concrete realities, all of this appears much less obvious. Consider, for instance, the case of a popularly elected leader of a decent, but not fully just, democratic society who is trying to make that society more just. He has a vision of where he would like to take the country, but also knows that

---

constraints on the concept of right." Note, however, that given Rawls' commitment to a political conception of justice, he cannot appeal to the truth of political constructivism to support the publicity condition. (See the discussion of the argument from political justification in chapter 3.)

[8] To invoke my earlier distinction, these considerations concern the civic bonds that obtain between citizens rather than content considerations.

[9] A "sincere" public justification is one in which people openly acknowledge what sorts of considerations are motivating (or motivated) them to take the political actions they are taking (or took). Note that while it is true that dishonest public justifications cannot be sincere, it does not follow that all honest public justifications are sincere. For it is possible for someone to take some political action, publicly offer considerations in favor of it that she genuinely believes to be valid, but, nonetheless, fail to be up front about what it is that is really motivating her to take it.

the country is not yet ready for his proposals. If this leader comes out and says publicly and honestly what his vision is, he will be lampooned in the newspapers and sent home at the next election. Since he knows this, he may decide to propose more modest reforms. These reforms, he may tell himself, will be a first step on the road toward the ultimate destination. The problem is that if the people find out that these modest reforms are simply the first step toward the more ambitious reforms, they will reject them. Given this, he must present these modest reforms as if they were the ultimate reforms. This will be tricky, for his opponents will naturally attack the modest reforms as a step on the road toward the unpopular ambitious reforms; and then, if he is to be successful, he will need to lie. He will need to make it appear that he does not endorse the more ambitious reforms.

It is not my purpose to suggest that the leader in this example acts rightly if he lies. To draw that conclusion we would need to know much more about the reforms. But it does seem plausible to say that he does not necessarily act wrongly. Most of us can, I submit, imagine a case where we would believe the leader in this example acts rightly.[10] If this is true, it calls into question the basic justification requirement. That requirement categorically rules out deceit. If citizens are always owed a sincere, honest, publicly accessible justification for the exercise of political power in their society, then the leader in the example must not lie, even if lying would help bring about important reforms.

Notwithstanding this objection, it might be thought that even if the basic justification requirement fails as a categorical rule, it is, nonetheless, a sound general maxim for political action in a democratic society. Here it could be urged that since most of the time it holds true, we ought to accept it. More precisely, it could be argued that political leaders in a democratic society must be sincere and honest about their political objectives in order for those objectives to be subject to public scrutiny. If the political objectives are not subject to public scrutiny, they will be more likely to lead to bad outcomes. This point combined with the other points about reciprocity and trust between rulers and ruled might lead us to think that we ought to accept the basic justification requirement, even if we concede that in some circumstances it would be right to violate it.

But there is a second objection to the basic justification requirement. As we have seen, the requirement demands that all citizens be given a sincere, honest, publicly accessible justification for political action. But it

---

[10] The point I am raising here has been elaborated in more general terms by Stuart Hampshire in his discussion of Machiavelli's morality. See *Innocence and Experience*, pp. 161–89.

is not clear what *public accessibility* amounts to. As a first approximation, let us say that a publicly accessible justification is one that appeals to reasons and evidence that can be publicly stated and evaluated. People who work to abolish capital punishment and justify their political action by appealing to a unique moral sense would not give others a publicly accessible justification.[11] In contrast, people who work to abolish capital punishment and justify their political action by appealing to a utilitarian argument would give others a publicly accessible justification. To be sure, other people may not accept their justification, but they would be able to understand it and evaluate it.

So far, so good. But what if one's justification were publicly accessible, but extremely complex and difficult? Suppose, for example, that one justified one's effort to abolish capital punishment by appealing to a world view that included, among other things, Einstein's theory of relativity. In this case it would be true that in one sense one's justification was one that could be publicly stated and evaluated. After all, one's reasons would in principle be publicly accessible. But given what we know about the cognitive capacities of the average citizen in a modern western society, it would not be plausible to say that this justification would be one that was *publicly understandable* for most citizens. And it might be thought that public accessibility implies public understandability; for what good is a publicly accessible justification that few can understand?

But if this is right, then it would be wrong to promote political action that could be justified only by appealing to considerations that could not be understood by all reasonable citizens; and this might exclude much political action that would otherwise be sound. Indeed, taken seriously, the standard of public understandability would seem to demand that we tailor our political justifications to the cognitive competence of the least competent reasonable citizen in our society. This is surely too stringent a demand.

For this reason, we might relax the standard of public understandability. We might say that to satisfy the publicity condition a political justification must be publicly accessible and publicly understandable to some proportion of the citizenry. Depending on how high the proportion is set, this would rule out extremely complex or convoluted justifications without placing severe constraints on acceptable justifications. With

---

[11] They could of course tell others about their unique moral sense; but when the others ask, "How does that give us a reason to abolish capital punishment?" all they would be able to say is that if the others had the moral sense, the others too would want to abolish capital punishment. But since they do not have it, it would be impossible for them to evaluate this claim.

some ingenuity, we might even be able to set the proportion at exactly the level that would be optimal for public discussion in our society. But there is a problem with this sensible idea. It would require us to violate the moral idea embedded in the basic justification requirement. That moral idea, to recall, is that *every* reasonable citizen is owed an honest, publicly accessible justification for political action. If we believe that public accessibility implies public understandability, then we cannot satisfy the basic justification requirement without imposing severe constraints on acceptable justifications for political action.

Thus, if we believe that public accessibility implies public understandability, then we have a good reason to reject the basic justification requirement. Perhaps, however, we should not believe this and we should hold on to the basic justification requirement. I propose to leave it an open matter whether the basic justification requirement includes both the standard of public accessibility and the standard of public understandability. These two standards give rise to two rival interpretations of the publicity condition. Whether both are included in the basic justification requirement is a question that need not be resolved here.[12]

Instead, I want to turn to a third interpretation of the publicity condition. This interpretation emerges from Rawls' more recent remarks on the subject. In *Political Liberalism* he introduces what he terms "the full publicity condition." From his description, it is clear that the full publicity condition goes beyond the standards of public accessibility and public understandability and includes a further standard, the standard of *public acceptability*. This standard rules out modes of reasoning, methods of inquiry and beliefs and values that are not shared or could not be accepted by all reasonable people.[13] As Rawls indicates, his original position is designed to help political liberalism satisfy this standard, for it rules out everything but commonly accepted modes of reasoning and shared values and beliefs.[14]

This more robust interpretation of the publicity condition sits well with Rawls' commitment to a certain ideal of social unity. This ideal

---

[12] For my part, I believe that the most plausible version of the publicity condition does not include either the standard of public accessibility or the standard of public understandability. All that it demands is that people be honest and sincere in their public political justifications. But I will not attempt to defend this much weaker version of the publicity condition here.

[13] J. Rawls, *Political Liberalism*, pp. 66–71. Also see Rawls' chapter on public reason in the same book.

[14] I assume that by commonly accepted modes of reasoning Rawls means those modes of reasoning that are both widely shared *and* sound. For example, the fact that a very large number of people accept some fallacious mode of reasoning would not get it included in the set of commonly accepted modes of reasoning. But Rawls is not explicit on this point.

gives voice to the aspiration to make the social world, to the greatest degree possible, "acceptable at the tribunal of each person's understanding."[15] As we shall see later, this ideal is related to a distinctive value that Rawls terms "full autonomy." For now I want to stress that what Rawls calls the full publicity condition represents a third and distinct interpretation of the publicity condition. It is also important to stress that it differs fundamentally from the other two interpretations. This is true because the first two interpretations – the one based on the standard of public accessibility, the other based on the standard of public accessibility *and* the standard of public understandability – refer to the manner or mode in which a political justification is presented. They make no reference to the content of the political justification in question. This is not to say that they place no constraints on the content of the political justification. As we have seen, the first interpretation rules out deceit and the second rules out extremely complex justifications. But if the publicity condition is sound, then when it is violated, those who have a complaint, according to the first or second interpretations, must base their complaint on how the political justification was presented to them. For instance, they must object that they were lied to or that they were not given a justification that they could understand. If they object that the political justification they were given was unsound, but publicly accessible and understandable, then they may have a valid objection, but it would have nothing to do with the publicity condition, at least as it is understood according to the first or second interpretations.

With the third interpretation, matters are different. The standard of public acceptability is a standard that imposes restrictions on the content of acceptable political justifications. It maintains that if a reasonable person could reject the political justification that is given to her, then the publicity condition is violated. Here the person with the complaint does not (necessarily)[16] refer to the manner or mode in which the political justification is presented. It is possible for her to concede that the justification is fully accessible and understandable, but still object that it is one that she can reasonably reject; and, in saying this, she would be referring to the content of the values and beliefs that are invoked in the political justification. If this is right, then the third interpretation of the publicity condition is significantly different from the first two. It goes beyond the moral idea expressed in the basic justification requirement

---

[15] J. Rawls, "Reply to Habermas," p. 146 n28. Here Rawls paraphrases and endorses a similar claim made by J. Waldron, *Liberal Rights*, p. 61.

[16] The third interpretation of the publicity condition includes the first two. That is why the qualifier "necessarily" is called for.

and imposes a standard aimed at the content of acceptable political justifications.

Let me now summarize the main points made in this section. There are at least three interpretations of the publicity condition. They are:

> PC (1) Acceptable political justifications must satisfy the standard of public accessibility.
>
> PC (2) Acceptable political justifications must satisfy both the standard of public accessibility and the standard of public understandability.
>
> PC (3) Acceptable political justifications must satisfy the standard of public accessibility, the standard of public understandability and the standard of public acceptability.

In *A Theory of Justice* Rawls endorsed PC (1) and possibly PC (2). He now endorses PC (3). PC (1) and PC (2) impose restrictions on the manner or mode in which a political justification is presented. PC (3) goes beyond these restrictions and adds a restriction on the content of the beliefs and values that may figure in an acceptable political justification.

I have argued that PC (1) and PC (2) are not obviously correct. If they are understood as conditions that impose categorical restrictions on acceptable political justifications, then we have some reason to reject them. But even if PC (1) and PC (2) are sound, it does not follow that PC (3) is sound.

Reconsidering the transparency argument

In the transparency argument the first premise states that "To be well ordered, a modern western society must be regulated by a conception of justice that fully satisfies the publicity condition." It should now be clear that the first premise is ambiguous. As stated, it does not tell us which interpretation of the publicity condition must be fully satisfied in order for a modern western society to be well ordered.

This ambiguity is significant. It is not possible to assess the transparency argument unless we determine which interpretation of the publicity condition is referred to in premise (a). If either PC (1) or PC (2) is plugged into premise (a), the transparency argument is not sound. Its soundness is secured, if at all, only by PC (3).

The reason for this is not hard to see. The second premise in the transparency argument connects the publicity condition to the third principle of restraint. It states that "For the publicity condition to be fully satisfied in a modern western society, citizens must accept and act in accordance with the third principle of restraint." Recall that the third principle of restraint demands that citizens refrain from basing their political arguments on reasons or considerations that are controversial or not publicly accessible. As I explained in chapter 2, "controversial" refers to values and beliefs that could be reasonably rejected by others; and, as I explained above in this chapter, "publicly accessible" refers to reasons and evidence that can be publicly stated and evaluated. Neither PC (1) nor PC (2) covers both of these ideas. PC (1) imposes a standard of public accessibility that would rule out reasons and evidence that could not be publicly stated and evaluated and PC (2) imposes a further standard that would rule out reasons and evidence that could not be understood by all reasonable citizens. Neither interpretation of the publicity condition, however, imposes any standard that would rule out controversial values and beliefs. Thus, it is possible to fully satisfy the publicity condition according to PC (1) or PC (2) and still not accept or act in accord with the third principle of restraint.

However, if PC (3) is plugged into premise (a), then premise (b) is true and the transparency argument has a shot at being a sound argument. As we have seen, this interpretation of the publicity condition imposes three standards: the standard of public accessibility, the standard of public understandability and the standard of public acceptability. These three standards cover both ideas expressed by the third principle of restraint. For the publicity condition to be fully satisfied, according to PC (3), citizens must refrain from basing their political arguments on controversial reasons or considerations not at present commonly accepted.[17]

We can now state the dilemma that confronts the transparency argument. If we decide to use PC (3) – what Rawls calls the "full publicity condition" – then premise (b) is true. But in this case premise (a) still calls for justification. For to assert that the publicity condition requires that political justification be acceptable to all reasonable people is to assert the conclusion of which the argument is in pursuit. This would show that the transparency argument is valid, but trivial. On the other hand, if we decide to use a weaker interpretation of the publicity condition like PC (1) or PC (2), then premise (a) could be non-trivially justified. It could be justified by the moral idea expressed in the basic justification requirement. But in this case, premise (b) would no longer be true. For, given this weaker interpretation of the publicity condition, citizens do not have to accept the third principle of restraint in order for it to be fully satisfied.

The transparency argument gets its force by moving back and forth between different interpretations of the publicity condition. In this way,

---

[17] For convenience throughout this chapter I have not insisted on the distinction between narrow and comprehensive restraint.

it looks as if it provides an argument for the third principle of restraint. But once we carefully distinguish between the different interpretations of the publicity condition, it becomes clear that it provides no such argument. From the claim that political justifications should be publicly accessible and publicly understandable we cannot derive the further claim that they must be publicly acceptable, where this means that they must be ones that no reasonable citizen could reject.[18]

Public justification and moral demands

To shore up the transparency argument Rawls needs independent support for PC (3). Can such support be found? To answer this question, I will first look at an argument that Rawls does not make, but that some may find compelling. I will then consider an argument that is implicit in Rawls' recent work. We shall see that neither argument is persuasive.

The first argument begins with the thought that public justification captures an important truth about the nature of morality.[19] The idea behind the thought is this: when we make moral demands on others, we need to give them reasons for why they should comply with those demands. If we offer them no reasons, we are not justifying our demands to them. We are simply asserting that they should do what we think they ought to do. However, in such cases, we are not making *moral* demands on others, for to make moral demands on others we must justify those demands to them. In short, offering reasons for a moral demand is a necessary part of it. Without justifying reasons, the demand is not a moral demand.

This idea can be summarized as follows:

(a) To make a moral demand on a person we must give him reasons for complying with the demand.

By itself, (a) does not tell us very much about public justification. But now consider this further thought: to give a person a reason for

---

[18] The movement back and forth between different interpretations of the publicity condition is also present in the work of others who endorse a version of the transparency argument. Jeremy Waldron in "Theoretical Foundations of Liberalism," for example, claims that "society should be a *transparent* order, in the sense that its workings and principles should be well-known and available for public apprehension and scrutiny"(p. 58); and he suggests that this idea lends support to "the liberal strategy" of searching "for underlying interests and beliefs shared in common which may be appealed to in the justification of our institutional arrangements"(p. 56). But the first quoted remarks pertain to PC (2), while the second pertain to PC (3).

[19] For a version of this argument see G. Gaus, *Justificatory Liberalism*, pp. 123–41. Gaus, however, is not interested in defending all the limits that Rawls includes in the limits of public reason. See his critique of the "reasonable people thesis" on pp. 31–36.

complying with a demand we must show him that his current system of reasons and beliefs commits him to it. We must, in other words, show him that from his own standpoint he has a reason to comply with the demand. Building this into (a) we get:

(b) To make a moral demand on a person we must show him that his current system of reasons and beliefs gives him a reason to comply with the demand.

This puts us on a path that leads to public justification. For in politics we make moral demands not just on specific persons, but on all of our fellow citizens. And if (b) is true, we will only be able to make moral demands on others in politics if we offer them a special type of public justification – a justification that addresses the standpoints of all. This, in turn, appears to lend support for the limits of public reason, for it is plausible to think that the only way we can offer this type of public justification is to respect these limits. Thus, if this argument is correct, it looks as if it provides independent support for PC (3).

But is the argument correct? Quite plainly, its crucial step is from (a) to (b). The question is whether we have good reason to take this step. Consider this objection. We can make a moral demand on a person if we offer her reasons that we sincerely believe are sound, even if she is incapable of appreciating their force. Suppose, for example, that we are fully justified[20] in thinking that the person has a moral reason to comply with some demand. When this is true, and when we press the demand on her, do we not make a moral demand?

This objection has force, but it is not decisive. A proponent of the argument under consideration could defuse it by rejecting the possibility of external reasons.[21] If all reasons are internal reasons, then we do not offer someone a reason for complying with a demand that we make on her if we do not provide a reason that is in some way related to her current system of reasons and beliefs.[22] Similarly, if there are no external reasons, justifying moral demands requires that we show others that from their own standpoints they have a reason to comply with the demands.

---

[20] Recall from chapter 4 that full justification requires both subjective and objective justification.

[21] This is the move that Gaus takes. See *Justificatory Liberalism*, p. 141.

[22] For discussion of internal and external reasons see B. Williams, "Internal and External Reasons." According to Williams, an internal reason is a reason that is related in some way to a person's "subjective motivational set" and an external reason is one that is not. I am using the phrase "a person's current system of reasons and beliefs" in roughly the same way that Williams uses subjective motivational set. In this context, however, nothing important turns on this use of terminology.

The rejection of external reasons, therefore, knocks down the objection. But the plausibility of this move plainly rests on the plausibility of rejecting external reasons. If it can be shown that at least some external reasons exist, the objection would remain standing.[23] However, I shall not try to show this here. The topic is much too big for present concerns. Instead, I will show that even if we ought to accept (a) and (b), we can and should reject PC (3). This, in turn, will show that the argument under consideration cannot be relied on to shore up the transparency argument.

To see why this is so, return to the objection mentioned above. We can now supplement it. Suppose that someone (call him X) is fully justified in making a demand (call it D) on another person (call her Y), and suppose that the only way X will be able to get Y to comply with D is to make the demand. If we assume that (a) and (b) are true, and if we assume that Y has no reason to comply with D given her current system of reasons and beliefs, then we must conclude that X cannot make a *moral* demand on Y to do D. However, even assuming all of this, it would still be fully intelligible for X to ask himself whether he has compelling moral reasons to refrain from making the demand on Y. This is a first-person moral question. It cannot be answered by attending to the nature of Y's current system of reasons and beliefs or by reflecting on what it means to make a moral demand on another person.

Since, by stipulation, X is fully justified in thinking that Y ought to comply with D, X needs to be given a reason why he ought to refrain from making the demand on Y. And for this reason to provide support for PC (3) it must follow from a general principle of the following form: *if one cannot justify one's demands to another person, one ought to refrain from advancing them.* This principle, if sound, would provide X with a compelling reason to refrain from advancing demand D on Y. More generally, it would show that all citizens have a compelling reason to refrain from making demands on others that could not be publicly justified to them.

But is this principle sound? It evidently rests on a moral intuition about treating others with respect. The intuition can be expressed in different ways, but the gist of it is that we should not make demands on others if we cannot justify those demands to them because doing so fails to treat them as persons or as ends in themselves.

This, however, is just another version of an argument that we have

---

[23] For a modest defense of external reasons, and one that I have some sympathy for, see J. McDowell, "Might There Be External Reasons?"

already considered and found wanting. In chapter 4 we saw that the democratic idea of toleration cannot be defended by appeal to a principle of respect. The reason for this, we saw, is that it is implausible to think that the civility consideration always takes precedence over content considerations, no matter what is at stake.[24] This same line of thought applies to the present argument. Even if there are moral costs to making demands on others that cannot be justified to them, it is a mistake to assume that these costs always outweigh the costs of not making the demands. Sometimes people will rightly conclude that they must make demands – and attempt to enforce them – on others even when these demands cannot be justified to all.

The point to keep in mind here is that while maintaining civility may be a genuine moral consideration, it is not the only or the most important one. When it does not outweigh all other considerations, citizens do not act wrongly when they advance justifications for their demands that cannot be justified to all. If this is right, we must conclude that the argument under consideration cannot provide independent support for PC (3) – the claim that acceptable public justifications must be ones that satisfy the standards of public accessibility, public understandability and public acceptability.

The appeal to full autonomy

Let us turn, then, to a second argument that might be able to strengthen the case for PC (3). As I mentioned above, this argument is implicit in Rawls' recent work. The argument appeals to a value Rawls terms "full autonomy." Properly understood, this value appears to give the transparency argument just the support it needs.

According to Rawls, full autonomy is "realized in public life by affirming the political principles of justice and enjoying the protections of the basic rights and liberties; it is also realized by participating in society's public affairs and sharing in its collective self-determination over time."[25] It is achieved when all citizens recognize and identify with the principles of justice that regulate the basic structure of their society. This collective identification is an exercise of collective self-determination. Rawls is careful to distinguish it from other understandings of autonomy.

This idea of a shared political life does not invoke Kant's idea of autonomy, or

---

[24] Recall that the civility consideration refers to the civic bonds that obtain between citizens. It is satisfied when the political order is regulated by principles that all reasonably accept.

[25] J. Rawls, *Political Liberalism*, pp. 77–78.

Mill's idea of individuality, as moral values belonging to a comprehensive doctrine. The appeal is rather to the political value of a public life conducted on terms that all reasonable citizens can accept as fair.[26]

This makes it plain that full autonomy is a value achieved by all or by none. It is, we might say, a non-excludable good. Thus, the political life of fully autonomous citizens is shared not just in the weak sense that all participate in it, but in the strong sense that all identify with its governing principles.

It is not hard to feel the attraction of this value. The ideal of a shared political life has affinities with the older ideal of government by consent. It expresses the hope that political society can be made more like a club or a voluntary association in which its members freely accept the rules that guide and constrain their conduct. This is not to suggest that Rawls is under any illusions that actual consent is a realistic possibility in modern western societies. Political communities, he writes, are closed social systems that we enter by birth and exit by death.[27] But a fully autonomous political society would realize many of the values of voluntary participation.

More to the issue at hand, Rawls contends that, given reasonable pluralism, in order for the value of full autonomy to be realized in modern western societies conceptions of justice must not refer to controversial reasons or considerations. "This leads to," he writes, "the ideal of democratic citizens settling their fundamental differences in accordance with an idea of public reason."[28] Plainly, this ideal includes the standard of public acceptability.

Thus reference to the value of full autonomy does indeed appear to provide support for the transparency argument. It grounds an independent reason for accepting PC (3). Nonetheless, two objections can be brought against it. These objections seriously weaken the power of this value to provide support for the transparency argument.

The first objection denies outright that the value of full autonomy is practically realizable. Like Rousseau's vision of a political community governed by the general will, a community of fully autonomous citizens looks suspiciously utopian given the diversity and complexity of modern western societies. As such, it cannot be assumed to be a sound ideal for guiding political action. It may be that the pursuit of the unattainable value of full autonomy would obstruct the realization of the best attainable state of affairs.

Interestingly, Rawls now denies that the two principles of justice he defended in *A Theory of Justice* are uniquely reasonable. He now

[26] Ibid. p. 98.   [27] Ibid. p. 40.   [28] Ibid. p. 98.

concedes that it is "inevitable and often desirable that citizens have different views as to the most appropriate political conception; for the public political culture is bound to contain different fundamental ideas that can be developed in different ways."[29] This concession adds credence to the first objection; for it is in tension with the value of full autonomy which is "realized by citizens when they act from principles of justice that specify the fair terms of cooperation they would give to themselves when fairly represented as free and equal persons."[30] Described as such, full autonomy presupposes a uniquely correct set of principles that all citizens could acknowledge as the ones they would accept under ideal conditions.[31] So Rawls himself may be coming to realize that this value is utopian.

Alternatively, he may believe that full autonomy is realized when all citizens agree that their society is a legitimate one.[32] But this amounts to a considerable watering down of the value. In a society in which all agree that the political order is legitimate they might still disagree about whether it is fully just and these disagreements might be intense. As Rawls himself admits, laws "passed by solid majorities [in democratic societies] are legitimate, even though many protest and correctly judge them unjust or otherwise wrong."[33] This moves us some distance away from the ideal of a political order in which all citizens "fully comprehend and endorse" its constitution and laws.[34]

The force of the first objection depends on an estimate of what is realistically achievable given the conditions of modern western societies. The second objection is more fundamental. It denies that full autonomy has unconditional value.

Unconditional values are values which are valuable in themselves. In contrast, conditional values are values whose value is dependent on the realization of some other value or set of values. The virtues of kindness and self-command bring out this distinction. The virtue of kindness has unconditional value. To explain why an act of kindness is valuable we do not need to refer to other virtues. The same is not true of the virtue of self-command. The disposition to be true to oneself, to act in accordance with one's deepest commitments and attitudes, does not have unconditional value. Whether or not it has value depends on the content of a

---

[29] Ibid. p. 227.   [30] Ibid. p. 77.

[31] In *A Theory of Justice* Rawls claims that "in a well-ordered society citizens hold the *same* principles of right"(pp. 447–48). In *Political Liberalism* he claims that in a well-ordered society "everyone accepts, and knows that everyone else accepts, the *very same* principles of justice" (p. 35, emphasis added).

[32] That is, in a legitimate, but not necessarily well-ordered, society.

[33] J. Rawls, "Reply to Habermas," p. 175.

[34] Ibid. p. 155 (describing the value of full autonomy).

person's deepest commitments and attitudes. The self-command of the good person has value whereas the self-command of the evil one does not. To show, then, that full autonomy has unconditional value one needs to show that its value is not dependent on some other value. One must show that it is more like the virtue of kindness than like self-command.

There are good reasons to think this cannot be shown. Full autonomy is realized when all citizens identify with the principles of justice that govern the basic structure of the society in which they live. But this collective identification is not necessarily a valuable thing. It depends on the soundness of the principles of justice that are collectively affirmed. To take an extreme example suppose German citizens in 1935 unanimously affirmed the ideals of the Nazi government. This act of collective identification would have no value. Indeed, it would rightly be regarded as a bad thing, as something which reflected poorly on German society. But if this is right, then the value of full autonomy is dependent on other values.

It will be objected that it is inconceivable that the ideals of the Nazi government could have been collectively affirmed. This may be true; but it misses the point. The point is that an unjust political order is not made better simply by the fact that its citizens identify with its governing principles. This holds true not only of the Nazi example, but of less extreme examples as well.

This is not to deny that a fully autonomous just political order may be, other things equal, a better political order than a just political order that does not realize full autonomy. Full autonomy may be valuable; but it is only valuable if it can be secured in the right way on the right terms. It is only valuable on the assumption that the political order in question is just. In this respect, it is like the virtue of self-command. It has conditional value only.

Against this, it might be argued that the value of full autonomy comes into play only after a political community becomes reasonably well-ordered. Beyond this threshold, it has unconditional as well as conditional value. It might then be claimed that in some circumstances it could be right to prefer a fully autonomous political order to a political order that was more just but not fully autonomous. But even if this were true, Rawls would still need to show that modern western societies have passed the relevant threshold. This is something he has not done. In the absence of such a demonstration, the claim is unpersuasive.

This can best be seen by returning to the perspective of the model citizen. If the model citizen believes that she can best advance the correct conception of justice by making political arguments that are based on controversial ideals and values, then the fact that her activity might impede the realization of the value of full autonomy should not move her. She should say: "The first and primary task is to establish justice. After that, we can worry about full autonomy. But it would be foolish to sacrifice justice for full autonomy." It would be foolish because the value of the latter is parasitic on the value of the former.

Rawls might object that this misdescribes the value of full autonomy. He might claim that full autonomy is not a conditional value; but rather a constituent element of a just society. It does not depend on justice; it is part of the content of justice. But this claim requires support. And it is hard to see how Rawls could provide it. We have already seen that he cannot claim that a political order that is based on principles that some citizens could reasonably reject *for that reason* treats those citizens with intolerance or disrespect. That argument was considered and rejected in chapter 4. And without it, we have no reason to think that full autonomy is a constituent element of a just political order. But even, *pace* this last point, if we accept that full autonomy is a constituent element of a just political order, it would not follow that it takes precedence over all other considerations. That would require yet another argument; and it is doubtful whether any such argument could succeed.

For these reasons, the appeal to full autonomy cannot provide the needed support for PC (3). Even if the model citizen ought to accept PC (1) or PC (2) because of the moral idea expressed in the basic justification requirement, it does not follow that he or she ought to accept PC (3). And, as I have emphasized, without PC (3) the transparency argument collapses.

It is time to take stock. I began by pointing out that to justify the principles of restraint one needs to present reasons that address the perspective of a model citizen participating in the politics of a modern western society. I then considered a range of arguments that attempt to provide such reasons – the pragmatic argument, the argument from political justification, the argument from democratic toleration and the transparency argument. All of these arguments, I have tried to show, are unsuccessful.

Do these arguments, while unpersuasive on their own, nonetheless add up to a convincing case when put together? They do not for the following reason. All the arguments suffer from the same fundamental defect. That defect is the failure to come fully to grips with the fact that citizens not only argue about the implications of their shared commitments, but also about the degree to which those commitments should be changed. This requires them to move beyond shared values and to advance and argue for controversial political ends, even when these ends could be reasonably rejected by some people. Ultimately, it is the failure to account for this dimension of citizenship that renders all the arguments for the bracketing strategy unconvincing. And since the arguments share this defect, they cannot complement one another in ways that would make the sum greater than the parts.

It is of course possible that some other argument for the bracketing strategy, one that I have not considered, might fare better. But since the arguments I have considered are the ones advanced by the most talented proponents of the bracketing strategy, their failure provides good inductive support for the belief that it cannot succeed.

In rejecting the bracketing strategy I have not tried to show that it leads to unsound political judgments. For all that I have said, the bracketing strategy might yield correct substantive results. But I have argued that its distinguishing feature – the idea that citizens have compelling reasons to recognize and comply with the principles of restraint – is not rationally grounded. Since this feature is not rationally grounded, the bracketing strategy lacks justificatory force. It leaves us with no good explanation for why we ought to cordon off political morality from our best understanding of human flourishing.

This negative conclusion has a constructive upshot. It suggests that a better account of liberal political morality – one with greater justificatory force – would draw freely on our best understanding of a good life. Whether such an account is available and what its character would be remain to be seen.

Part II

Autonomy and perfectionism

Throughout Part one I invoked the perspective of a model citizen of a modern western society. I used this character as a foil to help bring out the problems with the bracketing strategy. But no light was shed on the content of his or her views. All we know about him or her is that he or she rejects the bracketing strategy.

In the remainder of this book I argue that such a citizen should endorse a particular perfectionist account of political morality, one that gives the value of personal autonomy pride of place. I also argue that a strong commitment to personal autonomy is not incompatible with perfectionist political action designed to promote good and discourage bad pursuits.

The account of political morality I defend is incomplete. The focus is squarely on the value of personal autonomy. Other values are not discussed, except indirectly.[1] The account also does not specify in any detail what institutional arrangements best promote autonomy. Despite these (severe) limits, it does seek to show that autonomy-based political morality is rationally well-grounded and that it qualifies as a form of perfectionism. In this way, the account complements the argument of Part I. It further substantiates the thesis that liberal perfectionism has a stronger claim to acceptance than the best account of anti-perfectionist political morality.

---

[1] In particular, I do not address the important question of how egalitarian an autonomy-based account of political morality should be.

6   Personal autonomy and its value (I)

As I mentioned in the introduction, a liberal perfectionist theory is a perfectionist theory that holds that personal autonomy is a central component of human flourishing. Accordingly, a large part of the defense of such a theory must consist in making it clear what autonomy refers to and what justifies its value.

This chapter and the next present an account of the nature and status of personal autonomy. The account gives answers to three questions: (1) What are the constituent elements of this ideal? (2) What considerations account for its value? (3) How important is it for political morality? The three questions are distinct; but, as we shall see, the answers given to each inform the answers given to the other two.

Introduction

Even a casual glance at the literature on the topic will suggest that there is not a shared understanding of autonomy.[1] Different writers use the concept in different ways.[2] Here I am not interested in cataloguing how it has functioned in the philosophical literature or in describing how it is used in everyday discourse. I hope to present a sound account of the concept. This objective is primarily critical, not descriptive. As a result, the plausibility of my account of autonomy turns, in the end, on how good my arguments are for its value and importance.

Still, to cut short potential misunderstandings, I begin with some stipulative remarks. Personal autonomy does not refer to *metaphysical autonomy*. No effort will be made here to shed light on, much less resolve, the vexatious problem of free will. Personal autonomy also does not refer to *Kantian autonomy*. No effort will be made here to determine

---

[1] I use the terms "personal autonomy", "autonomy" and "self-determination" interchangeably.

[2] For a survey of how the concept has been used in recent political and moral philosophy, see G. Dworkin, *The Theory and Practice of Autonomy*, esp. pp. 5–6, and the essays collected in J. Christman, *The Inner Citadel*.

whether autonomy is a property of the will that is necessary for moral action. Nor, finally, does personal autonomy refer to a *moral right*. It does not mark a region or domain in which each person has a moral claim to be free to govern him- or herself.[3] The value of personal autonomy may justify giving people various rights to govern themselves in various ways; but it is not itself a moral right.

Furthermore, as I will depict it, personal autonomy is not a predicate that applies to individual preferences. People, not preferences, are autonomous; and in order to know whether a person is autonomous we will need to know something about his or her personal history. This is not meant to imply that the manner in which preferences are formed has no bearing at all on the degree to which people are autonomous. It is merely to insist that autonomy is a diachronic, not a synchronic, predicate. It applies to ongoing styles of choice and decision-making, manifesting itself over time by the ways in which people conduct their lives.

So depicted, personal autonomy is best described as a character ideal.[4] It is the ideal of people charting their own course through life, fashioning their character by self-consciously choosing projects and taking up commitments from a wide range of eligible alternatives, and making something out of their lives according to their own understanding of what is valuable and worth doing. Those who realize this ideal take charge of their affairs. They discover, or at least try to discover, what they are cut out for and what will bring them fulfillment and satisfaction. They neither drift through life, aimlessly moving from one object of desire to another, nor adopt projects and pursuits wholesale from others. In short, autonomous people[5] have a strong sense of their own identity and actively participate in the determination of their own lives.

Having said this, it is important not to confuse this ideal with other distinct character ideals. Some people lead monochromatic lives. Each pursuit they undertake is self-consciously integrated into an overarching plan of life. From the "age of reason" onward they know what they must do and they go about devising the best means to achieve their fixed objectives. Such people fully realize the ideal of the rationally planned

---

[3] This sense of autonomy is what Feinberg calls "personal sovereignty." See *Harm to Self*, pp. 27–51. Also see R. Nozick's characterization in *Philosophical Explanations*, pp. 498–504.

[4] I am not alone in describing autonomy as a character ideal. See S. Benn, *A Theory of Freedom*, and J. Raz, *The Morality of Freedom*.

[5] By "autonomous people" I mean people who realize autonomy to some substantial degree. It is true that people can be autonomous for some portions of their life and non-autonomous for others; but, for simplicity's sake, I will not dwell on this complication.

life;[6] but this ideal, whatever its merits, is not the ideal of personal autonomy. Not all people have goals and projects that express a dominant theme or fit into a single pattern. Some embrace a variety of pursuits, making no effort to harmonize them; others try out some pursuits only to discard them for radically different ones as their self-image changes. Unless the idea of a rational life-plan is stretched pretty far, these people do not have one. Nonetheless, they can be autonomous.[7]

Similarly, some people are critical self-examiners. Reflecting on and deliberating about their identity, they realize the Socratic ideal of the examined life. Self-reflective people are often autonomous, but autonomous people are not marked by their inclination to engage in critical self-examination. To be sure, the realization of autonomy requires the presence of an independent mind, one that is capable of altering its convictions and commitments for reasons of its own. Such a mind, however, need not be a particularly reflective one. It is no contradiction to say of someone that he was both unreflective and an active shaper of his own life.

Finally, consider the character type that Mill celebrates in *On Liberty*. Mill admires the eccentric person, the one who has the imagination and the strength of character to live his or her life against the grain. As Mill pointed out, people like this are often valuable to the societies in which they live. They suggest new ways of thinking and living; and quite often they realize the ideal of personal autonomy to a high degree. But eccentricity, like critical reflection, is not the imprint of the autonomous person. People can realize the character ideal of autonomy while fully endorsing the customs and conventions of their time and place.

Distinguishing personal autonomy from these other character ideals helps bring it into sharper focus. But the description of the ideal is still too abstract; and the abstract description allows for considerable variation, depending on how the constituent elements of the ideal are refined and specified. In a moment I shall attempt to remedy this defect. But, first, something should be said about autonomy's value.

Autonomy is an intrinsic value. It is intrinsically good for people to make their own choices about how to lead their lives. It is intrinsically good for them to adopt and pursue projects, not because others have tricked or coerced them into adopting or pursuing them or because they

---

[6] See J. Rawls, *A Theory of Justice*, part III, esp. pp. 407–16.

[7] Under the influence of Rawls many modern writers identify the autonomous life with the unified life. See, e.g., R. Young, "Autonomy and the Inner Self." For exceptions see J. Raz, *The Morality of Freedom*, p. 370 and J. Glover, *I: The Philosophy and Psychology of Personal Identity*, p. 135.

have no other worthwhile options to choose from; but because, according to their own lights, the pursuits are worth adopting and pursuing.

More strongly, autonomy is not just one intrinsic value among many; it is one of special importance. For most people it is, or so I shall argue, a central component of a fully good life. However well their lives may go, if they do not realize this ideal to some substantial degree, they will fail to live a fully good life.[8] This does not mean that personal autonomy is the only component of a fully good life. Far from it. By itself, and in isolation from other components, it has no value. Its value is dependent on the presence of these other components.[9] Still, this dependence does not show that autonomy has no intrinsic value or that it is not a central component of a fully good life.[10]

In addition to being intrinsically valuable, the realization of autonomy has instrumental value. It contributes significantly to the achievement of a further ideal, the ideal of self-development. Those who achieve self-development fully realize their talents and potentialities. They choose and successfully pursue projects that fit their nature, agree with their innate proclivities and bring to fruition their skills and capacities as they emerge from the interaction of their native endowments and their culture. In common parlance, such people "fulfill their promise."

Not everyone who realizes the ideal of autonomy achieves self-development. It is a further excellence that may or may not be realized. Conversely, to achieve self-development it is not necessary to be autonomous. It is possible to slip, or have others steer one, into a way of life that best develops one's talents and capacities. This being the case the connection between personal autonomy and self-development is not conceptual. The two ideals can come apart. But this conceptual independence does not show that autonomy is not instrumentally valuable to the realization of self-development. Even if no conceptual link connects the two ideals, there is good reason to think that there are contingent connections between them. Other things equal, autonomous people are more likely to achieve self-development than their non-autonomous counterparts.

To the extent, then, that the achievement of self-development contributes to a fully good life, the realization of personal autonomy is valuable as a means to the achievement of this ideal. This provides a

[8] As will become clear in the discussion that ensues, this claim requires some qualification.

[9] Borrowing terminology from G. E. Moore, we can say that autonomy is an element in an "organic whole" (the fully good life); and that it is the value of this organic whole that explains its value. G. E. Moore, *Principia Ethica*, chapter VI.

[10] *Pace* Moore, intrinsic values need not be goods that would be valuable in isolation from everything else. I say a bit more about this below.

further reason for valuing it. Not only is it a central component of a fully good life, but it also contributes to the achievement of a further excellence.

These are strong claims. If true, they have important implications for political morality. The rejection of the bracketing strategy in Part I of this book suggests that the general thesis of perfectionism may be correct. This is the thesis that political authorities should take an active role in creating and maintaining social conditions that best enable their subjects to lead valuable and worthwhile lives. If autonomy is a central component of a fully good life, and if we ought to accept the general thesis of perfectionism, then it would follow that political authorities should take an active role in creating and maintaining social conditions that help their subjects realize this ideal.

But do we really have good reasons for thinking that autonomy is a central component of a fully good life? Answering this question will occupy us for much of the remainder of this chapter and the next. However, the immediate task is to make the ideal of autonomy more determinate.

The constituent elements of personal autonomy

Personal autonomy is a complex character ideal consisting of a number of constituent elements. To make the ideal more determinate we need to identify and describe these elements. Three general desiderata should guide this undertaking. First, any characterization of personal autonomy should show that it bears some resemblance to the root idea of self-government. As many have pointed out, the etymology of the word "autonomy" can be traced back to the Greek terms *auto*, which means "self," and *nomos*, which means (roughly) "law." Applied to persons, the word most naturally refers to people who make their own decisions and are not dictated to by others. An adequate characterization of autonomy must show it to be a plausible interpretation of this root idea.

Second, a specification of the constituent elements should put the ideal of autonomy in a favorable light. It should make the ideal one that has at least a shot at being something that could be a central component of a fully good life. This means that the constituent elements of autonomy must not be specified in such a way as to make them incompatible with much of what gives meaning and value to human life. Conversely, and third, autonomy should be specified in such a way that it, nonetheless, remains a distinct ideal. There is a temptation in political philosophy to pack all good things into the same ideal. Doing this certainly would guarantee that autonomy was valuable, but it would divest it of its integrity. To retain its integrity, autonomy must be incompatible with some ways of life and compatible with a range of vices and shortcomings.

Bearing these desiderata in mind, I will now try to identify with more precision the capacities, skills, virtues and conditions that comprise the ideal. I claimed above that autonomy is the ideal of people charting their own course through life, fashioning their character by self-consciously choosing projects and taking up commitments from a wide range of eligible alternatives, and making something out of their lives according to their own understanding of what is valuable and worth doing. This general description suggests that autonomous people need (a) the capacity to choose projects and sustain commitments, (b) the independence necessary to chart their own course through life and to develop their own understanding of what is valuable and worth doing, (c) the self-consciousness and vigor to take control of their affairs and (d) an environment that provides them with a wide range of eligible pursuits to choose from. For ease of exposition, I will organize my remarks around these four basic elements; but of course each element could be broken down still further.

The first element refers to the general capacities necessary for project pursuit. The autonomous person fashions his character by choosing and pursuing projects, where projects are understood broadly to include commitments, relationships and goals. To do this he must possess a range of cognitive skills. Chief among them are the capacity to conceive of alternative projects, the capacity to form complex intentions and the capacity to plan ahead. Such a person must also have some skill in evaluating different courses of action according to how well they would further his projects. Otherwise, these projects will be doomed to failure. This is not to say that to be a project pursuer one must be successful in all or most of one's endeavors. Failure is a real possibility in many pursuits. But it does suggest that to be autonomous one must at least have the capacities necessary for successful project pursuit, even if most of one's projects end in failure.

In addition to these cognitive skills, a project pursuer must not suffer from psychological compulsions that severely inhibit his ability to translate decisions into actions. This separates him from the paranoiac, the compulsive neurotic, the schizophrenic and perhaps the psychopath. In different ways each of these afflictions undermine a person's ability to engage in self-directed action, an ability essential to project pursuit.[11]

---

[11] For a more detailed discussion of how these afflictions undermine self-directed action, see S. Benn, *A Theory of Freedom*, pp. 155–69.

Finally, the capacities for project pursuit include virtues such as the mental resolve to make decisions and the strength of character to stick to them once they have been made. Project pursuers are not continually paralyzed by the thought that they may be missing out on something or that they may be closing off other options if they decide to adopt a project or take on a commitment. Nor are they perpetually incapable of sticking to any pursuit they settle on, fluttering from one endeavor to the next without ever really engaging in any of them.

Of course not all project pursuers need these virtues to the same degree. For some the life that best suits their nature is one of incessant variety and spontaneity. Since their projects are short-lived, they do not need to be particularly good at sustaining commitments. But most people are not like this. Most of us have at least a few long-term projects (a career, a marriage, a complex hobby, etc.); and commonly these projects are central to our sense of who we are. For this reason, the strength of character necessary to sustain commitments is an important virtue for the autonomous person.

These capacities, skills and virtues make it possible to pursue projects. But to be autonomous one must not only possess these capacities, one must actually exercise them; and must exercise them in such a way as to make one's life one's own. To do this one needs a measure of independence from others. The second element mentioned above calls attention to this. People need to be independent if they are to chart their own course through life. But what does this independence consist of?

Start with some easy cases. If others imprison you for a long period of time, forcibly preventing you from engaging in a wide range of actions, then, quite conclusively, your ability to chart your own course through life is sharply diminished. Less conclusively, but still clearly, if others credibly inform you that if you continue to engage in your preferred way of life, they will lock you up, then this will impede your ability to chart your own course through life.

These two cases involve coercion.[12] They show how coercion militates against self-determination by obstructing the coerced person's ability to pursue his projects, thus undermining his ability to fashion his own life. So it is natural to conclude from this that independence requires, at the very least, freedom from the coercion of others. But while this conclusion is substantially correct, it does not tell the full story about coercion and independence.

Consider a more complicated case. Suppose you are about to give fifty

---

[12] I follow Frankfurt in holding that "When P coerces Q into doing A, then Q does not do A freely or of his own free will." See "Coercion and Moral Responsibility," pp. 44–45.

dollars to your favorite charity, as you have done every month for the past ten years, when a gunman appears on the scene and makes an unusual, but sincere, demand: "Give fifty dollars to that charity right now or I will kill you." Here you are subject to coercion, but you are not prevented from engaging in your projects. The gunman demands that you do what you would have done anyway.

If your autonomy is invaded in this case, it must be for some reason other than the one mentioned above – that coercion prevents its victims from engaging in the projects that they want to engage in. But it is not clear what this other reason could be.

Consider one last case, one that comes from Nozick. Suppose two people are trapped in their houses. Neither is able to leave because they are aware that if they do there is a high probability that they will be killed by an electric shock. The difference between them is that one is trapped because there is a very dangerous lightning storm hovering over his house (situation 1), while the other is trapped because a neighbor has credibly threatened to electrocute her if she leaves (situation 2). Nozick thinks that the person in situation 2, but not the person in situation 1, is coerced; for while both are equally obstructed, only the latter is subject to the will of another. Nozick explains:

In the lightning situation [situation 1], your will keeps you indoors – no other's motives and intentions are as closely connected to your act. Whereas in the threat situation [situation 2], it is another person's will that is operative.[13]

This explanation suggests an answer to the case about the gunman. If what is distinctive of coercion is not that the victim is obstructed from doing what he or she wants to, but rather that he or she is subjected to the will of another, and if it is this fact that explains why coercion invades autonomy, then we have an explanation for why the gunman invades your autonomy (in the above case).

But this explanation leaves us in the dark about why being subjected to the will of another is so damaging to personal autonomy. If an act is made less one's own, why does it matter *how* it is made less one's own? If it is brought about by natural circumstances, is this not just as bad as if it were brought about by the coercive interference of another?

Faced with this query, we do well to shift the focus to the subjective reactions (or the likely subjective reactions) of the victims. The person in situation 1 in all likelihood would harbor no resentment toward anyone. He would feel that he simply was the victim of bad fortune. But the person in situation 2 would almost certainly harbor resentment. She

---

[13] R. Nozick, *Philosophical Explanations*, p. 49.

would know that her will had been obstructed not by random chance, but by the deliberate, intentional actions of another person. And she would also know that she had been singled out for such treatment; for, presumably, the threatener does not go around making this threat to everyone.

Assuming that these subjective experiences are bad for those who experience them, this would explain why it is worse to be coerced than to be obstructed by one's natural environment. But could it explain how coercion could frustrate one's autonomy more than mere obstruction? It could do so only if the experience of resentment and the knowledge that one had been singled out had wider ramifications for one's ability to lead one's life according to one's own terms. This could occur if coercion damaged the victim's sense of self-worth, thereby undermining or weakening his resolve to pursue his projects and carry on with his life. If this happened, it would be worse, from the standpoint of autonomy, for the victim to be coerced than to be obstructed to the same extent by natural circumstances.

Of course the realization of this possibility rests on contingent psychological connections that do not hold true for all people in all circumstances. But while contingent, the connections might be important. And in modern western societies they are likely to be fairly strong. In these societies people have a strong sense that they are entitled to lead their lives on their own terms. As a result, in these societies at least, coercion is often perceived by the victims as an especially insulting sign of disrespect.

This goes some distance toward explaining the normative significance of coercion for personal autonomy. If people are to realize this ideal, they need to be relatively free from the coercive interference of others, particularly the types of coercive interference that would substantially restrict their ability to pursue their projects or would have deleterious effects on their enduring sense of self-worth.

I have spent a fair amount of space discussing coercion, since it is widely thought to be the most blatant form of interference with people's independence.[14] But freedom from coercion, significant as it is, does not exhaust the requirements of independence. There are other modes of

---

[14] As my discussion suggests, this widespread view may be an exaggeration. In some cases coercion may not diminish a person's autonomy at all. If it does not substantially restrict his ability to lead his life on his own terms and if it does not undermine his sense of self-worth, then it will not diminish his autonomy. It does not follow, of course, that there are no other reasons for opposing such coercion.

It is also worth pointing out that, under some circumstances, coercion can enhance a person's autonomy; e.g. when he is forcibly prevented from doing something that would destroy his general capacity to be autonomous. Such cases raise special problems that I will not tackle here.

influence that undermine the independence necessary for (or conducive to) the realization of personal autonomy. Many of these can be grouped under the broad heading of manipulation. In general, manipulation occurs when an agent bypasses or distorts another's rational decision-making faculties in order to get her to do (or refrain from doing) what the manipulator wants her to do (or refrain from doing). As this general description allows, manipulation can occur either "behind the back" or "in front of the face" of the manipulated person. Hypnotizing someone against her will would be an example of the former; overtly appealing to a weakness of this person in order to get her to do what you want would be an example of the latter.

Manipulation, like coercion, subjects the victim to the will of another. But there is an important difference between manipulation and coercion. Coercion alters a person's option set. It makes one option an option that cannot be refused. Manipulation, by contrast, operates on the very wants and desires of the victim. It implants or stimulates desires in him in order to get him to do what the manipulator wants. This undermines autonomy to the extent that it prevents a person from acting on the basis of his own reasons and wants. Autonomy requires not only that we make choices and decisions, but also that our choices and decisions be based on reasons and wants that we identify – or would identify – as our own.[15]

For this reason, freedom from manipulation, like freedom from coercion, is central to independence. However, even if we are not coerced or manipulated by anyone, we can still fail to be sufficiently independent from others to be autonomous. This is true because a lack of sufficient independence can result from a failure in ourselves. To take an extreme example, I might be in the grip of a powerful unconscious drive to emulate what other people around me say and do.[16] Here I would fail to be sufficiently independent from others, even if I were completely free from coercion and manipulation.

No doubt this is an extreme case; but people fail to be sufficiently independent in other, less extreme, ways. To be autonomous a person must display a distinctive virtue. I shall call it the virtue of *independent-mindedness*. Care must be taken in describing this virtue. As everyone knows, people live in communities and their values, beliefs and tastes are

[15] The hypothetical "would" in this sentence raises some hard questions. A full treatment of manipulation and its significance for autonomy would need to specify the conditions under which it would be appropriate to say of a person that he would (or would not) identify with particular reasons or wants that others have played a causal role in producing in him.

[16] See J. Elster's distinction between "conformity" and "conformism" in *Sour Grapes*, p. 23.

influenced by those with whom they live. No one chooses the country, the culture or the family into which he or she is born. Nor does anyone consent to the web of attachments that first form his or her character. A description of the virtue of independent-mindedness that ran afoul of these elementary facts would turn personal autonomy into a chimera.

The possession of this virtue, then, does not make the absurd demand that people be free from all social influences. Rather, it concerns the myriad ways in which they respond to their social environment. Those who have this virtue work with the cultural resources available to them to form their own judgments about how they should lead their lives. In describing what he terms "authenticity" Feinberg comes close to painting an accurate portrait of the person who exhibits this virtue.

[He] can and does alter his convictions for reasons of his own, and does this without guilt or anxiety. [He] will buy his clothes in part to match his purse, his physical characteristics, and his functions; he will select his life-style to match his temperament, and his political attitudes to fit his ideals and interests. He cannot be loftily indifferent to the reactions of others, but he is willing to be moved by other considerations too.[17]

Feinberg's description captures the gist of the virtue. Independent-minded people form their own judgments and act for reasons of their own. However, Feinberg overstates matters slightly. Independent-minded people do not have to form their own judgments and act for reasons of their own in every area of their lives. Someone who chooses his projects for reasons of his own, but who does not care about fashion and is happy to wear the clothes that everyone else is wearing would not fail to possess the virtue. Self-determination is the ideal of people shaping their lives by choosing projects that reflect their understanding of what is valuable and worth doing. The virtue of independent-mindedness is necessary if people are to make these self-determining choices, but possession of the virtue does not mandate independence in all choices.

As this last remark indicates, it is important not to read too much into this virtue. Several further points reinforce this. First, independent-mindedness does not require emotional aloofness. Rugged individualists who pride themselves on remaining free of all attachments do not necessarily possess it. Likewise, those enmeshed in social relationships are not barred from it. Second, the virtue of independent-mindedness does not require a rebellious attitude toward authority. As several writers have shown, it is reasonable to defer to the judgment of others when they are experts in the matter in question or when doing so

---

[17] J. Feinberg, *Harm to Self*, p. 33.

facilitates valuable social cooperation.[18] Those who possess the virtue of independent-mindedness can act reasonably in this regard. Finally, the virtue does not require a general distrust of custom or tradition. For reasons of their own, people can and often do choose to live according to the customs and traditions of their time and place. Indeed, it should surprise no one that many find customary ways suit them. The customs and traditions people are most familiar with are precisely the ones that have most shaped their nature.

Drawing these points together, it can be said that to be sufficiently independent from others to realize the ideal of autonomy one must possess the virtue of independent-mindedness and one must be substantially free from the coercion and manipulation of others. This is still fairly abstract. But it is not possible to fix precisely and generally how independent-minded people must be or how free from coercion and manipulation they must be if they are to be autonomous. This is not possible since the answers vary from person to person, depending on their nature and circumstances.

The third element of personal autonomy refers to the vigor and self-consciousness necessary for self-directed action. As I have been describing it, autonomy is the ideal of active, self-conscious self-direction. But we need to know more about what type of activity and what type of self-consciousness must be present.

In shaping their lives, autonomous people have a sense that they freely make life-determining choices. They see themselves as choosers, planners, initiators of action; and they view the options before them as genuine options. Put slightly differently, and somewhat more formally, autonomous people satisfy two awareness conditions: they are aware of themselves as being the type of people who can make choices and decisions (and have made them in the past) *and* they are aware that the objects of their choices and decisions are options for them (and have been in the past).

These awareness conditions are modest. They define the minimally necessary sense in which an autonomous person is a self-conscious chooser. Those who do not satisfy them cannot realize the ideal of autonomy, for that ideal just is the ideal of people determining their lives by self-consciously choosing projects and taking on commitments. But while modest, the conditions are not toothless. They distinguish the self-conscious chooser from those who have come to believe, rightly or wrongly, that their lives are overwhelmed by forces beyond their control

---

[18] See J. Raz, "Authority, Law and Morality," and J. Finnis, "The Authority of Law in the Predicament of Contemporary Social Theory."

and from those who have come to believe, rightly or wrongly, that they have no genuine options open to them – that, so to speak, all their bridges have been burned and all their ships have been sunk.

Does self-determination require more than this modest level of self-awareness? Linking autonomy with articulate self-understanding, many have proposed further awareness conditions that require a person to identify with his higher self or with his second-order preferences.[19] This view is rejected here. By elevating the importance of certain cognitive virtues, it moves autonomy too close to the Socratic ideal of the examined life. Since philosophers are in the business of critical reflection, it is perhaps understandable that they are inclined to describe autonomy in these terms. But this yields an account of personal autonomy that threatens to put it beyond the grasp of those who have no skill in the hyper-rational activities of self-examination. This is implausible. People can and often do self-consciously fashion their lives without engaging in these activities. Even if the cognitive virtues associated with critical self-interpretation are genuine virtues, they are not essential to personal autonomy.

Up to this point nothing has been said about the vigor necessary for autonomous self-direction. Autonomous people do not merely view themselves as beings capable of self-conscious choice. They not only satisfy the awareness conditions stated above, but *actively* take charge of their lives. This requires vigor. In discussing the capacities for project pursuit I noted several types of psychological afflictions – neuroses, paranoia, schizophrenia, etc. – that undermine self-directed action. Less extreme forms of these afflictions are germane to the present context. These include world-weariness, emotional distress, depression, laziness and perhaps a growing sense of the meaninglessness of the world and one's place in it. These less severe, but much more common, afflictions sap people's strength, inhibiting their ability to plan their lives and to translate their decisions into actions. If they are present throughout long stretches of life, they undermine self-determination.

In the main, the absence of these afflictions suffices for the vigor necessary for self-directed action. Normally, people who view themselves as self-conscious choosers do take control of their lives unless they are prevented from doing so either by internal afflictions or external circumstances. In all likelihood, there is a psychological connection between the awareness conditions and the absence of these afflictions. Those who suffer from acute world-weariness or severe depression or an over-

---

[19] See, for example, C. Taylor, "What is Human Agency?" and G. Dworkin, "The Concept of Autonomy."

whelming sense of the absurdity of life are likely to view themselves as passive objects under the sway of forces outside their control. Feeling helpless before events, they cease to think of themselves as active agents in the world.

This is not to deny that there are some who do not suffer from these afflictions and who view themselves as beings capable of self-conscious choice, but who, nonetheless, prefer to drift through life or just lack the energy to take charge of their affairs. It is not necessary to identify the causes of the lack of vigor in their lives to conclude that they too fail to realize the ideal of autonomy.

Consider, finally, the fourth element. Even those who have the capacities for project pursuit, are sufficiently independent from others and have the self-consciousness and vigor necessary for self-directed action will have difficulty realizing autonomy if their social environment does not provide them with a wide range of eligible pursuits to choose from. Let us call this last element the *option requirement*.[20]

The significance of the option requirement is obvious. Choice presupposes options. For us to be in a position to shape our lives according to our own lights we need access to a range of pursuits to choose from. Otherwise, our "choices" will not be choices at all. To invoke a metaphor: options are the cloth out of which autonomous people cut their lives and – at least up to a point – the larger and more varied the cloth, the better the finished product.[21]

Fully understanding the option requirement demands answers to two questions. First, what are options? Second, what counts as a wide range? Options refer to opportunities to engage in projects, commitments, ways of life, and, more generally, courses of action. Roughly, they divide into two groups: comprehensive and peripheral. *Comprehensive options* are those that are fundamental or central to our sense of identity. They provide the organizing framework within which further choices and decisions are made. *Peripheral options* either fall within this framework or are not related to comprehensive pursuits. An example may help clarify the distinction. The decision to lead a Christian life would be a comprehensive pursuit. The decision to attend a particular church would be a peripheral pursuit within its framework and the decision to take a vacation to the Grand Canyon would be a peripheral pursuit not related to it.

Some people may have few comprehensive pursuits. As I noted earlier,

---

[20] More than most writers on the subject, Raz has stressed the importance of what I am calling the option requirement. See *The Morality of Freedom*, pp. 369–99. I draw on some of his discussion below.

[21] Better in the sense of being more autonomous, not necessarily better *tout court*.

some may choose to lead a life of continual spontaneity and variety, and such a life may not sit well with engagement in comprehensive pursuits. But for most people these pursuits are the ones most central to their self-determination; peripheral pursuits either have much less significance or acquire significance only by being related in the appropriate way to their comprehensive pursuits.

By and large, both comprehensive and peripheral pursuits are provided or constituted by the social practices of the societies in which people live. The option to open up a small business, to enlist in the military, to get married, to join a church, to travel or to take up an interest in astronomy are options only for those who live in social environments which make possible these particular ways of acting. This is not to say that all options are dependent on social practices for their existence. Some options, like the option to have children, are natural in the sense that all normal human beings, no matter what society they live in, will have some knowledge of it. But options like this are the exception, not the rule.

The option requirement is satisfied if a society provides its members with a wide range of options to choose from. This brings us to the second question – what does it mean to say that a range of options is wide? Before tackling this question, we should note that the option requirement can be personalized. We can ask whether a range of options is sufficiently wide for a given person. Alternatively, the option requirement can be taken to apply to all people in a society. On this second understanding, it is possible for a person to be autonomous even if the society in which she lives does not satisfy the option requirement. Her society may provide her with a sufficiently wide range of options, while failing to provide others with such a range.[22]

Unless otherwise indicated, I will henceforth intend the second understanding when I refer to the option requirement. But it will be helpful to begin thinking about the matter by working with the personalized understanding. When does a person have access to a sufficiently wide range of options? The first point to make is that it is not just the number of options open to him that matters. Having access to two options that are significantly different may be better than having access to ten options that are very much alike. So to be sufficiently wide a person's option set must include a range of significantly different options. The second point is that a person must have at least some options that are, from his point of view, worthy of choice. If he has access to a large number of significantly different options, but none of them are options that he could

---

[22] This helps explain how it is possible for a person to realize autonomy in a society that is not autonomy-supporting.

imagine himself wholeheartedly engaging in, then he does not have a sufficiently wide range to be autonomous.[23] The third point follows on the heels of the second. An option set must include some options that do not require a person to violate moral constraints or fail to live up to his or her moral duties.[24]

Beyond this, a person's option set should include options that give him the opportunity to develop his talents and capacities.[25] Since people have capacities to do a bewilderingly large number of things, some way must be found to limit this requirement. Towards this goal, it is helpful to distinguish capacities and talents from ambitions and desires. The latter two differ from the former two in that they require more specific circumstances for their satisfaction. Suppose Mary wants to be a concert pianist. The fulfillment of this ambition requires the presence of a relatively well-defined, particularized option. But if this option is not present, it does not follow that Mary will not be able to develop her musical talents. She may find that her talents can be developed in other ways, e.g. by mastering another musical instrument. This is true of capacities and talents in general. Most of them can be developed in different ways.

So long as talents and capacities are not confused with particular ambitions and desires there is little reason to think that it will be impossible to provide people with a range of options that is sufficiently wide to allow them to develop their talents and capacities. However, this distinction raises a problem of its own. It may be easy for children to channel their talents and capacities toward options that are available to them; and, for this reason, it may be plausible to hold that the development of their talents and capacities does not require the presence of one

---

[23] It may be asked, what if people have outrageous views about what types of options would qualify as worthy of choice? Suppose they believe they must have the option of being a slave-owner, an Olympic sprinter or the spouse of a glamorous movie star. All other options have no value in their eyes. Would this show that their option sets, no matter how wide, would not be sufficient for them if they did not include one of these particular options? So long as their beliefs are sincere, I am inclined to think it would. To be autonomous one must have access to options that one genuinely believes are worth pursuing. It does not follow, however, that these people would have a strong claim on others to provide them with these options.

[24] See J. Raz, *The Morality of Freedom*, p. 380.

[25] It may be objected that this condition is unnecessary. If a person has access to a set of options that allow him to lead a satisfying life, why should it matter whether the set includes options that would allow him to develop his capacities and talents? The answer is that for most people a satisfying life is bound up with projects and goals that draw on their capacities and talents. And even those who have no inclination to develop their talents and capacities to any significant extent will often believe that a satisfying life requires at least having the opportunity to do so. Of course it is possible that there are some people who do not need options to develop their talents and capacities to be autonomous. But here I am interested in the general case.

set of particularized options rather than another. But this is much less plausible for adults. Adults will have invested time and energy in particular options; and this investment will, in some cases, make those options indispensable to the future development of their talents.

This problem suggests an additional condition. *In order for people to have access to a sufficiently wide range of options they must not only have access to options that would allow them to develop their capacities and talents, but also to particular options that have become indispensable to this development.* This makes it more difficult to satisfy the option requirement. If it is true that people, by investing time and energy in a particular option, can make it indispensable to their autonomy, then the option requirement, under some circumstances, will not be fully satisfiable. Maintaining an important option for some may prevent others from having access to a sufficiently wide range. In such cases the autonomy of some will be pitted against the autonomy of others and no resolution will allow all to have access to a sufficiently wide range of options.

This poses an important problem for a political theory that takes autonomy seriously.[26] Rather than try to resolve the problem here (which would take an extended discussion), I will merely point out that the option requirement will often be satisfied in degrees. The more people in a society who have access to a sufficiently wide range of options, the more the option requirement will be satisfied in that society. And, it is worth adding, in an ideally well-ordered society the option requirement would be fully satisfied.

Putting all this together, we arrive at the following formulation. The option requirement is satisfied to varying degrees. The degree to which it is satisfied depends on the number of people who have access to a sufficiently wide range of options. A range of options is sufficiently wide for a person if it consists of significantly different options that are deemed by him to be worthy of choice, if the pursuit of these options does not require him to act immorally, and if the options provide him with opportunities for developing his talents and capacities.

This completes the discussion of the four basic elements that comprise the ideal of personal autonomy. As I have described them, they define a distinct character ideal that is clearly related to the root idea of self-government. Autonomous people actively and self-consciously take charge of their affairs and are not subject to excessive coercion or manipulation from others. Moreover, the realization of the ideal is compatible with a wide range of ways of life. It does not, although this

[26] In saying this, I do not mean to imply that this type of problem is unique to political theories that take autonomy seriously. Other political theories will have their own distributional problems to contend with.

144 Autonomy and perfectionism

will require more discussion, conflict with much of what gives value and meaning to life. Finally, as described here, autonomy falls short of a complete ideal of the good life. Autonomous people are not necessarily moral, wise, prudent, happy or fulfilled.

One final point. Several of the elements discussed above can be realized to varying extents. For example, people can be more or less free from coercion and they can have access to a wider or narrower range of options. This suggests that personal autonomy is itself realized in degrees. This is correct; but it is also true that each of the constituent elements has a threshold, and to be autonomous a person must satisfy the threshold with respect to each element. For this reason, I will write as if there is a clear dividing line between autonomous and non-autonomous people. This is not entirely accurate, since the realization of the ideal comes in degrees and the line is vague; but so long as this is borne in mind no confusion should result.

Six value claims

In characterizing personal autonomy I have kept one eye on what makes it valuable; in discussing its value we must now keep one eye on how it has been characterized. The description of the ideal and the arguments for its value must fit together.

I have claimed that autonomy is a central component of a fully good life. This is a strong claim, but stronger claims have been made on its behalf. In this section I distinguish six claims about its value. Grasping them helps one understand the senses in which autonomy is and is not a valuable character ideal.

The six claims are:

(1) Autonomy is instrumentally valuable. Its realization facilitates the realization of other (weighty) goods.
(2) Autonomy is intrinsically valuable. Its realization is valuable for its own sake.
(3) Autonomy is a central component of a fully good life.
(4) Autonomy is unconditionally valuable.
(5) All people have a conclusive reason to realize the ideal of autonomy.
(6) If a person does not realize the ideal of autonomy, his life has no value.

I have already suggested that (1), (2) and (3) are true. But these claims should not be confused with or thought to entail (4), (5) or (6). Indeed, I will argue that these latter claims are false. Personal autonomy is not unconditionally valuable; it is not an ideal that all people, no matter what their circumstances are, have conclusive reason to realize; and it is not the source of value in the sense that if one fails to be autonomous one's life can have no value.

Whether or not I am right to reject these claims, one cannot refute (1), (2) or (3) by presenting a counterexample to (4), (5) or (6). This is worth keeping in mind. It renders nugatory some objections that are sometimes brought against arguments for the truth of (1), (2) and (3).

The intrinsic value of autonomy

We need to establish (3). This claim has sufficient strength to support the judgment that modern western societies have compelling reasons to promote the character ideal of autonomy. And this is the ultimate judgment we are after. But I will start by focusing on the arguments for the weaker (1) and (2). This, I hope, will provide some insight into how the stronger (3) could be true.

In this section I discuss an argument for (2); and in the next section I discuss an argument for (1). According to (2), the realization of autonomy is intrinsically valuable. Intrinsic value can be understood in terms of one of two locutions. It is sometimes said that if something is intrinsically valuable, then it is *"valuable in itself."* At other times it is said that if something is intrinsically valuable, then it is *"valued for its own sake."* However, these two locutions are not equivalent. The former refers to the source of value. It implies that an intrinsically valuable thing gets its value from itself, not from something else. The latter refers to the way in which a thing is valued. It implies that an intrinsically valuable thing is valued for its own sake and not for the sake of something else.[27]

How, then, should we interpret the claim that autonomy is an intrinsic value? In characterizing autonomy I took care to describe it in such a way that it would not be misunderstood as a complete ideal. I also took care to describe it as a constituent component of a larger whole. And I claimed that its value derives from its contribution to this larger whole (the fully good life). So understood, the realization of autonomy is not an ultimate end. It does not have value in itself. But it may, and I shall argue that it should, be valued for its own sake.

It is a good question whether any argument could conclusively establish this. If autonomy is intrinsically valuable in the sense that it is valuable for its own sake, how could this be demonstrated? One response would be to say that it needs no demonstration. Autonomy, it might be

---

[27] For a discussion of the differences between these two locutions, see C. Korsgaard, "Two Distinctions in Goodness."

held, is self-evidently valuable. All one must do is understand the ideal – bring it into clear view – and one will see its intrinsic worth. But this response is not satisfying when one is confronted with an interlocutor who both appears to understand what personal autonomy is and denies that it is valuable for its own sake.[28]

The problem, then, remains of how to argue for the intrinsic value of autonomy. The problem is formidable, for if autonomy is indeed valuable for its own sake, then it will not be possible to show that this is true by showing how it serves some other value. Still, the problem is not insurmountable. One way to argue for the intrinsic value of autonomy is to appeal to intuitions about particular cases and then to show that the intuitions are best explained by the truth of the claim that autonomy is intrinsically valuable. This is the method I will adopt.[29]

Consider the following case. Suppose I know that you are wise and that you have an excellent understanding of what is good for me. You know my talents, temperament and vulnerabilities and you know what types of projects would best suit my nature. Further suppose I know that you are a person of good will who cares about my well-being. Given these facts, we can ask: Would my life go better if I let you take control of it? Would it be a better life if I always turned to you for direction as to what I should do before I took up any project or commitment?

Most of us strongly think the answers to these questions are "no." It can be reasonable to defer to the judgment of others some of the time in some circumstances; but a person who surrendered his or her judgment in all contexts would not lead a fully good human life. This intuition is explained by the idea that it is intrinsically good for people to take charge of their own affairs and lead their lives on their own terms, even when others could do a better job of it.

But some may object. "The intuition in this case is not to be trusted. In the real world it is extremely unlikely that there is anyone with the wisdom, knowledge and good will necessary to run my life better than I could run it. We are led to judge the case under consideration in the way that we do because we are influenced by the types of judgments we would make in more realistic scenarios." If this is right, the fact that we naturally resist the idea that I should let you take control of my life may

---

[28] While not satisfying, this type of response may be appropriate in some contexts. There may exist bedrock values and ideals, values and ideals that cannot be justified by reference to other considerations. If so, these values and ideals would simply have to be grasped or perceived by those who came to understand them. Moreover, the failure of some to grasp or perceive them would not in any way show that they were not real.

[29] This method will not yield a demonstrative proof. Someone who shares none of the intuitions can resist the conclusion. But very few arguments in political philosophy yield demonstrative proofs.

be explained by the fact that the suppositions behind the case are unrealistic.

It is not clear that this objection succeeds. But, for the sake of argument, let us grant it. Let us suppose that if we saw matters clearly, and set aside our preconceptions, we would agree that the right judgment in this case is that I ought to let you take control of my life.

Consider now a second, related, case. In this case we have to judge the lives of two people. Person A is wise and has self-knowledge. He chooses projects that suit his nature and reflect his understanding of what is valuable and worthwhile. Person A leads a good, morally decent, life. Person B is also wise and has self-knowledge. But she finds the process of decision-making irksome and does not enjoy making important life decisions. Fortunately, person B has a friend with the requisite wisdom, knowledge and good will to make these decisions for her. Person B lets this friend take over her affairs and she leads a good, morally decent life.

In this second case it can be asked whether Person A and Person B lead equally good lives? Once again, most of us strongly think "no." Even if we think that Person B leads a good life, and even if we concede that Person B leads a better life than people who do a worse job of running their own affairs, we think that Person B lacks something important that Person A has. Person B leads a good life, but she does not lead her own life, whereas Person A leads a good life that is his own. This makes Person A's life better. And this intuition is best explained by the truth of the claim that autonomy is an intrinsic value.

This intuition can be further fleshed out by considering why it is good for people to lead their own lives. By taking charge of their affairs and charting their own course through life, people give meaning to their lives. They impart significance to it. This does not mean that those like Person B who let others run their affairs live meaningless lives. Their lives have meaning; but the meaning is not something they give to it themselves. So, on this view, it is valuable for people to lead their own lives because it is valuable for them to give meaning to their own lives.

This prompts two further questions. First, why is it valuable for people to give meaning to their own lives? So long as their lives are meaningful, why should it matter whether they are the ones giving it meaning? Second, is it not possible for people to give meaning to their lives non-autonomously?

The first question is the more difficult one. I believe that the answer to it is that giving meaning to one's life is essential to having a character. Let me explain. In one sense, all people have a character. Their character is determined by their biological nature and the environmental circumstances that have shaped them. Even a slave who from birth has been under the constant control of a master has a character in this passive sense. But there is another sense in which such a slave has no character. Since he has played no part in fashioning who he is, he has no character that is his own. The slave's character, to the extent that he has one, is determined solely by what happens to him, not by what he does. It is valuable for people to give meaning to their lives because it is valuable for them to have a character in this active sense. By engaging in some projects and taking on some commitments, we make ourselves one type of person rather than another. And it is very plausible to think that having a character (in this active sense) is intrinsically good.

Of course the slave referred to above is an extreme case. He is non-autonomous, but it does not follow that autonomy is necessary if people are to have a character in the active sense. Most non-autonomous people have more independence than this slave. This brings us to the second question. Is it not possible for people to give meaning to their lives non-autonomously? To answer this question we must recall that autonomy comes in degrees. Likewise, the lack of autonomy comes in degrees. To the extent that people let others run their affairs or simply drift through life without making decisions they resemble the slave. To that extent, then, they do not have a character in the active sense. The reason for focusing on the slave is simply to bring out more clearly and vividly the main point. It is valuable for people to give meaning to their lives because it is valuable for them to have a character in the active sense. To varying degrees non-autonomous people fail to have this type of character.

This provides further support for the intuition that it is intrinsically good for people to lead their own lives. But the cases considered so far call attention only to the independence and, to a lesser degree, the self-consciousness and vigor necessary for a person to be autonomous. They show that it is intrinsically good for people to take charge of their affairs and not merely follow the judgments of others. But the cases do not illuminate the importance of the option requirement. They show that it is intrinsically good for people to take charge of their affairs, not that it is intrinsically good for them to do so while engaging in projects from among a wide range of options. So it may be thought that the intuitions that I have been drawing on do not yet provide support for the claim that autonomy is intrinsically valuable.

Consider a third case.[30] This one invites us to compare the goodness of a person's life under two sets of circumstances.

[30] I have benefited from Hurka's discussion of a similar case. See T. Hurka, *Perfectionism*, p. 150.

Situation 1 Sally has two significantly different options, X and Y. Both are valuable. Sally chooses option X.

Situation 2 Sally has eight significantly different options. All eight are valuable. These options include X and Y and six others. Sally chooses option X.

Almost everyone agrees that Sally is better off in situation 2 than in situation 1. She has a wider range of choice and this can only put her in a better position.[31] But since she chooses option X in both situations, the judgment that she is better off in situation 2 than in situation 1 cannot be supported by the claim that in situation 2 her wider range of choice allows her to choose an option that better suits her.

To support this judgment there must be something independently good about having a wider range of options. It is not merely that having a wider range of options is better because it typically better enables us to get what we want, it must also be true that having a wider range of options is valuable for its own sake. This thought can be sharpened. In situation 1 Sally both chooses option X and chooses not to choose option Y. In situation 2 she chooses option X and chooses not to choose seven significantly different other options. From this we can infer that in situation 2 Sally is *more responsible* for the state of affairs that obtains than she is in situation 1. In both situations option X is chosen; but in situation 2 Sally is responsible for the non-realization of seven alternatives, whereas in situation 1 she is responsible for the non-realization of only one alternative. For this reason Sally is more responsible for the resulting state of affairs in situation 2 than in situation 1.

The intuition that Sally's choice in situation 2 is more valuable than her choice in situation 1 is best explained by the claim that autonomy is an intrinsic value. If autonomy is intrinsically valuable, then it is good for people to be more responsible for the states of affairs that their choices bring about (so long as those states of affairs are valuable). This greater responsibility reflects a greater exercise of self-determination; for self-determination is a function not only of what we choose to do with our lives, but also of what we choose not to do with them. Having access to (and being aware that one has access to) a wide range of options makes us more responsible for our choices in the sense that it makes our choices more our own. Reflection on this case, then, adds further support for the view that autonomy is an intrinsic value.

The first two cases suggest that it is intrinsically good for people to take charge of their affairs and run their own lives. The third case suggests that it is intrinsically good for people to make choices from

---

[31] This is true, but only up to a point. See chapter 8 below.

among a wide range of options. The claim that autonomy is an intrinsic value best accounts for the intuitions in all three cases. This gives us reason to believe that the claim is true.

The instrumental value of autonomy

According to claim (1), autonomy is an instrumental value. It is a valuable character ideal because it helps us achieve other (weighty) things of value. This claim does not compete with (2). Many goods are both intrinsically and instrumentally valuable.

Realizing autonomy might help people achieve many other values; but here I am interested in only one. This is the ideal of self-development. This ideal warrants attention because a case can be made that it is a good of considerable weight. If this case stands up, then a demonstration that autonomy is instrumentally valuable in achieving self-development would show that autonomy is an important value itself.

Before I discuss the good of self-development in more detail, a preliminary point needs stressing. The claim that "A is instrumentally valuable in achieving B" can be interpreted to mean either "A is an indispensable condition for the achievement of B" or "A facilitates the achievement of B." In this context I am appealing to the latter interpretation. Autonomy facilitates, but is not an indispensable condition for, the achievement of self-development. This is a consequence of the point made above. Autonomy and self-development are not conceptually linked. It is possible to realize one without realizing the other.

Self-development refers to the development of a person's talents and capacities. We say of someone who has achieved self-development that he or she has "realized his or her potential" or "fulfilled his or her promise." However, this fairly straightforward idea gives rise to two puzzles that must be solved if the ideal of self-development is to be coherent.

The first puzzle is how to make sense of the idea that we have determinate talents and capacities. According to Mill and von Humboldt, we have natural potentialities that unfold and come to fruition under appropriate social conditions. But this suggestion is not very convincing. Social conditions do not simply nourish or provide space for the development of talents and capacities. They also constitute them. Once this is recognized, it may seem that our talents and capacities are not determinate; and if they are not determinate, it may seem that self-development is not possible.

The solution to this puzzle is to reject both the view that we have fully determinate natural potentialities and the view that social conditions completely constitute our talents and capacities. The correct view lies in between these two extremes. People's talents are a product of their genetic endowment, their cultural surroundings and their own efforts to develop different aspects of their personality. Some of them are fixed at birth, others grow out of the ones fixed at birth and still others are acquired willy-nilly as people wend their way through life. While it is a mistake to think that all of a person's talents are determinate and invariant, it remains true that at any particular point in a person's life he or she can intelligibly ask him- or herself what his or her talents and capacities are; and he or she can intelligibly guide his or her conduct by considering what would best develop them. This is all that is needed for the idea of self-development to make sense.

The second puzzle emerges from the recognition that some talents are for vicious activities. Some people have a skill for gratuitously offending others. Is this the type of thing that should be developed if a person is to achieve self-development? If the answer is "no," then only valuable potentialities can be talents and capacities; and this is straightforwardly implausible. But if the answer is "yes," then the value of self-development is compromised, for surely the full realization of wicked talents could not be valuable. The response to this dilemma is to concede that talents can be vicious and wicked, but deny that this undercuts the value of self-development. It is good for us to develop our talents and capacities if they, by and large, enable us to do valuable things. For those whose talents are for wicked or degrading activities, self-development is not a good.[32] They are better off not developing them.[33] This implies that self-development is a conditional good.

But the fact that a good is a conditional good does not mean that it could not be a very important good or even a necessary component of a fully good life. So long as this is understood, the claim that self-development is a conditional good should not be thought to compromise its value. People have reason to develop their talents and they have reason to cultivate good, rather than bad, aspects of their character. The former reason is parasitic on the latter, but it remains a reason, nonetheless.

Resolving these puzzles helps show that self-development is a coherent ideal. But one final point needs to be made before we consider the

---

[32] For self-development to be a good it must also be true that a person has talents and capacities whose development would have some intelligible point. Developing a talent for standing on one's head, for example, might have no value.

[33] Some may think otherwise: the issue is a contested one. Some may say that it would be better for others if such people did not develop their talents, but it would be better *for them* if they did. I cannot defend my judgment here. But see W. Quinn, "Rationality and the Human Good" for the outlines of a defense.

relationship between it and autonomy. This point relates to the atheticism of self-development. Self-development demands energy and vigor; for while it is possible for one's talents and capacities to unfold effortlessly, this is not the normal case. Most people must strive to fulfill their promise. This arouses the suspicion that self-development is incompatible with the passive enjoyment of life. It conjures up the image of someone ceaselessly struggling to develop his or her talents to the maximum possible extent, leaving little time for the simple pleasures of leisure and relaxation.

However, one should not read too much into self-development. Like other components of a good life, it is not all that matters. A fully good life contains a range of goods that must be balanced against one another. Depending on their nature and temperament, different people will not unreasonably balance these goods in different ways. All that self-development demands is that people develop their talents and capacities to some significant degree.

I have claimed that autonomy is instrumentally valuable to self-development in the sense that the realization of the former facilitates the achievement of the latter. Two arguments substantiate this claim. The first one draws on the independence and vigor that mark the autonomous person. The second one draws on the option requirement.

The first argument builds on the Millian idea that people generally are in a better position than others to know what projects would best develop their talents. Few have perfect self-knowledge, but most know more about themselves than others do. This would not matter much if people all had the same talents and capacities. For if this were true, it would not be unreasonable to follow the lead of others, particularly if one had good reason to think that they knew what they were doing. But, while people share some common capacities and abilities, they differ markedly in others; and to achieve self-development they need to develop their distinctive abilities as well as the ones that they share with everyone else.

For these reasons, people who form their own judgments and act for reasons of their own are, other things being equal, better able to develop their talents than those who either take their cues from others or drift passively through life. This is not an exceptionless claim. There are some who know straight away what their talents are and how they could best be developed. Mozart may have known in childhood that he should pursue a life of music and he may have been driven by innate impulses to develop his talents. For him, autonomy may not have been instrumentally valuable for self-development. But most people are not like this. They do not know straight away what their talents are or how they can best be realized. For them, this knowledge comes, if it comes at all, only from a process of trial and error in which they try out different pursuits.

Speaking generally, then, to develop their talents and capacities, people need to take up a range of pursuits and they need to be able to evaluate whether they can succeed in them and whether the pursuits call for talents and dispositions which they in fact possess.[34] Given this, it is plausible to believe that the independence and vigor that mark the autonomous person will be instrumentally valuable to the achievement of self-development.[35]

This argument can be clarified and strengthened by considering two objections to it, both of which merit comment. The first one holds that the argument rests on an unrealistic picture of how people come to acquire and pursue projects. According to this objection, people do not try out different pursuits and then settle on the ones that they judge best fit their nature; but rather, given the limited time they have on this earth and given the fact that any projects they take up will partially constitute who they are, they must, for the most part, stick with projects that either first strike them as worthwhile or that they have been guided into taking up by others. The trial and error process mentioned in the argument, therefore, fails to correspond to the way that people actually lead their lives.

In responding to this objection we do not need to deny the obvious – almost everyone has projects that he or she adopted without going through a process of trial and error. Nor is it necessary to deny the evident fact that some projects may be of such a nature that it is not feasible or morally permissible for people to drop them and pursue others. For example, if a parent, after bringing a child into the world, decides that parenting does not suit him, he is not free to abandon this project and do something else.

Conceding all of this, however, does not in the least undermine the argument in question. This argument is based on two contingent, empirically defeasible, but nonetheless plausible propositions:

[34] More specifically, people need to ask themselves a whole range of questions. Consider the list provided by Daniel Dennett. "Among the questions facing a sophisticated self-controlling agent are: could I revise my basic projects and goals in such a way as to improve my chances of satisfaction? Are there grand strategies or policies that are better than my current ones? Is there a style of operation that would suit my goals better than my current style? Will my current policies tend to lead me into tight quarters with little room to maneuver and great risk of disaster? What should my general policy regarding risk be?" (*Elbow Room*, p. 86).
[35] Similar reasons led Mill to favor the active over the passive character. See *On Liberty*, pp. 55–56.

(a) People are in a better position than others to know what projects would best develop their talents.

(b) Therefore, if people autonomously choose and/or revise their projects with an eye toward developing their talents, they will be more likely to develop their talents than if they take their cues from others or drift passively through life.

The first objection does not challenge either proposition. It contends only that the space in which people can and do make decisions about which projects to take up, pursue and abandon is smaller than this argument may, at first blush, indicate. But while this may be on the mark, it is surely the case that there remain enough important decisions within this space for the argument, if sound, to be significant. This is borne out by the everyday occurrences, at least in modern western societies, of people changing their careers, taking up new hobbies and terminating personal relationships.

The second objection is more bold. It seeks to cast doubt on proposition (b) by denying that autonomous self-direction is generally conducive to self-development. Commenting critically on the third chapter of Mill's *On Liberty*, James Fitzjames Stephen expressed the basic idea behind this objection:

Habitual exertion is the greatest of all invigorators of character, and restraint and coercion in one form or another is the great stimulus to exertion.[36]

Stephen's point is that the motivation to achieve self-development depends on a vigorous and strong character and that this type of character is best cultivated not by leaving people free to lead their lives on their own terms, but rather by subjecting them to discipline and constraint.

If Stephen is right about this, then it will complicate the argument we have advanced. But would it refute it? It would not, for Stephen overlooks an important consequence of discipline and constraint, namely, that discipline and constraint can and often do close off routes to self-development. Even if, for a typical person, the motivation to develop her talents would be strengthened by coercion, it might still be true that coercion would prevent her from pursuing projects that would best develop her talents. So, even on the assumption that Stephen is right, we cannot conclude that discipline and constraint better promote self-development than leaving people free to lead their lives on their own terms. To draw that conclusion we would need to show that the advantages of discipline and constraint generally outweigh their disadvantages with regard to self-development.

---

[36] J. F. Stephen, *Liberty, Equality, Fraternity*, p. 31.

Nonetheless, Stephen's remarks do bring to light a potential problem for the account of autonomy presented here. As we have seen, autonomy is an ideal that consists of a number of different elements. Among these elements are the independence necessary for people to chart their own course through life and the vigor necessary for them actively to take control of their affairs. However, it may be that in some circumstances efforts to promote one of these elements (protecting people's independence from others) will impede the promotion of another element (strengthening their capacity or motivation to take charge of their affairs). When and if this occurs, it will not be clear what an autonomy-promoting society should do.

It is important to see, however, that this problem does not substantially threaten the claim that autonomy is instrumentally valuable to self-development. For, as we have seen, autonomy includes, as one of its constituent elements, the vigor necessary to take charge of one's affairs. So if Stephen is right that discipline and constraint are necessary if people are to have vigorous characters, then this poses a problem about *how* to promote autonomy – given that discipline and constraint may be both necessary to autonomy and inimical to it.[37] Yet the problem here, while it might be genuine, would not give us any reason to reject the first argument.

Having considered these objections, we can now turn to the second argument, which supplements the first one. Earlier I claimed that the option requirement (on the personalized understanding) is a precondition for the realization of personal autonomy. To be autonomous a person needs access to a wide range of pursuits. The argument presently under consideration maintains that having access to a wide range of pursuits facilitates self-development.[38]

To grasp its thrust, return to the earlier example concerning Sally. In situation 1 she has access to two options, while in situation 2 she has access to eight significantly different options. In discussing the intrinsic value of autonomy I stipulated that she chooses option X in both

---

[37] A natural response to this is to say that discipline and constraint are more appropriate in childhood when people's characters are first being formed and that independence from others is more appropriate as they get older and become more capable of governing themselves. But this response, while reasonable, may not completely resolve the problem.

[38] Like the first one, this argument has a Millian pedigree. See, for instance, *On Liberty*, p. 65: "Such are the differences among human beings in their sources of pleasure, their susceptibilities of pain, and the operation on them of different physical and moral agencies that, unless there is a corresponding diversity in their modes of life, they neither obtain their fair share of happiness, nor grow up to the mental, moral, and aesthetic stature of which their nature is capable." However, it is necessary to bear in mind that personal autonomy, as I have characterized it, is not the same thing as Mill's ideal of individuality.

situations. But this stipulation can be dropped. In many contexts when a person has access to a wider range of options she will choose a different option than she would have chosen if she had access to fewer options. The reason for this is that having access to a wider range of options increases the likelihood that one of the additional options will better suit her ideals, temperament or talents.

This is a fairly elementary point, but it reveals the strength of the second argument. If we assume that Sally is motivated to develop her talents and capacities, and if we assume that she is a reasonably good judge of what types of pursuits would develop them, then it follows that giving her access to a wider range of options would facilitate her self-development. Both of the assumptions in the antecedent of this conditional could be false. Sally might have no motivation to develop her talents or she might be notoriously bad at selecting pursuits that would develop them. But while the assumptions do not always hold, they are generally plausible. In the main, people are motivated to develop their talents; and, in the main, they are better judges than others of what pursuits would best develop them. This is sufficient to justify the claim advanced by the second argument.

This argument, like the first one, becomes stronger when coupled with some very plausible claims about individual diversity. We enter the world with diverse native endowments, inheriting different aptitudes and proclivities. As we grow up, we are exposed to different social influences. We then cultivate some aspects of our endowment and neglect others. This combination of genetic difference, diverse social influences and our own efforts to develop different aspects of our personality result in a wide range of characters. As common observation confirms, we differ in talents, dispositions and preferences.

Given this individual diversity, if most people in a society are to achieve self-development, then the society must contain a wide range of options. Since the same options will not suit all people, the society must provide all its members with a wide range. Otherwise, it will fail to provide them with adequate opportunities for self-development. Satisfying the option requirement, therefore, both promotes personal autonomy and facilitates self-development.

These two arguments vindicate the claim that autonomy is instrumentally valuable to the achievement of self-development. But it might be wondered how significant this claim is. It might be thought that self-development is an achievement, but one of no real consequence. If this were right, then the argument that autonomy facilitates self-development would not earn much for the value of autonomy.

To allay this worry we need to identify the considerations that account for the value of self-development. Since my primary topic in this chapter is autonomy, not self-development, my discussion here will be brief. Nevertheless, three considerations can be mentioned. They suggest that self-development is an ideal of considerable weight.

The first consideration draws on the intuition that a fully good human life is one which contains pursuits that give it depth. The achievement of self-development is one important way in which a person can lead such a life. By developing his talents and capacities, he can accomplish valuable things; and these accomplishments can add depth to his life, making it the kind of life that is worth living.

It is important not to exaggerate this consideration. Some may find that selfless devotion to their families gives their lives a depth that it would not have if they sought to develop their talents. Others may find this depth in a commitment to a particular cause or religion. The point is only that for many this sense of depth is intimately bound up with their own accomplishments; and to accomplish worthwhile things they generally need to develop their talents.[39]

The second consideration appeals to what Rawls has termed the "Aristotelian Principle." This principle states that "other things equal, human beings enjoy the exercise of their realized capacities (their innate or trained abilities), and this enjoyment increases the more the capacity is realized, or the greater its complexity."[40] If this principle accurately describes human psychology, it provides a powerful argument for self-development. People are constituted so as to derive enjoyment and satisfaction from the development of their talents.

The third consideration strengthens the second one. In propounding the Aristotelian Principle, Rawls writes as if he has donned the hat of an empirical psychologist. He asserts that this principle is "a deep psychological fact"[41] and that it "expresses a psychological law governing changes in the patterns of our desires."[42] These assertions may be correct; but in the absence of empirical evidence, evidence that Rawls does not provide, they cannot be confidently affirmed.[43] Interestingly,

---

[39] This is not always true. It is possible for some to accomplish much with little exertion. But, by and large, to accomplish something worthwhile people need to develop their talents.

[40] J. Rawls, *A Theory of Justice*, p. 426.

[41] Ibid. p. 432.   [42] Ibid. p. 427.

[43] This is the sum total of the evidence that Rawls provides. "[The Aristotelian Principle] seems to be borne out by many facts of everyday life, and by the behavior of children and some of the higher animals. Moreover, it appears to be susceptible to an evolutionary explanation. Natural selection must have favored creatures of whom this principle is true." Ibid. p. 431.

however, Rawls does not say much about the normative issue raised by the Aristotelian Principle. A natural question to ask is whether it is good for humans to be motivated in the ways prescribed by it.

Although Rawls does not directly address this question,[44] there are solid reasons for answering it affirmatively. For consider. When people develop their talents and capacities, everyone can benefit.[45] When an artist creates a beautiful painting, a scientist discovers a new truth about the physical world, an entrepreneur invents a new product or an athlete develops his or her prowess, all can share in these accomplishments. Of course not everyone who achieves self-development will accomplish something of great value. Most of us have limited talents; and, as a consequence, are not capable of great accomplishments. But the general point still holds. We have reason to encourage others to develop their talents because we often can share in their accomplishments; and even when these accomplishments are of no great moment, they still can enrich our lives.[46]

Adopting some more terminology from Rawls, we can say that the disposition to develop one's talents and capacities is a "*broadly based property*." That is, it is an attribute that it is rational for people to want one another to have.[47] It is plausible to believe that a good society would promote broadly based properties in its members, at least if doing so was possible and did not require violating any moral constraints. Assuming this is correct, we can infer that a good society would promote the disposition to develop one's talents; for there does not seem to be any reason to think that doing so would be impossible or would require the violation of any moral constraint.

It now should be clear how this consideration strengthens the second one. Even if the Aristotelian Principle does not express a deep psychological fact about human motivation, it may still be true that in a good society the motivation expressed by it would be fairly widespread. The

---

[44] Rawls does claim that the Aristotelian Principle when taken in conjunction with other general facts "accounts for our considered judgments of value" (ibid. p. 432). But he does not explain why this is so.

[45] Assuming their talents and capacities are for valuable things. Henceforth, I omit this qualification.

[46] This point is a natural extension of von Humboldt's defense of community. He claimed that "It is through a social union . . . that each is enabled to participate in the rich collective resources of all the others." *The Limits of State Action*, p. 16. (Quoted by J. Rawls in *A Theory of Justice*, pp. 523–24 n4.) The claim here is that this is true only to the extent that people actually develop their talents.

[47] In Rawls' words, they are "properties which it is rational to want in persons when they are viewed with respect to almost any of their social roles." See *A Theory of Justice*, pp. 435–37.

fact that people were motivated to develop their talents and capacities would then be seen as a social achievement, rather than a natural fact.

Taken together, these considerations reveal the normative significance of the ideal of self-development. They show how this ideal could be an important component of a fully good life for many people; and they suggest that in a good society many would derive enjoyment and satisfaction from the development of their talents. This, in turn, reveals the normative force of the claim that autonomy is instrumentally valuable to self-development. If the realization of autonomy facilitates the achievement of this further ideal, and if this further ideal has considerable weight, then there are strong reasons to be autonomous.

This, however, does not establish that autonomy is a central component of a fully good life. For all that I have said, it is possible for people to lead fully good lives without achieving self-development. It is also possible for them to achieve self-development without realizing autonomy. Thus claim (3) remains unsubstantiated. In the next chapter further considerations will be advanced in its support. But before embarking on that task, I want briefly to consider some counterexamples that pose no threat to (3).

Three cases

Demonstrating that a value is a central component of a fully good life does not establish that all people have a reason to realize it. Nor does it establish that people have a reason to realize it under all circumstances. With regard to personal autonomy, these points are borne out by consideration of the following cases.

> *Case I* As the result of a very poor upbringing, David has acquired a settled, vicious character. He is disposed to slight and harm others; and he is fully enmeshed in degrading pursuits. Short of a conversion experience, which does not seem in the offing, David will never acquire the habits and dispositions necessary to lead a morally decent life.

Does David have a reason to be or to become autonomous? I believe the answer is "no." While it is intrinsically valuable to make one's life more one's own, this is true only if one's pursuits are, by and large, valuable. David's pursuits are shameful. It is better for him if they are less his own. Similarly, while it is good for one to develop one's talents, this is true only if one's talents are for valuable activities. David's talents are bound up with his vicious character. It is better for him if they are left undeveloped.

Suppose this is right. Then David's "reason" to be autonomous is canceled.[48] However, it is important not to draw the wrong lesson from this case. The fact that David is not that unusual a character – there are, after all, people like him – and the fact that he has no reason to be autonomous shows that autonomy is not a value all people have reason to realize. It shows that autonomy is a conditional good.[49] But it does not show that autonomy is not a central component of a fully good life, for not all people are in a position to live a fully good life. David's bad upbringing has put such a life outside his reach. The best he can do is lead the least bad life available to him. Case I, then, refutes claims (4) and (5); but it provides no reason to be suspicious of (3).

> *Case II* Through bad genetic luck, Jane suffers from an unusual nervous condition. Important decisions fill her with extremely painful anxiety. Fortunately, she has friends who are willing to run her affairs for her and ensure that she has a relatively stress-free life.

Clearly, Jane is better off not being autonomous. Her life goes better because her friends run her affairs. Jane has a reason to be autonomous, but her reason is overridden by her need to avoid painful anxiety. Like case I, this case refutes (4) and (5). And since there is no reason to think that Jane's projects, even though they are not autonomously engaged in, could add no value to her life,[50] case II refutes (6) as well. But it does not give us any reason to be suspicious of (3), for it is plausible to believe that Jane's nervous condition puts a fully good life outside her reach.

> *Case III* Mark lived a tragic life. He fully realized the ideal of autonomy and pursued valuable projects; but because of bad fortune his projects all ended in failure. Looking back on Mark's life, we realize that he would have been better off had he not been autonomous. Had he stayed in his home town,

---

[48] In the next chapter I argue that the social forms of modern western societies establish a tight connection between being autonomous and leading a good life. If this argument is sound, it might be the case that David has a reason to be autonomous after all. But I do not think this is true. Given David's character, even if he lives in an autonomy-supporting environment, it is better for him not to be autonomous. This raises some tricky questions that I will not try to answer. Fortunately, to make the point I am seeking to make here, we do not need answers to them.

[49] In holding that autonomy is a conditional good I follow J. Raz, *The Morality of Freedom*, pp. 411–12. It might be objected that autonomy has a value all its own, irrespective of whether it is realized in the pursuit of valuable or base pursuits. But I have suggested that autonomy is a component of a larger whole (the fully good life); and that it derives its value from its contribution to that larger whole. If this more general view is correct, the objection is mistaken.

[50] See the discussion of the endorsement thesis in chapter 8 below.

taken over his father's job, and simply followed the unimaginative advice of those around him he would have lived a more successful life.

The judgment that Mark's life was made worse by his being autonomous is made in retrospect. It would not have been possible for Mark to know this fact about himself as a young man. Indeed, it would have been unreasonable for someone to advise him not to become autonomous because of the possibility that his autonomously chosen projects could end in failure. Still, it remains true that Mark would have been better off not being autonomous.

This shows that autonomy does not always make a life go better. But, once again, it does not show that autonomy is not a central component of a fully good life. In Mark's case bad luck put a fully good life outside his reach.

These three cases illustrate the Aristotelian idea that a fully good life is not in the cards for all people. Bad upbringing, unfortunate physical or mental endowments and bad luck can make it impossible for some to lead a fully good life. Acknowledging the truth of this idea does not cast any doubt on the value of personal autonomy. However, it does raise an important issue. As we have seen, even if autonomy is a central component of a fully good life, it does not follow that all people have a reason to realize it. And, assuming sound political morality is concerned with the flourishing of all people, not just those who are lucky enough to lead fully good lives, does this not call into question the claim that political authorities ought to take an active role in promoting personal autonomy?

To answer this question we must know more about the social conditions of modern western societies and how they relate to the character ideal of autonomy. This is the main subject of the next chapter.

7   Personal autonomy and its value (II)

In the previous chapter I argued that personal autonomy has both intrinsic and instrumental value. But many ideals have intrinsic and instrumental value. We need to know why it is appropriate to elevate autonomy to a central component of a fully good life.

This chapter presses the argument for autonomy further. It does so by confronting an important objection that can be brought against autonomy-based political morality. This objection I will call the *pluralist objection*. It holds that autonomy is only one good among many; and that it, accordingly, does not warrant any special standing in the scale of values. The reason for focusing on this objection should be evident. If it can be defeated, then the door will be open to accepting the claim that autonomy is a central component of a fully good life.

The argument of this chapter unrolls in seven sections. I begin, in the first two sections, by discussing in more detail the pluralist objection and the problem it poses for a strong commitment to autonomy. In an effort to come to grips with this problem I argue, in the third section, that there are features of modern western societies that make autonomy an ideal of special importance. Then, in the fourth section I respond to some objections to this argument; and in the fifth section I show that this dependence of the value of autonomy on particular social conditions does not compromise its value. In the penultimate section, I ask whether this argument applies with equal force to people who live in non-autonomous groups; and, finally, in the last section, I conclude that the pluralist objection fails.

The pluralist objection

Expounding the doctrine of value pluralism, Isaiah Berlin has written

The world that we encounter in ordinary experience is one in which we are faced with choices between ends equally ultimate, and claims equally absolute, the realization of some of which must inevitably involve the sacrifice of others.[1]

[1] I. Berlin, "Two Concepts of Liberty," p. 168.

This famous passage does not imply that value pluralism calls into question a strong commitment to autonomy, and Berlin has never made such a claim. But others who are sympathetic to Berlin's views have pressed the point. Thus, in his study of Berlin's thought, John Gray writes:

Autonomy-based liberalism . . . elevates a controversial and questionable ideal of life uncritically and unduly. There are many excellent lives that are not especially autonomous, and which liberal societies can shelter.[2]

Gray's remarks splendidly capture the basic thrust of the pluralist objection. The objection maintains that the realization of autonomy is incompatible with some human lives that are fully good. It is important not to confuse this claim with the different (and stronger) claim that the autonomous life is less good than a life that does not realize autonomy. The pluralist objection insists only that there are some lives that are both *incompatible* and *incommensurable* with fully good autonomous lives. This claim can be expressed as follows:

(a) There is at least one kind of human life that is of equal or incommensurable value with a fully good autonomous life *and* is incompatible with it.

This claim implies a second one.

(b) The realization of autonomy is not a necessary component of a fully good human life.

Claim (b), in turn, provides support for a third claim.

(c) Autonomy deserves no privileged position in a sound account of political morality.

As a first statement, let us take the pluralist objection to be the conjunction of these three claims. Its name derives from its foundational commitment to the idea that there is a wide plurality of incompatible kinds of human lives that are fully good. As I have presented it, the pluralist objection does not try to establish the truth of this idea. It presupposes it.[3]

So one way to make short work of the pluralist objection would be to reject this presupposition. If only one kind of human life were fully good, the objection would collapse. A second way to attack the objection would be to accept the presupposition, but deny (a). Along these lines,

---

[2] J. Gray, *Berlin*, p. 32.

[3] Berlin (and Gray following him) do claim that the "ordinary resources of empirical observation" provide evidence for the truth of value pluralism in the sense that it best explains our moral and evaluative experience. See I. Berlin, "Two Concepts of Liberty," p. 169, and J. Gray, *Berlin*, pp. 62–64. But, even if this were true, it would fall short of a full defense of the doctrine, since it does not address the important issue of whether our experience should be left in the state we find it.

one could argue that while there is a plurality of kinds of fully good human lives, all of them are compatible with the ideal of autonomy. If successful, this argument would also defeat the objection.

In what follows I will not pursue either of these strategies. My plan of attack will be to block the inference from (b) to (c).

An initial clarification

But first a clarification is in order. Recall that this book is concerned with the political morality of modern western societies. I have suggested that we leave it an open matter whether, and to what extent, this political morality is binding on other societies. Some may be skeptical of this suggestion. They may fear that restricting the scope of the argument in this way compromises the claims here advanced. This is an important worry; and something will be said about it shortly. For now we need to take account of an ambiguity that emerges from this restriction.

Claim (b) can be read to mean either (b1) or (b2)

(b1) The realization of autonomy is not a necessary component of a fully good life.

(b2) The realization of autonomy is not a necessary component of a fully good life for people who live in modern western societies.

The difference between the two claims is that (b1), but not (b2), would be falsified if it were true that people could lead fully good non-autonomous lives in societies other than modern western ones. Since (a) implies (b1), but not (b2), the pluralist objection can be reformulated as follows: (b2) is true. (b2) provides strong support for (c). Therefore, we ought to accept (c).

The social forms of modern western societies

I want to begin analyzing the pluralist objection by asking the question, is (b2) really true? Joseph Raz has recently advanced an important argument that puts it in doubt.[4] To answer our question, we need to take a close look at this argument.

For reasons that will become apparent, I shall call Raz's argument the *social forms argument*. In this section I describe it in some detail; in the next I respond to some objections that can be raised against it.

Raz contends that valuable ideals are not independent of the social forms that exist in particular societies. There is, he claims, a tight

---

[4] J. Raz, *The Morality of Freedom*, pp. 390–95.

interconnection between them. Building on this general thought, he argues that once we come to an understanding of the social forms that predominate in modern western societies, we will see that personal autonomy is not just one ideal among many for people who live in these societies, but one that is intimately bound up with a fully good life.[5] This would show that even if (b1) were true, (b2) would be false.

To assess Raz's argument we need to know more about social forms in general and the social forms of modern western societies in particular. Social forms refer to the "forms of behavior" which are "widely practiced" in a society.[6] As such, they cover a wide range of phenomena. They encompass not only economic conditions, such as the nature of the labor market, but also social practices such as the institutionalization of occupations or conventions regulating the relations between the sexes. Moreover, and importantly, social forms also include established moral codes and "the shared beliefs, folklore, high culture, collectively shared metaphors and imagination" found in a society.[7]

So described, the social forms of a society determine (to a large extent) the nature and range of the relationships, projects and options available to its members. This is true for a number of reasons. First, many projects and options are brought into existence by particular social forms. One cannot play football unless a social form has emerged that defines this pursuit. Second, pursuits that exist in different societies acquire a different significance in the lives of those who take them up depending on the nature of the social forms that predominate in their society. Leading a Christian life has a different significance for those who live in religious societies than it does for those who live in secular ones. Third, the opportunities for experimentation are sharply circumscribed by social forms. People often invent new pursuits and new ways of acting; but these are, for the most part, variations on existing social forms.

Understanding these points provides the key to understanding why it is plausible to claim that there is a tight interconnection between social forms and valuable ideals. If the social forms of a society determine to a large extent the nature and range of the relationships, projects and options available to its members; and if the flourishing of people is bound up with their engagement in relationships, projects and options (a not implausible assumption), then it follows that the social forms of a society will determine the possibilities for human flourishing within it.

---

[5] Ibid. p. 394: "[In modern western societies] the value of autonomy is a fact of life . . . we can prosper in [such societies] only if we can be successfully autonomous."

[6] The description in this and the next couple of paragraphs draw on Raz's discussion in ibid. pp. 308–13.

[7] Ibid. p. 311.

This does not imply that all judgments of human flourishing are relative to a particular social context. But it does imply that the opportunities people have to lead good lives are determined and shaped by the social forms that predominate in their society.

With this in mind, we can turn now to what is distinctive about the social forms of modern western societies. In contrast with other types of societies, the social forms of modern western societies are marked by a high degree of technological innovation and social mobility. They are relatively dynamic and pluralistic; and in many areas of life they celebrate individual choice and initiative. As such, the social forms of these societies put certain demands on their members. In Raz's words they "call for an ability to cope with changing technological, economic and social conditions, for an ability to adjust, to acquire new skills, to move from one subculture to another, to come to terms with new scientific and moral views."[8]

In a moment I will discuss the significance of these sociological facts for the ideal of autonomy. But, first, it may be helpful if we characterize more precisely the features of modern western societies that distinguish them from other societies. As I mentioned in the introduction to this book, six features stand out.[9]

(1) *Geographic mobility* People in modern western societies change their place of residence more often than people in many other societies.[10] Children not infrequently leave their home town and settle elsewhere. Adults often do not stay in the same place throughout their working lives. The reasons for this are many and complex; but a primary reason is that people often need to move in order to find adequate or better work. The result of this geographic mobility is that communities and neighborhoods in modern western societies are not as stable and permanent as they are (or have been) in many other societies.

(2) *Technological and economic innovation* Virtually all societies make innovations in their productive forces, but in modern western societies these innovations are rapid, often transforming entire industries in a relatively short period of time. New technologies demand new skills; and people in these societies often must make

---

[8] Ibid. pp. 369–70.
[9] For a more detailed discussion of some of the distinguishing features of modern western societies, see E. Gellner, *Conditions of Liberty*, P. Berger, *The Capitalist Revolution*, and M. Walzer's discussion of the "Four Mobilities" in "The Communitarian Critique of Liberalism." Perhaps none of the features discussed here is unique to modern western societies, but their conjunction is unique to these societies.
[10] But not more than all societies. There have been, of course, nomadic tribes which have members that change their place of residence more often than people who live in modern western societies.

adjustments to technological change, either by switching their line of work or by participating in retraining programs.

(3) *Familial and social mobility* In general, people in modern western societies have a less stable family life than those in many other societies. Rates of divorce and remarriage are often higher in these societies than in others. In all likelihood, this is due in part to other mobilities, geographic and economic; but also it is a consequence of the widespread belief (in these societies) that marriage should be based on individual choice. Perhaps as a consequence of this belief people in modern western societies are more likely to marry across class, ethnic, and religious lines.

(4) *Secularization* Modern western societies are secular in the following specific sense – they do not contain a single, authoritative religion that is supported and enforced by the state. Accordingly, in these societies, there is a differentiation between political and religious authority.

(5) *Pluralism* Modern western societies contain a wide plurality of religious and philosophical views. These societies also contain a range of non-political associations and groups which are united by common interests or shared regional or ethnic identities.

(6) *A commitment to human rights* Modern western societies profess a commitment to human rights and make some reasonably sincere effort to respect them. These rights include those associated with freedom of conscience, freedom of association, freedom of movement, freedom to own personal property and the freedom to emigrate. Importantly, these rights are individual rights. They grant individuals protection from various types of interference from political authorities and from others.

These six features characterize an ideal type. They distinguish modern western societies from centralized tyrannies like the former Soviet Union, theocentric societies like some now found in the Islamic world, pre-industrial societies, and those societies ruled by authoritarian dictatorships which may have modern economies, but which suppress pluralism and do not respect human rights. Of course not all societies that might plausibly be classified as modern western will exhibit each of these six features or have them to the same degree. But, as I pointed out in the introduction, to understand the social conditions of modern western societies it helps to have in mind a paradigm case – like that of the United States – in which all six features are clearly present.

Reflecting on these features, some have claimed that liberalism (understood as a political theory that gives personal autonomy and individual liberty pride of place) is, in simplest terms, the theoretical justification for the social conditions of modern western societies.[11] As we shall see, this is not entirely accurate; but it does correctly suggest that there is an important connection between them and the value of personal autonomy. Succinctly, the connection can be expressed as follows: *to flourish in societies marked by these six features people need to realize the ideal of personal autonomy at least to some substantial degree.*[12]

There are many reasons for thinking the connection holds true. To prosper in these societies people must possess a distinctive set of skills. Without them, their lives are vulnerable to being taken over by events. These skills are similar to those that mark the autonomous person. They are the skills needed to form new projects and make revisions in old ones, to make adjustments to a rapidly changing economic environment and to reflect independently on the welter of options thrown one's way. In less dynamic, less mobile societies these skills would be less important. But, given the environment in which people in modern western societies find themselves, they acquire special significance. For consider. Geographic, technological and social mobilities force people to make choices about how to lead their lives. They must decide where to live, what job to take and who to live with; and they must be capable of revising their goals and plans when circumstances require or when events lead them into tight quarters. To be successful in such a mobile environment they will also need to come to an understanding about what types of options best suit their nature and talents. Unlike those in more traditional, less dynamic societies they will fare less well if they simply emulate those in their immediate social milieu.

The pluralism and secularization of modern western societies provide further evidential support for the claim that there is an important connection between the value of autonomy and the social conditions of these societies. Since there is not a single, authoritatively enforced religion in modern western societies, it is more difficult for people in these societies to rely on religious authority in deciding what to believe and how to lead their lives. The existence of a plurality of incompatible ways of life exerts pressure on them to develop convictions of their own.[13] This is not to deny that conformism is possible in these societies.

---

[11] M. Walzer, "The Communitarian Critique of Liberalism," p. 12.

[12] Compare this with J. Raz, *The Morality of Freedom*, p. 391: "For those who live in an autonomy-supporting environment there is no choice but to be autonomous: there is no other way to prosper in such a society."

[13] On this point see Peter Berger's discussion of religious pluralism in *The Sacred Canopy*, esp. pp. 138–39. Berger argues that when a society contains a number of rival religious groups, each group must compete for the allegiance of members in the society. As a result, many religious organizations become, at least in part, "marketing agencies." In

It no doubt is. The claim is that conformism is a less viable strategy in societies that contain rifts and divisions than in ones that do not.

This point can be expressed slightly differently. There is a double link between pluralism and autonomy. On the one hand, autonomy presupposes pluralism; for if a public environment does not provide its members with a rich and varied range of options then it will not be possible for them to chart their own course through life. But, on the other hand, the existence of a plurality of incompatible ways of life demands that people define themselves and decide how to lead their lives without relying on shared authority. Autonomy presupposes pluralism, but pluralism puts pressure on people to be autonomous.[14]

Consider, finally, the relationship between human rights and autonomy. Modern western societies grant individual citizens various protections against being used or interfered with by others. While there is considerable disagreement about the proper extension of these protections, there is near unanimous agreement that certain ways of treating people are unjustifiable. It is, for example, widely accepted that people should not be tortured, persecuted for their religious or ethnic background, censored or imprisoned for their political opinions or prevented from forming associations with others who share similar interests or concerns. All of these protections are protections for *individuals*. They give individual people some room to lead their lives free from the interference of others.

Note that I am not here concerned with the correct justification for human rights. I am merely calling attention to the fact that in modern western societies commitment to these rights is a constitutive part of the social conditions. The belief in them and in their importance is a social fact. This is significant; for belief in and respect for human rights helps contribute to a culture which celebrates and protects individual choice and discretion. And this is precisely the type of culture which favors the autonomous life.

Each of the six features listed above helps vindicate the claim that autonomy is a value of special importance for people in modern western societies. Because of the social forms predominant in these societies people need to be autonomous in order to flourish. The social forms argument, therefore, provides a ground for rejecting (b2).

---

this way, the man in the street is made all too aware that he has a choice in this fundamental matter.

[14] On this see S. Macedo, *Liberal Virtues*, p. 238: "living in a pluralistic society widens the options that people typically have available to them, persons living in such societies must choose more often and are encouraged to reflect more deeply than those living in societies with few real alternatives."

Two objections

Some will think that the social forms argument overstates its case. Two objections to this effect can be brought against it. To further clarify the argument I want to pause and consider them.

The first objection draws attention to the fact that people in modern western societies sometimes do choose to lead relatively non-autonomous lives. For example, they join convents or enlist in the military for life. And at least some of those who do this appear to lead good lives. Does this not show that one can lead a fully good life in these societies without realizing the ideal of autonomy?[15]

This objection overlooks something important. People in modern western societies who lead relatively non-autonomous lives can choose to lead these lives. This fact is important, for it transforms the nature of the way of life they engage in. The self-conscious decision to become a nun or have a career in the military is not incompatible with the ideal of autonomy. It is true that these ways of life may not allow a person to be maximally autonomous. But the social forms argument does not claim that a necessary component of a fully good life is that a person be as autonomous as possible.[16]

No doubt some people in modern western societies who lead such lives do fail to realize autonomy. Those who join a convent or pursue a military career because they have no other options or because they have been forced to do so or because they simply follow the judgment of others do not lead autonomous lives. But their lack of autonomy is not a result of their engagement in these particular pursuits; it is a result of how they pursue them. And here it is plausible to think that they do lead less good lives. They fail to be autonomous, even though the way of life they have chosen is not incompatible with autonomy.

The point here is subtle, and perhaps requires further comment. To refute the social forms argument one needs to present a way of life that is both fully good and incompatible with autonomy. This is true because if the way of life is compatible with autonomy, then it is plausible to claim (for the reasons given in the last chapter) that autonomy would make that life better. But if the social forms of modern western societies affect the nature and significance of all pursuits and options in them, then this will be difficult to do. The examples of a nun or a career military man bear this out. Given the social forms of modern western societies, both

---

[15] See J. Gray, *Berlin*, pp. 32–33.
[16] In chapter 8 below I provide reasons for rejecting the maximizing claim.

ways of life are compatible with autonomy and so neither refute the social forms argument.

The second objection is more empirically minded. It maintains that the skills needed to prosper in modern western societies – the ability to change jobs, move to different areas of the country, adjust to changing technology, etc. – are compatible with many non-autonomous ways of life. As evidence for this view, those who press this objection point to the experiences of contemporary Asian cultures. These cultures have adopted many of the economic institutions of the West without abandoning a commitment to cultural traditions which place little value on personal autonomy. This shows, the objectors claim, that there is no tight connection between modern social conditions and the ideal of personal autonomy.[17]

This objection rests heavily on the empirical claim that contemporary Asian societies have successfully grafted a modern economy on to cultural traditions which discourage autonomy. It is not clear how correct this claim is. The relevant question to ask is not "Are the social forms of contemporary Asian societies less autonomy-supporting than those of modern western societies?", but "Would the social forms of these societies be even less autonomy-supporting if they had not adopted western economic institutions?" And there is some evidence to answer this latter question in the affirmative.[18] But to turn back this objection it is not necessary to refute the empirical claim on which it is based. Even if the claim were true, the objection would have limited force.

The reason for this should be plain. As we have seen, the social forms of a society are not simply a function of the type of economy it has. Non-economic features are of equal or greater importance. The social mobility, pluralism, secularization and respect for human rights that mark modern western societies are all constitutive parts of the social forms of these societies and they all contribute to making autonomy an ideal of special importance in them. In societies which do not have all of the general features of modern western societies autonomy may be less central to flourishing. Thus, one can agree with Ernest Gellner that it is "perfectly possible to run a successful modern industrial society pervaded by a communalistic or family spirit with an authoritarian state presiding over it"[19] without thereby abandoning the claim that autonomy is a

---

[17] See B. Parekh, "Superior People: The Narrowness of Liberalism from Mill to Rawls."

[18] See P. Berger, *The Capitalist Revolution*, pp. 140–71. Perhaps, as Berger tentatively suggests, the communalism of East Asian societies is in the process of being gradually weakened by the adoption of modernizing economic conditions.

[19] E. Gellner, "The Conditions of Liberty," p. 199.

necessary component of a fully good life for those who live in modern western societies.

Conventionalism

Let's review the argument so far. In response to the pluralist objection I have argued that there are features of modern western societies that give us reason to think that autonomy is a necessary component of a fully good life for people living in them. This argument, which I have called the social forms argument, calls into question (b2); and, in so doing, undermines the pluralist objection. I then considered and rejected two objections that can be brought against it.

Now it is time to address the worry briefly alluded to earlier, a worry that may be all the more pressing in the light of the responses I have given to the objections. The social forms argument is indexed to modern western societies. Accordingly, even if it is valid, it cannot establish that autonomy is a necessary component of a fully good life for all people in all societies. By itself, this need not occasion concern. As I have made plain, my subject in this book is the political morality of modern western societies. But some may think that the modesty of the conclusion established by the social forms argument undermines autonomy's claim to be a fundamental value.

In this vein, they may object:

An adequate defense of the value of autonomy must show that all societies have reason to undertake reforms to facilitate the autonomous development of their members. If their existing social forms are not autonomy-supporting, then we must show (to our satisfaction at least) that they have reason to change them. This is true because if we cannot establish this, then it follows that the value of autonomy is relative to social forms. And if this is the case, then it follows that we cannot justify our social forms by reference to the fact that they are autonomy-supporting.

It is vital to see that this objection misfires. The social forms argument does not purport to establish that autonomy is a value. It is an argument that purports to show that autonomy has *special standing* under certain social conditions. As such, the argument presupposes the value of autonomy. In the last chapter I advanced arguments to show that autonomy has intrinsic and instrumental value. The social forms argument builds on these arguments. It does not replace them. Therefore, there is no basis for claiming that the value of autonomy is relative to social forms. If it is a value, it is a value for all people, even for those who live in societies with social forms very different from those of modern western societies.

Be this as it may, this response will not completely assuage the worry under consideration. For it can be pointed out that, according to the social forms argument, even if the value of autonomy is not relative to social forms, its importance or standing in the scale of values is largely conventional. The objection, then, could be restated as follows:

According to the social forms argument, autonomy has special standing only in certain types of societies. But this leaves the value without a sturdy enough foundation for it to warrant a central place in political morality. For if the special standing of autonomy is relative to social forms, then it cannot be said unqualifiedly that political authorities (in modern western societies) have strong reasons to protect and promote personal autonomy. It could just as well be said that they have strong reasons to change the character of these social forms and promote non-autonomous ways of life.

So formulated, the objection cannot be dismissed as confused. Two replies are in order.

The first reply begins with a reminder. The pluralist objection does not maintain that the autonomous life is less good than some non-autonomous lives. It holds merely that not all lives that are fully good are compatible with autonomy. So, taken on its own terms, the pluralist objection does not show that modern western societies have a reason to change the character of their social forms so as to make them less supportive of autonomy. From the possibility that some ways of life are fully good, incompatible with autonomy and incapable of being sustained in modern western societies, one cannot infer that there is a reason to change the social forms of these societies so as to make them more hospitable to non-autonomous ways of life. To draw that conclusion one would need to show that some non-autonomous way of life is superior to the autonomous ways of life supported by the social forms of modern western societies. But this is something the pluralist objector does not – and cannot – establish.[20]

Proponents of this objection, then, can provide no reason why the general character of the social forms of modern western societies ought to be changed. There are, in contrast, very good reasons for not changing their general character. People have an interest in living in an environment that is familiar and understandable to them. Change, particularly the type of change needed to transform the general character of the social

---

[20] Some critics of the social life of modern western societies have advanced this stronger claim. See, for example, A. MacIntyre, *After Virtue*. My concern in this chapter is not with these critics, but with those who advance the pluralist objection. However, a full defense of the social forms argument would need to show that the social forms of modern western societies do not give rise to pathologies that offset the values they support and sustain. While I believe this is true, I will not undertake the prodigious task of trying to establish it here.

forms of a society, would be very disruptive. Since disruption almost always brings costs, we should not change the character of our social forms unless we have a compelling reason for doing so.

This simple point upholds a conservative conclusion. *So long as we believe that our social forms are as good as, or rationally incommensurable with, other possible social forms, we should not change them.* Rather, in this case, it is entirely legitimate to take them as a starting point in thinking about the content of political morality. This conclusion does not imply that there is never good reason to reform any aspect of the social forms in our society. It holds only that we have no good reason to change their general character simply because there might exist (or could conceivably exist) other equally good social forms.[21] This neutralizes the objection in question.

But this reply, while effective, does not address all of the concerns that give rise to the worry. The worry is that once we link the special standing of the value of autonomy to particular social forms we compromise its claim to be a fundamental value. The first reply shows that this need not overly trouble *us*, as members of modern western societies. For we can plausibly take the general character of the social forms of our societies as starting points for reflection on the content of political morality. But this still leaves us with the question of what we should think about the political morality that is appropriate for other societies with different social forms, those either that have existed in the past or exist now elsewhere in the world. And the worry resurfaces here. For if we say that a political morality that gives autonomy a central place in the scale of values is valid for us, but not for others, have we not conceded too much? By shrinking the domain in which it applies, have we not transformed our political morality into "an anemic, parochial, and ultimately trivial ideology"[22]?

The second reply speaks to these concerns. But what I have to say here is sketchy, and I do not pretend to address all the issues that need to be addressed. My remarks are put forward more in the nature of a suggestion as to the form a convincing response to these concerns might take. Very simply put, the thrust of the reply is this: some of the features of modern western societies that make them autonomy-supporting are independently valuable. If this is true, then to the extent that we have

---

[21] Compare this conservative reply with Raz's claim that "Normal politics, to our relief, is not concerned with large scale social design. Its business is to conduct our affairs within the existing, though ever-changing (in part because of political interventions) social structures." "Facing Up," p. 1228. See also, in a somewhat different context, Popper's defense of piecemeal social engineering in *The Open Society and its Enemies*, pp. 157–68.

[22] J. Feinberg, *Harmless Wrongdoing*, p. 333.

reason to value these features, we have reason to value autonomy as an ideal. The argument here is structurally similar to one advanced by Charles Taylor in his paper "Atomism,"[23] and it may be helpful to begin by contrasting it with Taylor's argument. Taylor sought to show that the autonomous individual (the person who realizes the ideal of personal autonomy) can only exist in a certain type of social matrix, one that contains institutions, practices and attitudes that sustain this ideal. From this he reasoned, quite plausibly, to the conclusion that if one values the ideal of autonomy one must also value the social matrix that sustains it and makes it possible.

The argument that I am advancing here turns this argument around. It contends that if we value, and if we have good reason to value, the social forms of modern western societies, then we have reason to cherish and support the ideal of autonomy that these social forms sustain. What is crucial to this argument is the idea that the social forms of modern western societies, or at least some important aspects of them, can be justified independently of their contribution to the ideal of personal autonomy. To the extent that this is true, we and others have reason to affirm these social forms, and to the extent that we and others have reason to affirm them, we and others have reason to conceive of personal autonomy as a central element of human flourishing. This would take much of the sting out of the charge that the social forms argument turns autonomy-based political morality into a merely parochial ideology.

There is, however, no single strand of argument that establishes these claims. We must look at the features of modern western societies one by one to see if any plausible independent justification can be given for them. With this in mind, I start with the commitment to human rights. Respect for human rights gives individual people some space to lead their lives on their own terms. When these rights are recognized and respected, they transform the social forms of a society, making the public environment more hospitable to autonomous ways of life. But there is good reason to believe that the recognition and respect of these rights constitutes moral progress in itself, over and above the contribution it makes to the realization of personal autonomy. As many have pointed out, the justification for human rights is morally overdetermined. They can be justified by reference to positive goods like happiness, knowledge and freedom or by reference to the minimization of evils like misery, ignorance and cruelty.[24] One does not need to decide which of these justifications is the best one to conclude that the recognition and respect

---

[23] C. Taylor, "Atomism."

[24] See T. Nagel, "Personal Rights and Public Space." Nagel himself grounds human rights in the "inviolability" of persons.

for human rights has value independent of its contribution to personal autonomy. And one does not have to value autonomy highly to believe that societies which do not respect human rights are deservedly subject to criticism.

These points are not undercut by the fact that one important justification for human rights is that they protect autonomy. If this were the only justification for them, then it would not be possible to appeal to them in order to respond to the worry under consideration. The argument in this case would indeed be circular. But, as we have just seen, there are many plausible justifications for human rights. One can rationally value their recognition without thereby embracing the character ideal of personal autonomy. So there is good reason to think that this feature of modern western societies is independently valuable.

The same can be said about the pluralism characteristic of these societies. As I have pointed out, modern western societies contain a wide range of religious and philosophical doctrines. They also contain a wide range of non-political associations in which people come together to pursue different ways of life. Assuming the doctrine of value pluralism is true, this feature of modern western societies is itself commendable. Pluralistic societies express an important truth about value: people can lead different and incompatible lives without being in error. By not imposing a single way of life on all, these societies respond appropriately to the nature of value and the limits of reason.[25]

Furthermore, and importantly, if this is right, it exposes a fault line in the pluralist objection. Suppose that we have before us a society with two salient features. It has social forms that are not autonomy-supporting and it contains members who do not accept the doctrine of value pluralism. Suppose now that the people in this society gradually come to accept this doctrine. This would affect the character of the social forms in their society in two related ways. First, it would transform the shared evaluative beliefs of the society. Second, it would make ineligible some justifications for certain social practices in the society; namely, those justifications that rest on assumptions about the rational superiority of one way of life.

In all likelihood, the upshot of these changes would be that the society would gradually become more pluralistic. Recognizing the truth of value pluralism, its members would be psychologically less inclined to suppress the emergence of new ways of life. Over time this would transform the social forms of the society, making them more supportive of autonomous ways of life. This is true for the reason mentioned earlier. There is a

[25] On this point see B. Williams, "Introduction," pp. xvii–xviii.

double link between pluralism and autonomy. Autonomy presupposes pluralism, but pluralism puts pressure on people to be autonomous.

Against this, proponents of the pluralist objection might argue that it is not necessarily a good thing for people to come to accept the doctrine of value pluralism. But this would be a strange claim for them to make, since they spend much energy urging others to accept the doctrine. Alternatively, they might claim that people could come to accept the doctrine and yet remain just as committed to preserving a non-pluralistic culture. This is logically possible. The claim I make is that acceptance of value pluralism puts psychological pressure on people to welcome, not suppress, the emergence of different ways of life.

The fault line in the pluralist objection should now be in view. To the extent that people accept the foundational idea on which it is based they will be more inclined to respect, rather than suppress, different ways of life; and this, in turn, will have an impact on the character of the social forms in their society, making them more supportive of autonomy. But as the social forms of a society become more autonomy-supporting, the pluralist objection loses its force. It becomes less plausible to hold that the autonomous life is just one valuable way of life among many.

For these reasons, the pluralism that marks modern western societies is independently valuable. Assuming value pluralism is true, these societies have come to a better understanding of value than those that discourage or suppress diversity. The same point can be expressed negatively. Assuming value pluralism is true, the emergence of a plurality of ways of life is best interpreted as the natural result of free practical reason under favorable conditions. As such, it is plausible to think that it can be overcome only by the "oppressive use of state power."[26] If so, then those who oppose state oppression must welcome pluralism. And to the extent that pluralism contributes to a public environment supportive of autonomy, they must also welcome autonomy.

Consider, lastly, the secularization of modern western societies. As noted above, secularization is understood here in a specific sense. It refers to the fact that in these societies there is no single, authoritative religion enforced by the state. Consequently, in these societies, there is a differentiation of religious and political authority.

Is this feature of modern western societies independently valuable? The answer is "yes" if it represents a true understanding of the role that religion should play in social life. If God either does not exist or has no plan for how we should organize political life, then this understanding of religion is correct. And if it is correct, it is good for a society to have it. It

[26] For this phrase see J. Rawls, *Political Liberalism*, p. 37.

is a good thing, other things being equal, for political life not to be organized around false doctrines about divine purposes.

We want (and should want) our political life to be based on true doctrines about the world. This reason is not conclusive. It may be that secularization brings social pathologies in train. But truthfulness is an important value. It gives us reason to believe that the secularization that marks modern western societies is good in its own right, independent of its contribution to an autonomy-supporting public environment.[27]

A good case, then, can be made for thinking that several features of modern western societies – respect for human rights, pluralism and secularization – are valuable for reasons that do not derive from the ideal of autonomy. Because they are independently valuable we have reason not to change them so as to make our social forms less supportive of autonomy. It may be that a similar case can be made for some of the other features that characterize modern western societies, but I shall not try to show this here. My main concern has been to make plausible the argument behind these more specific claims. This argument, if sound, shows that we have reason to value the ideal of autonomy because we have reason to value the social forms that sustain it. There is nothing circular about this reasoning. The realization of autonomy has value, but it is not the only source of value. Other considerations may vindicate the social forms that make it a central element of human flourishing.

This reply supplements the first one. It provides further support for the idea that the reason-giving force of autonomy is not compromised by acceptance of the claim that it acquires special standing only under certain social conditions. This should go some distance toward allaying the worry that the social forms argument makes autonomy a conventional, and therefore normatively non-fundamental, value. Still, as I conceded above, this reply is not conclusive. The comparison and evaluation of radically different social forms raises very large issues, issues that I have not begun to deal with adequately.[28] Therefore, on the basis of what has been said here, it cannot be concluded that a fully good life is possible only in a society with autonomy-supporting social forms.

In light of this, some readers may remain unsatisfied. They may yearn for a stronger defense of autonomy, one that would demonstrate that (b1) is false – i.e. that all societies that do not respect and promote

---

[27] Here I am assuming, but do not try to demonstrate, that this understanding of religion is indeed correct. However, a full defense of this claim would need to justify this assumption.

[28] For some of the issues that would need to be addressed see B. Williams' discussion of the "relativism of distance" in *Ethics and the Limits of Philosophy*, pp. 156–73. One reason why I have not tried to give a full treatment of these issues here is that if I did this, I would have had to have done little else.

autonomy are deficient and that people in them fail to lead fully good lives. But while I have not shown that (b1) is false, it should not escape notice that if it is false, then the claims I have made are only strengthened. The social forms argument holds that autonomy is a necessary component of a fully good life for people living in modern western societies. If (b1) were false, the conclusion of the social forms argument would not be imperiled. That is why, at least in the present context, it is safe to suspend judgment on its truth.

Non-autonomous subgroups

Up to this point nothing has been said about subgroups within modern western societies whose way of life is unreceptive to autonomy.[29] If the social forms argument is sound, the members of these subgroups ought to fare less well than others. Living in a larger environment inhospitable to their way of life, it should be more difficult for them to flourish.

This might not be true if these subgroups could inhabit their own world, effectively withdrawing from the larger culture and living in an environment with different social forms. But there are substantial limits to the extent to which any subgroup can insulate itself from the larger culture. The social forms of modern western societies not only set the conditions for the well-being of those who live in the dominant culture, they also alter the environments of groups which strive to sustain non-autonomous ways of life. In various ways and for various reasons, subgroups come into contact with the larger culture and this interaction transforms their way of life.

This reveals why modern western societies cannot simply "shelter" non-autonomous ways of life. They can take measures to ensure the survival of some of them. They can tolerate them; but they cannot create a public environment for them in which they can flourish. Life in a non-autonomous subgroup of a modern western society is not the same as life in a society whose social forms do not support autonomy. It is much harder to prosper in the former than in the latter.

Reflection on this point has led Raz to advance a strong claim: "For those who live in an autonomy-supporting environment there is no choice but to be autonomous: *there is no other way to prosper in such a society*."[30] If this claim is correct, it refutes the pluralist objection. But perhaps the claim is too strong. Perhaps, while difficult, it remains

---

[29] Examples of such subgroups include the Amish community in America, the Muslim community in Great Britain and various immigrant communities and religious sects.

[30] J. Raz, *The Morality of Freedom*, p. 391.

possible for a person to flourish in a non-autonomous subgroup in a modern western society.[31]

At the beginning of this chapter I claimed that my strategy in defusing the pluralist objection would be to challenge the inference from (b) to (c). To do this it is not necessary to refute (b). Accordingly, for argumentative purposes, let us concede that there is at least one non-autonomous subgroup in a modern western society that allows at least one of its members to live a fully good life. This would be enough to establish the truth of (b2).

It is important to see that even with this concession the social forms argument defeats the pluralist objection. As I argued in the last section, if we do not have good reason to change the general character of our social forms, we ought to take them for granted when thinking about the content of political morality.[32] When we do this, we will find that the best way to promote the well-being of people is to create and sustain conditions that help them realize the ideal of autonomy. The possibility that there exist a small number of people who would fare better by living non-autonomously does not threaten this conclusion. It merely shows that it is not possible for every person in these societies to live in a social environment that best promotes his or her well-being. Those who would do better in a non-autonomy-supporting public environment cannot plausibly claim that the social forms of their society should be transformed at great cost to everyone else so that they could live in an environment that better suits them.[33]

The mistake in the pluralist objection, therefore, is the move from (b2) to (c). Even if (b2) were true – that is, even if it were not true that autonomy is a necessary component of a fully good life for all people in modern western societies – it would not follow that this would provide strong support for (c) – that is, the claim that autonomy deserves no privileged standing in a sound account of political morality. Given the character of the social forms of modern western societies, a fully good life will include the realization of autonomy, at least for the vast majority of people. This vindicates autonomy's claim to be a value of special standing.

---

[31] Raz appears to concede as much when he considers the possibility of a non-autonomous subgroup that enables its members "to have an adequate and satisfying life." Ibid. p. 423.

[32] That is, we ought to take their general character for granted.

[33] Recall the three characters discussed at the end of chapter 6 above. David, Jane and Mark would lead better lives if they lived in non-autonomy-supporting environments. This is true because of special facts about them. But their plight would not show that the societies in which they live would have compelling reason to change the character of their social forms to make them less autonomy-supporting.

But while this defeats the pluralist objection, it leaves unanswered the difficult question of how non-autonomous subgroups ought to be treated by the larger societies which contain them. A complete discussion of this question falls outside the confines of this chapter.[34] But a few general comments can be ventured. This should give some sense of how the question ought to be approached within a liberal perfectionist framework.

Critics of autonomy-based liberalism often charge it with failing to show proper respect for non-autonomous ways of life. The following complaint is representative.

> Autonomy-based liberalism ultimately contains no commitment to the value of diversity in and of itself. It justifies only those diverse forms of life which themselves value autonomy and thus makes toleration a pragmatic device – a temporary expedient – not a matter of principle.[35]

This charge prompts two questions. Is there truth in it? And, if so, should it occasion concern?

The social forms argument shows that, by and large, non-autonomous subgroups will not be able to provide their members with opportunities to lead fully good lives. Because of this it is generally a good thing if these subgroups do not survive. But it does not follow that there are no principled reasons for tolerating them. As I argued in chapter 4, the costs of repression or interference may exceed the costs of toleration. This is likely to be true in cases where people's well-being is deeply entwined with a non-autonomous way of life. Even if this life is not fully good, continued participation in it may be the best option open to them. This would ground a principled reason for tolerating the non-autonomous subgroup.[36]

So the above charge errs in suggesting that, on an autonomy-based account of political morality, there could be no principled rationale for tolerating non-autonomous subgroups; but it is substantially correct in suggesting that on this account of political morality diversity is not valued in and of itself. On an autonomy-based account of political morality diversity is valuable to the extent that it contributes to human flourishing. On this account, there is no good reason to preserve ways of life that impede human flourishing simply because their continued existence would contribute to a more diverse social world.

---

[34] For some relevant discussion, some of which I disagree with, see W. Kymlicka, *Multicultural Citizenship*.

[35] S. Mendus, *Toleration and the Limits of Liberalism*, p. 108.

[36] However, to the extent that it would be possible to provide younger members of the subgroup with opportunities to lead a fully good life, there would be a case for interference. For more on this see the discussion of civic education in chapter 9 below.

I believe that this is not a weakness, but a strength, of this account of political morality. The fact that it refuses to take diversity to be a good in and of itself reveals its commitment to humanism – the notion that ultimately it is the flourishing of human beings that matters.

Conclusion

This chapter has focused on the pluralist objection because this objection forcefully challenges the claim that personal autonomy is a central component of a fully good life. Now that this objection has been defeated, the door is open to accepting this claim.

Personal autonomy has intrinsic and instrumental value. For those ways of life that are compatible with it, its realization makes them better. But autonomy is not compatible with all ways of life. Some ways of life are constitutively incompatible with it.

This would pose a problem for an autonomy-based account of political morality only if the following claims were true

(1) Some ways of life, incompatible with autonomy, could still be fully good.
(2) Because of this, autonomy should not be given a central place in an account of political morality.

Whatever the truth of (1), the social forms argument shows (2) to be false. For the vast majority of people in modern western societies, personal autonomy is a central component of a fully good life. This provides support for the claim that political authorities in these societies have strong reasons to create and sustain conditions that best enable their subjects to lead autonomous lives.

8   Three mistakes about autonomy

Over the past two chapters, by describing and defending the ideal of autonomy, I have sought to provide constructive support for liberal perfectionism. In prosecuting my case I have done three things. I have defined autonomy as a distinctive character ideal. I have argued that its realization has intrinsic and instrumental value, and I have defended it from those who charge that it is merely one value among others, deserving no privileged position in a sound account of political morality.

I now want to discuss some of the limits to autonomy's value and importance. The reason for doing this is that sometimes a commitment to autonomy is understood to justify anti-perfectionism, and I want to show that this understanding is mistaken. Put more precisely, it is sometimes thought that if autonomy is a valid character ideal, then the best way for the state to promote the flourishing of its members is for it to refrain from using its power to promote good pursuits and discourage bad ones. This thought poses a challenge to liberal perfectionism. Very concisely expressed, the challenge consists in turning the "liberal" part of liberal perfectionism against the "perfectionist" part. By focusing on some of the limits to autonomy, I hope to show that the challenge can be met.

With this in mind, this chapter changes direction and addresses the claims of those who have tended not to undervalue, but overestimate, the importance of personal autonomy. The spotlight is put on three popular arguments that claim more for this ideal than it can deliver. The discussion of these arguments clarifies the status of autonomy *vis-à-vis* other values and casts further light on the relationship between autonomy and perfectionist political action.

The maximizing argument

The first argument to be considered holds that there is a conclusive reason to maximize autonomy. The rationale behind the argument is straightforward. If autonomy is indeed a value of special importance, then we ought to realize it to the highest degree possible. Let us call this the *maximizing argument*.

An immediate objection to this argument is that autonomy is not the sort of value that can be maximized. Even if it makes sense to speak of greater or lesser degrees of autonomy (as I claimed in chapter 6), the idea of maximization demands more quantitative precision than is possible in this area. For consider how the maximizing goal might be formulated. Suppose that it is said that the goal is to bring about social conditions such that as many people as possible in a given political community would be as autonomous as possible. So described, the goal would be incoherent for two connected reasons. First, as I have characterized it, autonomy is measured along several dimensions.[1] This creates a problem for maximization, since efforts to increase development along one dimension might well decrease development along another. This problem is compounded by the second reason. The goal contains two variables. We are instructed to maximize both the number of autonomous people in the political community and to maximize the autonomous development of each member. But, at least under some conditions, these two maxima would pull in opposite directions. When this occurred, the general injunction to maximize would break down.

These technical problems call into question the coherence of the maximizing argument. But perhaps with a clever enough reformulation the technical problems could be surmounted. For the sake of argument, then, let us assume that the maximizing argument can be made coherent. On this generous assumption, we can ask, is the maximization of autonomy a valid goal for political action?

It is not. To see why we need to recall that the value of autonomy derives from its contribution to a successful and fulfilling life. A substantial measure of autonomy is a central component of a fully good life. But not everyone has reason to achieve the same degree of autonomous development. The arguments advanced in chapters 6 and 7 allow for considerable variation with respect to individual talents, capacities, inclinations and temperament. And such factors are relevant to a determination of how much autonomy is necessary for a fully good life. It should occasion no surprise if some do not need to be as autonomous as others to lead a fully good life. Accordingly, holding that all people have reason to be autonomous does not commit one to the view that all people have reason to be autonomous to the same degree. This shows that the maximizing injunction is misguided. If there is no

---

[1] The dimensions correspond to the four basic elements of the ideal as described in chapter 6.

reason for people to be autonomous to the same degree, there is likewise no reason for them to be as autonomous as possible. They only have reason to be sufficiently autonomous, where sufficiency is a variable that is not constant across persons.[2]

Perhaps, however, the maximizing injunction should be understood to be relativized to each person. On this understanding, it holds that for each person, given his or her specific makeup (talents, capacities, temperament, etc.) he or she has a conclusive reason to be as autonomous as possible. This would imply that while it might be true that all people do not have reason to be autonomous to the same degree, they, nevertheless, all have reason to be as autonomous as they can be given their specific makeup. The person with the talent and temperament to be an actor or an actress may need to be more autonomous than the person with the talent and temperament to be a rural farmer, but both ought to be as autonomous as they can be given their distinctive talents and temperament (and perhaps the way of life their talents and temperament incline them toward).

But this view is not plausible either. And it is not plausible for a very simple reason. *Autonomy is not all that matters.* It is one, but only one, component of a fully good life. From this it is a short step to the conclusion that sometimes reasons to promote autonomy should give way to reasons to promote other ideals. Sometimes the pursuit of maximal autonomy will obstruct the pursuit of other goods, and sometimes these other goods will contribute more to a person's life than the increased autonomy. In such situations, the reason to maximize autonomy is defeated. The maximizing injunction, even when relativized to peoples' specific makeup, runs afoul of this basic truth.

This does not yet refute the maximizing argument. For friends of the argument can and will object that I have mischaracterized its basic thrust. The goal, they will say, is not to maximize autonomy, but rather to maximize the number of options open to people. This may or may not maximize their autonomy. But, so the objection will run, if we maximize the number of options open to them, then we will have done all that we realistically could hope to do for them.

This revised version of the maximizing argument may escape the above criticism. So before passing judgment on the maximizing argument as a whole, we need to look more closely at this version of it. To bring it into sharper focus it will help to introduce some terminology. According to the option requirement (see the discussion in chapter 6 above), a pre-

---

[2] In fact, as I pointed out in chapter 6, some people, in virtue of their personal circumstances, have no reason to be autonomous at all.

condition for the realization of personal autonomy is that a person have access to a wide range of eligible pursuits. Let us define a range of eligible pursuits that is sufficiently wide for that person to make the realization of personal autonomy genuinely possible for him as his *S option set*. This can be distinguished from the maximally wide set of eligible pursuits that it would be possible for this person to choose from, given the social and economic conditions of his society. Let us define this as his *M option set*.[3]

With this terminology, we can state more precisely the argument under consideration. It holds that either the S option set and the M option set are equivalent, in which case maximizing the options available to a person is necessary if one is to enable him to realize the ideal of autonomy *or* the S option set and the M option set are not equivalent, in which case increasing the options available to a person beyond his S option set and closer to his M option set could only enhance his personal autonomy. Either way, if we value personal autonomy, we have a reason to maximize the options available to people.

At first glance, the revised version of the maximizing argument looks more promising than the original. Upon closer examination, however, we will see that it fares no better. Begin by considering the first disjunct in the argument. This is the claim that the S option set and the M option set are equivalent. Simply put, this implies that to realize the ideal of autonomy a person must have access to the maximally wide range of eligible pursuits that it would be possible for him to choose from, given the social and economic conditions of his society. Such a requirement would make autonomy an extremely demanding ideal. Very few would ever achieve it. But this is not the main reason for rejecting it. The requirement is not only excessively demanding, it is counter-intuitive. It would imply that a person who charts his own course through life by self-consciously choosing projects and pursuits from among a wide and rich range of options would not be autonomous if it were true that it was possible for him to have chosen those projects from a range of options that was identical to the one he did choose from except that it included one additional option. This would remain true even if the one additional option were one that the person would have had no interest in taking up. Since this conclusion is manifestly false, the first disjunct in the revised maximizing argument must be rejected.

---

[3] Alternatively, the M option set could be defined as the maximally wide set of eligible pursuits that it would be possible for a person to choose from that was compatible with a like set for everyone else, given the social and economic conditions of his society. Since the point I make below holds true for this definition as well as the one in the text, it is not necessary for us to decide which one is better.

For this reason, proponents of the argument need to make their case by appealing to the second disjunct. This states that while the S option set and the M option set are not equivalent, increasing a person's access to options beyond that required by the S option set could only enhance his autonomy. The second disjunct, then, crucially presupposes that *more options never diminish a person's autonomy.*

Should this presupposition be accepted? Consider this counterexample. By proliferating the number of options a person has access to one can make him confused and disoriented. Beyond some point, increases in the number and range of options open to this person will almost certainly impair his ability to choose autonomously and intelligently. This counterexample shows that it is not, strictly speaking, true that adding options to a person's option set could never diminish his autonomy.[4]

Since the presupposition behind the second disjunct in the revised maximizing argument is false, we must reject the second disjunct; and since we have already rejected the first disjunct, the argument as a whole collapses. Yet doubts may persist. Perhaps this refutation proceeds too swiftly. Let us see, then, whether a stronger defense for the (revised) maximizing argument can be mounted.

In light of the counterexample, it might be thought that the presupposition considered above needs refinement. For example, it might be said that more options enhance a person's autonomy, but only up to some point. Beyond that point (call it the diminishing point), added options diminish autonomy by confusing the person. Accordingly, it could be argued, the M option set should be redescribed as the option set that includes the largest number and widest range of options up to the diminishing point.

Given this refinement of the presupposition, the maximizing theorist could concede that for any given option set for a given person it is possible that it could be made worse by adding options to it. And he or she could make the case by appealing to a different claim; namely, that there is an option set for each person that is maximally best. Then the argument would run that each person ought to be given access to this option set; or, more modestly, that as many people as possible ought to be brought as close as possible to having access to their maximally best option set.

This argument evades the criticism directed against the unrefined presupposition. But it is not free from difficulties. One problem, which I shall mention but not discuss, concerns the issue of how the maximally

---

[4] For further discussion of this point see G. Dworkin, "Is More Choice Always Better?"

best option set for each person is to be defined. As several writers have argued, it may not be possible to make the types of comparative judgments between different possible option sets that would need to be made if one of them is to be selected as maximally best.[5] The best that we may be able to do is to identify a range of option sets that would serve a person's autonomy equally well.

Be this as it may, we can assume, once again, that this technical problem could be overcome with sufficient ingenuity. Yet even on this optimistic assumption, the argument still should be rejected. Like the first version of the maximizing argument considered above, this argument runs up against the fact that autonomy is not the only value that matters. Even if there were a maximally best option set for each person, and even if this argument established a coherent goal for political action, it would not follow that political authorities would have a conclusive reason to undertake this political action. At most, the argument would establish that there is a *prima facie* case for such action.

To sharpen this point I will introduce a distinction between two ways in which an option set might be thought to be maximally best. Let us say that an option set is *maximally best* if it is one that enables a person to realize the ideal of autonomy to a greater degree than any other possible option set. And let us say that an option set is *all-things-considered-best* if a person is likely to lead the best life she could lead if she had access to it. Working with this distinction, it is possible for an option set to be all-things-considered-best for a person without it also being maximally best for her. Suppose, for example, that if she had access to a range of options that was narrower than that provided by her maximally best option set (but still wide enough to enable her to realize autonomy to a substantial degree) she would lead a better life because she would be inclined to pursue options that were more valuable. In such a case this narrower option set would be her all-things-considered-best option set; and we should conclude that it is better for her to have access to this option set rather than to her maximally best one. We should conclude this for two reasons – autonomy is not the only component of a good life, and its value derives from its contribution to a fully good life.

This would not be true if autonomy had lexical priority over all other values. This would imply that a person's all-things-considered-best and maximally best option sets were equivalent. But there is no good reason

---

[5] See I. Berlin, *Four Essays on Liberty*, J. Gray, "On Negative and Positive Liberty," and R. Arneson, "Freedom and Desire." These writers are primarily concerned with measuring the contribution of option sets to negative freedom, not autonomy. But many of the problems they raise apply here as well.

to accept this view. I have argued that a substantial measure of autonomy is a central component of a fully good life; and I have claimed that in order for people to be autonomous they must have access to a wide range of options. These claims establish that people have a compelling interest in having access to a wide range of options. But from this one cannot infer the further claim that people have an important interest in having access to their maximally best option set. Moreover, this further claim is, on its face, implausible. If autonomy is only one component of a fully good life, then there is no reason to think that people have a particularly strong interest in having access to a maximally best option set, particularly if some other good or value could be significantly promoted by restricting their options.

This reinforces the conclusion arrived at earlier. People do not have a conclusive reason to be as autonomous as possible. Nor do they have a conclusive reason to have access to a maximally best option set. They have a compelling interest in being sufficiently autonomous and in having access to a sufficiently wide range of options.[6] That is all.

The endorsement thesis

Let us turn our attention now to a second argument that exaggerates autonomy's value. Some philosophers have suggested that some measure of autonomy is a necessary condition for any pursuit to be valuable to the person engaging in it. They claim that if someone is forced or tricked to engage in a pursuit that he deems valueless, then whether or not the pursuit is valuable, it cannot add value to his life. This, it is further said, follows from a general truth about value: *a person's life is improved only if he leads it from the inside and according to his own beliefs about what is worthwhile.*[7] I will call this the *endorsement thesis*, since it implies that a pursuit only adds value to a person's life if he endorses it.

The endorsement thesis is a strong thesis. It yields an equally strong conclusion about the value of autonomy. If it is true, then autonomous engagement is a necessary condition for any pursuit to contribute to the value of a person's life. This would imply that a person could never improve his or her life by non-autonomously engaging in a pursuit. Derivatively, it would imply that governments could not improve the

[6] Note that to reject the maximizing argument we do not need to have a precise account of what qualifies as sufficient autonomy or a sufficiently wide range of options.
[7] W. Kymlicka, *Contemporary Political Philosophy*, pp. 203–04. Kymlicka suggests that this truth about value is an important element in the liberal commitment to autonomy. It is this suggestion that I want to explore here.

lives of those subject to their power by inducing them to engage in pursuits non-autonomously.

We shall see that both the endorsement thesis and the conclusions that follow from it are too strong. But to see this we must first get a better grip on the endorsement thesis. In particular, we need to know what the phrase "living a life from the inside" amounts to. In thinking about this matter it will help to look at some examples. Consider the following:

(1) Sarah is "forced" to go to the theatre once a week. Her boss tells her that if she does not go, she will be fired from her job. And Sarah's job is very important to her.
(2) Unknown to Sarah, her psychiatrist has hypnotized her to take up an interest in the theatre. She goes to the theatre once a week.
(3) Sarah has the misfortune of living in a town where there is very little to do. The only form of entertainment available is the theatre. Out of boredom she goes to it once a week.
(4) Sarah goes to the theatre once a week. She has not thought much about why she goes to the theatre every week. Nor has she formed a belief about the value of going to the theatre. She goes simply because this is what has always been done in her family.

In none of these examples is Sarah's desire to go to the theatre based on a belief that doing so is a valuable activity. In (1) she goes because she is under a threat. In (2) she goes on the belief that it is a worthwhile activity, but the belief is not really hers, for it has been implanted in her by her psychiatrist. In (3) she goes because there is nothing else to do and in (4) she does so out of habit or tradition.

Does Sarah live her life from the inside in any of these examples? Proponents of the endorsement thesis have not provided a precise characterization of the notion of living a life from the inside. Let us assume that it is has something to do with the phenomenological experience of the agent, i.e. the agent has the experience of freely choosing to engage in the pursuit. Given this characterization, it is clear that in (1) Sarah does not live her life from the inside. She is threatened into doing something that she would otherwise not want to do. She can plausibly claim that she is being forced to follow the will of another.

But in (2) through (4) this is not the case. In (2) Sarah is manipulated by her psychiatrist, but she does not know this. From the "inside" it seems to her that she is going to the theatre because she believes that going to the theatre is a valuable activity. She is not aware that she has been manipulated to believe this. Similarly, in (3) it is hard to see how the absence of alternative forms of entertainment in her town has any effect on whether Sarah lives her life from the inside. She may lament the lack of alternative options, but this would not show that from the inside she feels she is not leading her life. And in (4) this is even more clearly the case. In following the habits of her parents and grandparents, Sarah leads her life from the inside.

It seems, then, that the requirement that a person live his or her life from the inside will not take us very far if we want to show that the requirement provides us with a reason to value autonomy. For the only thing it clearly rules out is coercion. If we coerce someone to do something, then, in doing it, he is not leading his life from the inside. But this falls short of an argument for autonomy. An autonomous life is more than a life free from coercion.

However, there is a second clause in the endorsement thesis. If a pursuit is to add value to a person's life, he not only must lead his life from the inside, he must also lead it according to his own beliefs about what is worthwhile. By emphasizing this second clause, it can be claimed that in examples (2), (3) and (4) Sarah does not endorse going to the theatre. She does not endorse it because in each example her desire to go to the theatre is not based on her belief that doing so is objectively worthwhile. Thus, according to the endorsement thesis, Sarah does not add value to her life in any of the four examples.

This brings us closer to an argument for autonomy. If it is true that not only coercion, but also manipulation, a lack of alternative options and a lack of independent judgment negate the value of a pursuit for the person engaging in it, then it is plausible to believe that some substantial measure of autonomy is a necessary condition for any valuable pursuit. But while this brings us closer to an argument for autonomy, it also begins to look much less credible. It is simply hard to believe that in none of the examples does Sarah's practice of going to the theatre add value to her life.

Intuitively, at least, there is an important difference between the first two and last two examples. In (1) and (2) Sarah is made to serve the will of another. She is compelled to go to the theatre because someone else wants her to do it. And it is often thought that compulsion, whether through coercive threats or manipulation, obliterates the value of the pursuit for the person who is compelled to engage in it. But in (3) and (4) matters are different. Sarah is not made to serve the will of another. She is not compelled by anyone. She, herself, willingly decides to go to the theatre. Here it is much less plausible to claim that her participation in the pursuit could add no value to her life.

The difference between the two types of examples may lie in Sarah's attitude toward the pursuit. In (1) Sarah likely feels resentment at being forced to go to the theatre and in (2) she would likely feel resentment when, and if, she found out she had been hypnotized. But in (3) and (4) it would be very odd if Sarah felt any resentment at all. As indicated, in these examples, she willingly goes to the theatre.

Whatever the precise rationale for the difference between the two types of examples, the difference seems real. To take it into account I will distinguish two interpretations of the endorsement thesis.

> *Strong interpretation* In order for a pursuit to add value to a person's life, the person must *actively* endorse the pursuit on the belief that it is valuable.
>
> *Weak interpretation* In order for a pursuit to add value to a person's life, the person must at least *passively* endorse the pursuit.

The adverbs "actively" and "passively" that distinguish the two interpretations mark the difference between *self-conscious engagement* and mere *willing engagement* in a pursuit. On the strong interpretation of the endorsement thesis, Sarah does not add value to her life in any of the four examples. However, on the weak interpretation, she adds value to her life in (3) and (4). This follows because on the weak interpretation the absence of active endorsement does not negate the value of the pursuit for the person engaging in it.

It now ought to be clear that in order for the endorsement thesis to provide an argument for autonomy we must accept the strong interpretation. The weak interpretation rules out only coercion and manipulation; and it is possible to believe that coercion and manipulation are evils even if one does not believe that autonomy is valuable.[8] Since we have already seen that the strong interpretation is implausible, we must conclude that the endorsement thesis does not provide an argument for autonomy.

Notwithstanding this negative conclusion, it may be thought that the weak interpretation, even though it falls short of providing an argument for autonomy, is still relevant to its value. For it remains true that coercion and manipulation undermine autonomy. So if it can be shown that coercing or manipulating a person to engage in a pursuit could never add value to that person's life, then, it may be thought, we have at least established a conclusion supportive of autonomy.

But even this more modest conclusion cannot be established. The weak interpretation of the endorsement thesis ought to be rejected. Even though it is weaker – and more plausible – than the strong interpretation, it is still too strong. To bring out the reasons for this judgment, I want to consider an example provided by Ronald Dworkin. Dworkin is a

---

[8] This is possible since some of the reasons why coercion and manipulation are evils do not derive from the ideal of personal autonomy.

proponent of the endorsement thesis,[9] but he is eager to show that accepting it does not rule out all cases of coercive paternalism. Here is his example:

> We know that a child who is forced to practice music is very likely to endorse the coercion by agreeing that it did, in fact, make his life better; if he does not, he has lost little ground in a life that makes no use of his training.[10]

In Dworkin's hands this example is used to support the more general claim that when coercive paternalism is likely to be subsequently endorsed by the coerced person and when it does not significantly constrict his choices if endorsement never comes, then it may be justified.

Here I will not investigate whether this general claim is correct. What interests me about the example is that, when it is thought through, it casts doubt on the endorsement thesis. Dworkin suggests that if the child does not subsequently come to agree that being forced to practice music made his life better, then it follows that he must have lived a life that made no use of his training; and, it follows from this, that he must not have benefited from being forced to practice music. There are two ideas here that need to be disentangled.

(a) In order for the child to benefit from being forced to practice music he must make use of the training later in life.
(b) If the child does not come to believe that being forced to practice music made his life better, then it did not.

(a) is suspect. It is possible for the child to benefit from being forced to practice music even if he makes no use of the training later in life. It may just be intrinsically good to have some training in music at some point in one's life. So (a) should be put to one side.

The endorsement thesis tells us that (b) is true. The musical training may benefit the child either intrinsically or because he makes use of it later in life, but either way it only does so if he comes to believe that it did so. This provokes the following worry. Is it not possible for the adult (who was once the child) to be mistaken about whether or not the forced musical training benefited him?

In thinking about this question we need to consider two perspectives from which an assessment could be made about whether a coerced pursuit adds value to the life of the coerced person. One perspective is the perspective of the person himself and here endorsement does seem to be the relevant criterion. The other perspective is that of the reasonable

---

[9] R. Dworkin, "Foundations of Liberal Equality," pp. 237–38, 262–67. It is hard to know whether Dworkin accepts the strong or weak interpretation of the endorsement thesis, since he appeals to "genuine endorsement" and it is not clear how strong he intends this notion to be.
[10] Ibid. pp. 265–66.

onlooker who sees the full effects of the coerced pursuit on the person's overall life and properly appreciates its value for that person's life.[11] Here the relevant criterion must be whether the coerced pursuit enriched the person's life or made it go better in some respect. In many cases, the assessments made from the two perspectives will coincide; but in some cases they may not. And if and when they do not coincide, we will need to decide which perspective is more fundamental.

There is a simple argument that suggests that the second perspective, the perspective of the reasonable onlooker, must be the more fundamental one. The argument is based on the thought that it must be possible (at least in some cases) for us to be mistaken about whether or not a particular pursuit, whether coerced or not, added value to our lives. If our endorsement determines the issue, then it is not possible for us to be mistaken. Our decision to endorse or not endorse would settle the matter. But this would make unintelligible a question we could surely put to ourselves; namely, "Did this pursuit add value to my life?" When we put this question to ourselves, we are not trying find out whether we have, in fact, endorsed the pursuit; we are trying to find out whether we *should* endorse it. And for this question to even make sense it must be allowed that we could be mistaken about it.[12] This entails the rejection of the idea that our say-so simply settles the matter. The second perspective, but not the first, can take account of this. From the perspective of a reasonable onlooker, it can be said both that a person believes that a particular pursuit added no value to his or her life and that he or she is mistaken in believing this.

It may be thought that a proponent of the endorsement thesis could resist this conclusion by appealing to hypothetical, as opposed to actual, endorsement. This may be what Dworkin has in mind when he refers to "genuine endorsement." Here the thought is that if a person has full information and if he is not suffering from some defect in rationality, then his endorsement does settle the matter whether a particular pursuit adds value to his life. It is important to see that if this standpoint, the standpoint of hypothetical endorsement, is to be distinct from the perspective of the reasonable onlooker, then the full information referred to cannot include information about the value of the pursuit in question.

[11] There are many possible specifications of this perspective depending on how the reasonable onlooker is described. The point I want to make, however, does not depend on any particular specification.

[12] Compare Wittgenstein's famous remarks on a private language: "One would like to say: whatever is going to seem right to me is right. And that only means that here we can't talk about 'right.'" *Philosophical Investigations*, no. 258.

If it did, then the hypothetical endorser would shade into the reasonable onlooker.

This has the consequence that the hypothetical endorser is in roughly the same position as the actual endorser in the sense that he too can ask whether the pursuit in question adds value to his life; and when he asks this question and deliberates over it, he will not be trying to figure out whether he, in fact, has endorsed it. Rather, he will be trying to figure out whether he should endorse it. And, as we saw above, if the hypothetical endorser takes this question seriously, then he must admit that he could be mistaken about the matter. The hypothetical endorser must admit that even with full information and no defects in rationality, he could fail to give all the relevant considerations the force they deserve.[13]

For this reason, the appeal to hypothetical endorsement does not save the endorsement thesis from the argument under consideration. We ought to conclude that the perspective of the reasonable onlooker is the correct standpoint for determining whether pursuits add value to the lives of those who engage in them.

Return now to Dworkin's example. From the standpoint of the reasonable onlooker it is possible that the adult, who was once the child forced to practice music, could be mistaken about whether this added value to his life. That is, it is possible that the adult may fail to grasp the value of the pursuit in question. Does this possibility refute the weak interpretation of the endorsement thesis? It might not if the assessments made from the perspective of the reasonable onlooker never conflict with the assessments made from the perspective of the person himself. But there is little reason to expect this perfect congruence between the two perspectives. It is a common fact of human life that people make mistakes in assessing their lives. We have no reason to think that they could never make mistakes in assessing whether or not a pursuit that they had been forced to engage in added value to their lives. If they not only could be mistaken, but, in fact, sometimes are mistaken in this

---

[13] One way to resist this line of argument would be to insist that value is parasitic on desire. Crudely, this view holds that we judge things to be valuable because we desire them; we do not desire them because we judge them to be valuable. If this view were correct, then it would not make sense to deliberate about whether a pursuit added value to one's life. One would simply need to consult one's desires. A full defense of the argument I am pressing would need to show that this view is mistaken. (For a refutation see J. Griffin, "Against the Taste Model.") However, the proponents of the endorsement thesis I have in mind – Kymlicka, Dworkin – do not accept this view. They believe that people can make mistakes about what is valuable. Their view is that endorsement is necessary, but not sufficient, for a pursuit to add value to the life of the person who engages in it. This is the view I am calling into question.

matter, then the weak interpretation of the endorsement thesis is false. And if it is false, then it can provide no support at all for autonomy.

Nonetheless, even if we ought to reject both interpretations of the endorsement thesis, there remain strong intuitions that continue to nourish it. Can these intuitions be accounted for without acceding to it? The rejection of the endorsement thesis follows from the recognition that value and belief in value can come apart. As we have seen, it is possible for a pursuit to add value to people's lives even if they never come to believe that it did. Suppose, for example, that a person lives in a country which requires him to spend a year in public service before entering college. It is possible that such a person may benefit from this experience even if he goes to his grave thinking that it was a waste of time. Despite this belief, he may have learned valuable things from this time in public service and may have improved his character in various ways. The fact that he refused to acknowledge these benefits would not show that they did not exist.[14]

However, it may be that if such a person not only went to his grave believing that the year spent in public service was a waste of time, but also harbored deep feelings of self-hatred because he was forced to do it, then it would be true that it did not add value to his life.[15] Here the claim is that the presence of certain negative affective responses toward a pursuit can negate the value of engaging in it. This claim has considerable plausibility. But notice that one can accept it without accepting the endorsement thesis, for not every time a person believes a pursuit adds no value to his life will he also harbor deep negative affective responses toward it. At best, the connection between the belief and these responses is contingent.

Moreover, there may be some pursuits for which it is true that a person must believe in their value if he or she is to get any value from them. Proponents of the endorsement thesis often appeal to the example of religious faith as support for their view.[16] They claim that if people are coerced into religion, they will get no value from it. If this is right, it establishes that there are some pursuits for which the endorsement thesis

---

[14] There is a further issue I have not discussed. Can a pursuit add value to a person's life even if, on balance, it would have been better for him to have done something else? If the answer is "no," then the only pursuits that could add value to our lives would be pursuits that were the best ones available to us. This is surely too strong. It makes sense to say "my career added value to my life, even though I could have chosen a career which added more value to my life." And if it makes sense to say this, then it makes sense to say that some pursuits can add value to my life even if it is true that engaging in them was not the best use of my time.

[15] This point was suggested to me by Joseph Raz.

[16] See R. Dworkin, "The Foundations of Liberal Equality," p. 238.

holds true. For them, it can be said that they are valuable only if they are believed to be valuable. But this tells us more about these particular pursuits than it does about value in general. Not all valuable pursuits are like religious practice. Some pursuits can add value to people's lives even if they do not endorse them in either the active or passive sense.

It is now possible to identify where the endorsement thesis goes wrong. It errs in moving from a consideration of the conditions of the value of particular types of pursuits to a thesis about the nature of value in general. It also fails to see that in many cases it is not the belief that a pursuit has no value, but the presence of certain negative affective responses toward it, that negates its value for the person engaging in it. Granted that we understand this, there is no bar to accepting some of the intuitions that lie behind the endorsement thesis. These intuitions can be affirmed without accepting the thesis.

Let me now summarize the general case against the endorsement thesis. The endorsement thesis is ambiguous. To clear up the ambiguity it is necessary to distinguish a strong from a weak interpretation. To get an argument for the value of autonomy, the strong interpretation is needed, but the strong interpretation is not plausible. Thus, the endorsement thesis provides no argument for the value of autonomy. Moreover, the weak interpretation of the endorsement thesis is also suspect. It cannot take account of the possibility that people may be mistaken in believing that a pursuit that they were forced to engage in added no value to their lives. So neither the strong nor the weak interpretation of the endorsement thesis warrant acceptance. Since neither warrant acceptance, neither provide support for autonomy.

The non-discrimination argument

I have rejected two arguments: the maximizing argument and the endorsement thesis. Both exaggerate the significance of autonomy and both are sometimes relied on to discredit perfectionism. Now consider one last argument. This argument bears more directly on the relationship between autonomy and perfectionist political action.

Before discussing it, we need to recall a distinction briefly alluded to in the introduction to this book (see page 6 note 8). This distinction concerns two types of perfectionist political action. Type (1) perfectionism holds that it is morally permissible for governments to promote, actively and intentionally, the ideal of autonomy. Type (2) perfectionism holds that – in addition to promoting autonomy – it is morally permissible for governments to favor, actively and intentionally, valuable pursuits over less valuable ones. Given this characterization, it follows that those who accept type (2) perfectionism will also accept type (1) perfectionism.[17] But it is possible to accept type (1) and reject type (2) perfectionism.[18]

Such a view is possible. But it is not immediately clear why anyone would want to endorse it. Once one has embraced type (1) perfectionism, thus conceding in principle the legitimacy of perfectionist political action, it would seem that there is nothing to prevent one from also embracing type (2) perfectionism.

However, some have argued that a proper understanding of autonomy shows that there are good reasons for rejecting type (2) perfectionism. They believe that type (2) perfectionism involves coercion or manipulation which, they further believe, invades the autonomy of those subject to it. I will call this the *non-discrimination argument*.[19] It yields the conclusion that any form of type (2) perfectionism is morally suspect because it discriminates in favor of some pursuits and against others, thus showing improper respect for personal autonomy.

To assess the non-discrimination argument we need to assess its central premise. This is the claim that type (2) perfectionism involves coercion or manipulation that invades autonomy. No doubt there are some forms of type (2) perfectionist political action that would objectionably involve coercion or manipulation. But the non-discrimination argument is after a more general conclusion. It seeks to rule out *all* forms of type (2) perfectionist political action. So, to assess it, it is fair to consider cases which seem intuitively to be least objectionable.

Consider this case. A government in a modern western society adopts a policy of offering a tax credit to all those who visit a natural park within a specified period of time. The idea behind the policy is that these tax credits will stimulate an appreciation of natural beauty. The government considers the possibility that some will go to the parks solely to get the tax break. But it believes that even this would be a good thing, since part of the rationale behind the policy is to expose more people to natural beauty, even if they ultimately do not come to appreciate it.

Several possible objections could be brought against such a policy. But here we are interested only in one objection, the objection that maintains

---

[17] Assuming, that is, that they believe that autonomy is a valuable ideal.

[18] Working with this distinction, we can divide contemporary liberal political philosophers into three rough camps. First, there are those who reject both type (1) and type (2) perfectionism and opt for some version of the bracketing strategy (Rawls, Nagel, Larmore). Second, there are those who accept type (1) perfectionism but reject type (2) perfectionism (Kymlicka, Waldron). And third, there are those who accept both type (1) and type (2) perfectionism (Raz).

[19] Proponents of the non-discrimination argument include J. Waldron, "Autonomy and Perfectionism," W. Kymlicka, *Contemporary Political Philosophy* and C. Nino, *The Ethics of Human Rights*, pp. 136–37.

that this policy would in some way invade the autonomy of people in this society. How might such an objection be pressed? Defenders of the non-discrimination argument often advance the following line of thought: "If the autonomy of people is to be respected, they must be left free to make their own decisions, so long as these decisions do not cause clear and direct harm to others. The freedom to make their own decisions includes the freedom to choose between different options which have not had their opportunity costs artificially tampered with by the government." This line of thought provides a justification for rejecting the above policy. When the governments gives tax credits to those who visit natural parks, it is tampering with the opportunity costs of this option *vis-à-vis* other possible options. So perhaps, in so doing, it invades the autonomy of its subjects.

This argument invites two questions. First, what does it mean to say that someone or some body tampers artificially with the opportunity costs of different options? Second, why should such tampering be thought to invade autonomy? Let me tackle the first question first. The opportunity costs of the different options available in a society are determined by the decisions and preferences of everyone in the society. Such costs are reflected in the market-clearing prices of different options. For example, it may cost $20 to go to a baseball game, $7 to go to a movie and $40 to go to the theatre. If we like we can call these costs "natural" since they are determined by the free decisions of everyone in the society. But the opportunity costs of options are also affected by what governments do. Either indirectly or directly, governments can use their considerable powers to influence the opportunity costs of different options. A government, for example, might impose a steeply progressive income tax which has the result of reducing inequality in income which, in turn, has the result of raising the prices of luxury items.[20] This would indirectly change the opportunity costs of such items. Alternatively, a government might simply levy a tax on luxury items, thereby directly raising their costs.

Proponents of the non-discrimination argument cannot claim that all government action that affects the natural opportunity costs of different options in a society is objectionable. This would lead straight to anarchism. Assuming anarchism is unacceptable, they must claim that it is only a particular type of government action that is objectionable because it artificially tampers with the opportunity costs of different

[20] Strictly speaking, such a tax would not raise the price of all luxury items. It would raise the price of luxury items which have high start-up production costs, but relatively low marginal production costs. A good example of such an item would be a luxury car like a Rolls Royce.

options. This is government action justified on the grounds that it favors some options over others because they are more valuable. So understood, artificial tampering with opportunity costs just is the *modus operandi* of type (2) perfectionist political action.

This raises the second question. Why should this be thought to be objectionable? Why, in other words, should we think that this type of artificial tampering with opportunity costs (if we want to call it that) necessarily invades autonomy?

Suppose your friend tells you that she will give you $50 if you go to a natural park this afternoon. Suppose further that your friend says this because she believes that the offer will induce you to discover and appreciate a value (the value of natural beauty) that you would otherwise overlook; or perhaps she thinks that you are aware of this value, but that you need some assistance if you are going to adequately appreciate it. There is no question that her generous offer would affect your opportunity costs of going to the park. But surely you could not object that your friend would be invading your autonomy by tampering with the opportunity costs of your options.[21] So if you cannot make this objection to your friend, why can you make it to your government?[22]

The answer must be that the government possesses powers that your friend does not have. The government, unlike your friend, has control over an enormous apparatus of coercive power. But while this response is surely true, it is hard to see how it undercuts the analogy. If your friend's offer does not invade your autonomy, then the government's tax credits should not either. The fact that the government has standing control over a large apparatus of coercive power is neither here nor there.[23]

It will be objected that the tax credits issued by the government will

---

[21] Under some circumstances, offers can be coercive or manipulative, particularly when they seek to exploit some weakness in those to whom they are directed. I do not deny this. I deny only that offers that affect the opportunity costs of different options are *ipso facto* coercive or manipulative.

[22] Waldron has suggested that when governments subsidize options to encourage their pursuit they illegitimately interfere with the moral deliberations of their subjects. (See "Autonomy and Perfectionism," pp. 1141–52.) But this fails to distinguish government action from similar action undertaken by others that is unobjectionable; e.g. generous offers made by friends. For further, but different, criticism of Waldron's view, see G. Sher, "Liberal Neutrality and the Value of Autonomy."

[23] Perhaps what distinguishes government action from an offer from a friend is that government action has a public meaning. As I pointed out in chapter 4, in some contexts government support for some pursuits might be understood as a public condemnation of other worthy pursuits. This would indeed provide a reason for taking a second look at the permissibility of the government action in question. But this consideration is out of place here for two reasons. First, it is not obvious that this meaning would invade anyone's autonomy; and, second, it is not plausible to claim that all government action that favors some pursuits over others would convey a harmful public message.

have to be paid in the end by somebody. Somebody's taxes will be higher as a consequence of the issuance of the tax credits. So here, it may be said, is where the government's coercive power comes into the picture. Your friend freely makes you an offer, but the government coercively collects taxes. Doesn't this undercut the analogy?

It should be kept in mind that people do not normally object to government taxation when the money is used to promote the common good. Friends of the non-discrimination argument do not claim that the mere fact that the government must raise its money coercively implies that everything that it does with the money invades the autonomy of its subjects. So the mere fact that the money that (in the end) pays for the tax credits is raised coercively does not entail that the policy of giving tax credits to people who visit natural parks invades their autonomy.

We still need an argument for that conclusion. Given this, the proponent of the non-discrimination argument might be tempted to defend the following thesis:

> *Coercion minimization thesis* Given that coercion invades the autonomy of people, governments must never engage in any coercion (whether directly or indirectly) unless such coercion is necessary for the protection and promotion of autonomy.

This thesis explains why it is wrong to issue the tax credits. Doing so is not necessary for the protection and promotion of autonomy. People can and do lead autonomous lives without ever setting foot in a natural park.

Yet, even though the coercion minimization thesis yields the judgment that the non-discrimination argument needs, it has two unacceptable consequences. First, it presumes either that autonomy is the only value or that it takes priority over every other value in all circumstances. But, as I suggested earlier, this presumption is implausible. At least in some circumstances, it ought to be permissible to use coercion to advance and sustain other values important to the common good. Second, the coercion minimization thesis is in tension with a proper understanding of the value of autonomy. We have seen that an autonomous life is valuable, if and only if, it is a life composed of pursuits that are, by and large, worthwhile and valuable. Given the conditional value of autonomy, it is a mistake to accept a thesis that has the consequence of ruling out all governmental efforts to promote valuable options over less valuable ones. For in doing so we lose sight of the fact that it is not an autonomous life that is ultimately valuable, but rather an autonomous life of valuable pursuits.

This gives us ample grounds for rejecting the coercion minimization thesis. And without this thesis, we still do not have an argument that shows that the proposed policy of issuing tax credits invades the autonomy of those subject to it. It still seems to be the case that if our friend can offer us money to go to a natural park without invading our autonomy, then our government can do it as well.

Rather than fight the battle at the level of principle, the proponent of the non-discrimination argument might retreat to the level of pragmatic politics. He might claim that while there is no principled reason to oppose type (2) perfectionism, there are all sorts of common sense reasons which tell against it. In this vein, he might ask, if we want to promote an appreciation of natural beauty, do we really want to entrust this job to politicians? Would it not be wiser to find ways to get people in civil society to do it themselves?[24]

There is surely some wisdom in this pragmatic objection. It may be true that in many contexts it is best to leave the government out of the business of evaluating options. Such judgments turn on the expected competence of political decision-makers. But even if it were true that modern governments never do a good job of evaluating options, this would remain a secondary matter. The primary issue is whether all forms of type (2) perfectionism necessarily invade the self-determination of individual people. The pragmatic objection does nothing to substantiate this idea. It might provide a reason for being suspicious of type (2) perfectionism in some contexts, but it does not demonstrate that such political action necessarily infringes autonomy.

In the absence of any compelling case for the non-discrimination argument, it must be rejected. This is a significant conclusion. The non-discrimination argument holds that there is a fundamental incompatibility between respect for autonomy and type (2) perfectionism. Its rejection shows that no such fundamental incompatibility exists.

At the same time, this conclusion should not itself be exaggerated. The rejection of the non-discrimination argument does not show that all forms of type (2) perfectionist political action are compatible with respect for autonomy. This clearly is not the case. Respect for autonomy does place constraints on type (2) perfectionist political action. The problem with the non-discrimination argument is that it turns this valid point into an ill-supported overstatement.

Conclusion

To sum up: I have investigated three ways in which the ideal of personal autonomy can be exaggerated. I have argued that there is no good reason

---

[24] This is the view that Kymlicka ultimately comes round to (*Contemporary Political Philosophy*, p. 219).

to think that autonomy should be maximized, that only autonomous pursuits add value to a person's life or that there is a fundamental incompatibility between respect for autonomy and type (2) perfectionism.

These conclusions cast further light on the relationship between autonomy and perfectionist political action. By highlighting the limits of autonomy, they remove some further grounds for rejecting perfectionism at the level of principle.

Since the three chapters on autonomy that come to an end here have discussed a wide range of issues, the following summary may be helpful.

Personal autonomy is the ideal of people charting their own course through life, fashioning their character by self-consciously choosing projects and taking up commitments from a wide range of eligible alternatives, and making something out of their lives according to their own understanding of what is valuable and worth doing.

This ideal is intrinsically valuable in the sense that it is valuable for its own sake. This supports the following conclusion. If two valuable lives are similar in all evaluatively relevant respects except that one realizes autonomy and the other does not, then the former is better than the latter. It is better because it manifests an additional perfection.

Personal autonomy also facilitates the achievement of a further excellence of considerable weight – the ideal of self-development. Autonomous people are more likely to achieve self-development than non-autonomous people.

Taken by themselves, these claims about autonomy do not show that it is a central component of human flourishing. However, given the social forms of modern western societies, there is good reason to think that the realization of this ideal is bound up with a fully good life, at least for the vast majority of people in these societies.

This claim is strong, but it is compatible with the rejection of some stronger claims. Autonomy is not unconditionally valuable; it is not an ideal that all people, no matter what their circumstances, have conclusive reason to realize; and it is not the source of value in the sense that if a person fails to be autonomous his or her life can have no value.

Establishing that personal autonomy is a central component of human flourishing provides support for liberal perfectionism; for liberal perfectionism is a perfectionist theory that holds that autonomy is a central component of human flourishing.

However, some have thought that a strong commitment to autonomy does not sit well with perfectionism. Three arguments are commonly invoked to bolster this view. They are the argument that autonomy should be maximized (the maximizing argument), the argument that the only pursuits that add value to a person's life are ones that he or she endorses (the endorsement thesis) and the argument that perfectionist political action invades autonomy by artificially tampering with the opportunity costs of people's options (the non-discrimination argument).

Since none of these arguments succeeds, there is good reason to think that a strong commitment to autonomy is compatible with perfectionism. This provides further support for liberal perfectionism.

9   Applications

So far the argument of this book has been fairly abstract. In chapters 2–5 I sought to discredit the bracketing strategy by calling into question its distinctive feature, a commitment to the principles of restraint. In chapters 6–8 I then tried to provide support for liberal perfectionism by arguing for the centrality of personal autonomy to human flourishing and by showing that a strong commitment to autonomy is fully compatible with perfectionism. Taken in conjunction, these arguments were intended to show that liberal perfectionism has greater justificatory force than the best account of anti-perfectionist political morality.

This concluding chapter brings the discussion down to earth by considering a range of public policy issues. The issues to be discussed will not be given the type of in-depth treatment they require. But my ambition in this chapter is not to defend conclusively any particular policy judgment.[1] I have two much more modest goals. First, to give some indication of how the perfectionist views defended in this book might differ from anti-perfectionist views at the level of concrete politics. Second, to expose some weaknesses and limits in anti-perfectionist arguments often invoked in public debate over policy issues.

Promoting autonomy

I have argued that personal autonomy warrants a central place in a sound account of political morality. But I have not said anything about how this ideal could be promoted through political action. Personal autonomy is not a tangible resource or a primary good that can be distributed by political authorities. It is a character ideal. How, then, might political societies promote it?

To get a better grip on this question it will help to distinguish *respecting* from *promoting* autonomy. To respect the autonomy of others

---

[1] This is not my way of taking back what I say. It is merely an acknowledgment that the issues discussed in this chapter call for more detailed discussion than I can give them here.

one must not illegitimately interfere with their decisions. In the main, this means that one must give them some space to lead their own lives and to pursue the projects that make up that life. It also means that one must not restrict their range of options to the point where they no longer have access to a sufficiently wide range, or interfere with the efforts of others to promote their autonomy.

Political authorities who respect the autonomy of their subjects comply with these injunctions. This imposes a general constraint on justified political action: political power must be exercised in ways that do not illegitimately interfere with the self-determination of those subject to it. Of course for the content of this general constraint to be reasonably determinate the adverb "illegitimately" must be specified.[2] But this vague statement can serve as a rough approximation.

Promoting autonomy, in contrast, requires more than merely complying with a series of negative injunctions. It calls for positive efforts to help others develop the capacities and skills needed to realize the ideal of autonomy as well as positive efforts to ensure that their environment gives them access to a rich and varied range of options. Such efforts should help them achieve autonomy, or at least they should be the type of efforts that would help typical people achieve autonomy under normal conditions.

Political authorities can play an important role in promoting autonomy. They can enact policies that cultivate the requisite skills and capacities, they can take steps to ensure that all their subjects have access to a sufficiently wide range of options and they can enforce legal rules that protect people from coercion and manipulation. All of these efforts, properly undertaken, will help their subjects achieve the character ideal of autonomy. However, it does not follow that political authorities have a general duty to ensure that all or any of their subjects become autonomous. There are limits to what can be done through political action. Even in a perfectly administered state, some would fail to be autonomous. Precisely because autonomy is (in part) a personal achievement it is something people themselves can fail to realize.

Notwithstanding this limit, autonomy-based perfectionist political action is important. Governments have duties to sustain a legal framework that facilitates the autonomous development of their subjects. These duties extend beyond the negative injunctions entailed by respect for autonomy and encompass positive efforts to promote it. This has the

---

[2] Sometimes morality requires that we obstruct the self-determination of some to protect the interests of others. This would be an instance of the legitimate obstruction of personal autonomy.

consequence that in some contexts political authorities should actively favor some ways of life over others.

To illustrate this point I want to discuss one issue of public policy. This concerns the education of the younger members of a political community. By focusing on this issue, I do not mean to suggest that it is the only instance of justified autonomy-based perfectionist political action. I focus on it because it is an important issue and it effectively brings out the contrast between liberal perfectionism and some prominent versions of anti-perfectionist liberalism.

> *Example 1* A small religious community in a modern western society refuses to send its children to state-accredited schools. They want to teach their children the skills necessary for their way of life and they want to insulate them from the outside world. The religious community is peaceful and it poses no threat to the larger social order. It simply asks to be left alone. But if its request is granted, then its younger members will not receive a liberal education and they will not be taught some of the skills necessary for an autonomous life.[3]

What should be done? The view to be defended here is that the society acts correctly if it requires this religious community to send its children to state-accredited schools.[4] Furthermore, I will argue that this position is best justified by direct appeal to the value of autonomy. The government acts correctly because it has a general duty to promote the autonomy of all children subject to its authority.

This position provokes two sorts of objections. From one direction some will claim that the government acts wrongly in requiring the community to send its children to state-accredited schools. These objectors will trumpet the values of pluralism and diversity.[5] From another direction some will agree that the government acts correctly in requiring the community to send its children to state-accredited schools, but will insist that this position can be justified without appeal to autonomy (or any other controversial ideal of human flourishing). These objectors will trumpet the values of shared democratic citizenship.[6]

[3] The reader familiar with American constitutional history will recognize that this hypothetical illustration raises issues similar to those raised in *Wisconsin v. Yoder, et al.*, 406 US 205 (1972). I discuss this example rather than the actual case so as to avoid addressing questions of constitutional law.
[4] In particular cases there may be considerations that tell against intervention. The position defended here is that there is a general presumptive case for intervention, providing the government does a tolerably good job in setting standards for school accreditation.
[5] See W. Galston, "Two Concepts of Liberalism."
[6] See John Rawls, *Political Liberalism*, and S. Macedo, "Liberal Civic Education and Religious Fundamentalism."

Both objections deserve serious consideration. Let me begin with the first one. The case for requiring this community to send its children to state-accredited schools is based on the government's general duty to protect and promote the interests of children. Left to their own community, the children in the above example will receive an education which prepares them for only one way of life. They will almost certainly not develop the skills and capacities necessary for an autonomous life. Nor will they have access to a rich and varied range of options when they become adults. At the "age of reason" their fate will be largely sealed. Having been educated to pursue one way of life, they will have little choice but to pursue it.

As I have argued, for both instrumental and intrinsic reasons, autonomy is a value of special importance. It is a central component of a fully good life. For this reason, the government has a duty to promote the autonomy of children, even when their parents wish to discourage it, providing there is some effective way to do it which is not ruled out by countervailing values.

Two such values are salient in this context. They are the parents' interest in shaping the lives of their children and the community's interest in self-reproduction. Both values are genuine. But, as we shall see, neither defeat the case for intervention.

Parents should be given latitude to influence the development of their children. This remains true even when it is known that they are not particularly wise or do not hold sound beliefs. The institution of the private family gives parents the opportunity to shape the values and ideals of their children. But it does not follow that they should have unlimited control over their lives and minds. Numerous restrictions on parental control are compatible with respect for the private family. Among the most obvious are restrictions on physical abuse, but many others are justified as well. The requirement that parents send their children to schools which will assist them in developing the capacities necessary to become autonomous is one further restriction. If, as I have argued, autonomy is a central component of a fully good life, this further restriction is justified.

It is important to stress that even with this restriction parents have significant opportunities to shape the values and ideals of their children. Compared with the influence of neighbors, strangers and public officials, they exert by far the dominant influence on the development of their children. Assuming that the institution of the private family is justified, this is entirely appropriate.

The response, then, to those who reject the position defended here by invoking the parental interest in shaping the values and ideals of children is to point out, first, that this interest is not absolute and, second, that even when parents are required to send their children to state-accredited schools, the interest is still substantially respected.[7]

The second countervailing value mentioned above concerns the community's interest in its self-reproduction. Like the parents' interest in the development of their children, this value is genuine. In the section below on perfectionism and culture I will discuss one type of political action justified by it. But this value does not defeat the case for requiring the children of our hypothetical community to attend state-accredited schools. The community's interest in self-reproduction, like the parents' interest in the education of their child, is not unlimited. The interest has value only if the community is worth sustaining. In general, three criteria are relevant to this judgment. First, the community must not sustain a degrading way of life. Second, the community must be morally decent (it must not oppress its members or those who do not belong to it). And, third, the community must be sustainable by the free decisions of its members.[8] The first two criteria are not in question here. We can assume that in example 1 the community's way of life is not degrading or morally indecent. The third criterion, however, bears directly on the issue and calls for further comment.

Recall that we are discussing a sub-community in a modern western society. This community exists in a larger environment that is constituted by social practices that favor individual choice. Given these background conditions, it is plausible to believe that if this community is to prosper it needs to be sustainable by the free choices of its members. This is what I sought to establish in chapter 7. The arguments there justify the third criterion. If a community is not sustainable by the free decisions of its members, then the larger society has no duty to take steps to ensure its survival.

From this there is a short argument that shows that the community's interest in self-reproduction does not defeat the case for requiring its members to attend state-accredited schools. The argument runs like this. If the children of the community are required to attend state-accredited schools, then one of two things will happen. Either the community will survive because enough of its younger members will return to the community after receiving their education or the community will not

---

[7] For a similar line of thought, one from which I have benefited, see J. Feinberg, "The Child's Right to an Open Future."

[8] By free decisions I do not mean particularly reflective decisions. I mean something more basic; namely, that members of the communities have more than one genuine option. The troubling aspect of the education that our hypothetical community wishes to give its younger members is that it prepares them for only one way of life.

survive because too many of its younger members will freely choose to pursue other ways of life. If the former occurs, the community's interest in self-reproduction is not frustrated.[9] But, if the latter occurs, then the community is not sustainable by the free choices of its members and it loses its claim to self-reproduction.

If this is right, neither countervailing value defeats the case for requiring the community to send its younger members to state-accredited schools. However, it might be thought that I have overlooked an important point. In chapter 7 I noted that for some who live in non-autonomous sub-communities the best life for them is continued participation in the non-autonomous way of life. Does this not undercut the case for requiring children of such communities to attend state-accredited schools?

I think not. There is an important difference between children and adults who live in these communities. Having spent most of their lives in these communities, adults have little choice but to continue participating in them. The conditions of their well-being are tied up with the way of life of the non-autonomous community. This explains how their reason for being autonomous can be canceled or overridden. The same is not true for children in these communities. The conditions of their well-being are largely indeterminate. They have, in a real sense, an open future. This being the case, the considerations which cancel or override their parents' reason to be autonomous do not come into play in their case, or at least do not have nearly as much force.

So far I have tried to demonstrate that the society acts rightly if it requires the hypothetical community to send its younger members to state-accredited schools. Many anti-perfectionists agree that this is the correct policy, but they argue that we do not need to rely on autonomy-based considerations to justify it. Instead, they claim, we can and should appeal to the values of democratic citizenship to make our case.[10] These values, they are quick to stress, are not perfectionist. They are not defended as constituent elements of a fully good life.

The view I have been defending will be strengthened if it can be shown that this argument is unconvincing. The argument can be set out as follows.

---

[9] Note that a community's interest in self-reproduction is not the same thing as its interest in resisting all changes in its practices. The latter interest is much weaker than the former. So it is no objection to point out that even if a community is sustainable by the free choices of its members, the requirement that its younger members be sent to state-accredited schools would likely result in changes in some of its practices.

[10] This argument is most clearly set out by S. Macedo in "Liberal Civic Education and Religious Fundamentalism." Also see J. Rawls, *Political Liberalism*, p. 200.

(a) If modern western societies are to function well, their citizens must possess a set of basic civic virtues.

(b) If citizens are to possess a set of basic civic virtues, then as children they must learn them.

(c) State-accredited schools teach, among other things, the basic civic virtues.

(d) Therefore, "each of us can reasonably be asked to surrender some control over our own children for the sake of reasonable common efforts to insure that all future citizens learn the minimal prerequisites of citizenship."[11]

This argument purports to show that we can rightly require children to attend state-accredited schools without invoking the value of personal autonomy.[12] We can justify the requirement by maintaining that the demands of common citizenship take precedence over the interests of sub-communities to protect and preserve their ways of life.

Despite its initial plausibility, this argument is flawed. Even if we should concede premises (b) and (c), we should not accept premise (a) as it stands. The reason for this is that premise (a) is ambiguous between (a1) and (a2):

(a1) If modern western societies are to function well, then *all* their citizens must possess a set of basic civic virtues.

(a2) If modern western societies are to function well, then a majority (or a preponderant majority) of their citizens must possess a set of basic civic virtues.

The flaw in the argument follows from this ambiguity. If we insert (a1) into the argument, then (d) follows. But (a1) is false. It is not true that for a modern western society to function well all of its citizens must possess a set of basic civic virtues. Alternatively, if we insert (a2) into the argument, then we have a much more plausible premise, but (d) does not follow. For the truth of premises (a2), (b) and (c) would not show that each of us has a duty to help "insure that *all* future citizens learn the minimal prerequisites of citizenship."

This is significant. In modern western societies non-autonomous sub-communities compose a distinct minority. Because of this it is reasonable to believe that a modern western society could exempt all those who wish to preserve their non-autonomous way of life by not educating their

---

[11] S. Macedo, "Liberal Civic Education and Religious Fundamentalism," pp. 485–86.

[12] In practice this may not make much of a difference. As Amy Gutmann has pointed out, there is a substantial convergence between an education that prepares one to be a good democratic citizen and one that prepares one to lead an autonomous life. See her "Civic Education and Social Diversity," p. 573.

children in state-accredited schools from the requirement that children be taught a set of basic civic virtues without thereby endangering itself. If the preponderant majority of children in the society receive instruction in civic virtue, it should not occasion concern that a few sub-communities pull their children out of school.[13]

So in example 1 we cannot conclude that considerations of civic virtue provide a sound rationale for requiring the community to send its younger members to state-accredited schools. We do not have a case against the claims of the parents and the community to educate their children as they see fit in virtue of the fact that we have an interest in the well-functioning of the political institutions of our society. That case supports the idea that schools should teach civic education. It falls short of demonstrating that all children must receive that education.[14]

Against this, it might be said that once a society started making exceptions for some groups, allowing them to keep their children out of state-accredited schools, then there would be no principled way to enforce the requirement that children in general attend such schools. The slope here, it might be said, would be too slippery.

But this point has force only if it is, in fact, true that if exceptions were granted, then there would be a flood of demands for further exceptions. In the present context this seems unlikely. The vast majority of citizens in modern western societies have no objection, and indeed may have a preference for, sending their children to state-accredited schools.[15]

So slippery slope worries will not be much help to proponents of this argument. To get the right result in this example we will need to appeal to the interests of the children. I have argued that the relevant interest is the child's interest in receiving an education that prepares him or her to realize the ideal of autonomy. If the community were permitted to pull its children out of state-accredited schools, this interest would be thwarted. Allowing communities to do this fails to pay due regard for the future well-being of children.

Perhaps there is some alternative line of argument that yields the same

[13] Compare this with the analogous case for tolerating the free expression of anti-democratic views. The advocacy of such views may encourage some citizens to reject the basic values of liberal democracy. But, so long as these citizens constitute a distinct minority, we should not fear for the survival or well-functioning of the liberal democratic state.

[14] This argument could be shored up by adding the civic republican claim that participation in public political life is a necessary element in any good life. This would provide a case for making sure that all children receive an education that teaches them basic civic virtues. But, whatever its plausibility, this civic republican claim is a perfectionist claim. It is not available to anti-perfectionist liberals.

[15] The argument also assumes that no reasoned discriminations could be made; but such discriminations are made all the time in the law. Consider, for instance, exemptions from military service on the basis of religious belief.

conclusion in this case. But I have tried to make it plain that an argument that appeals to autonomy has the best chance of succeeding. If this is right, example 1 illustrates and provides support for autonomy-based perfectionist political action.

Promoting the good

Autonomy-based political action is one type of perfectionist political action. But it is not the only type. Other types may conflict with or supplement it. In this section I examine government efforts to promote valuable pursuits. As we saw in chapter 8, some writers believe that autonomy-based perfectionism rules out all such efforts. This is a mistake. Respect for the value of autonomy places constraints on justified perfectionism, but it does not exclude all non-autonomy-based perfectionist political action.[16]

Still, there may be other reasons for rejecting these governmental efforts. Even if they do not conflict with respect for autonomy, they may not be justified. My strategy here will be to argue that there is no general principled reason for rejecting this type of perfectionism and to propose an example that has a shot at being justified.

The flagship argument for this type of perfectionism has already been discussed. It is based on the claim that the good life is not merely the autonomous life, but the autonomous life which consists, by and large, of valuable pursuits. This establishes a presumptive case for promoting valuable options and discouraging base ones. To the extent that the exercise of governmental power makes it more likely that those subject to it will embrace worthy pursuits and less likely that they will embrace unworthy pursuits, it is presumptively justified. The presumption of course is not indefeasible. If the exercise of governmental power runs roughshod over some other important value, then even if it is effective in increasing the likelihood that people will embrace worthy over unworthy pursuits, it might be unjustified.

With this in mind, consider a second example.

> *Example 2* In an effort to promote and stimulate appreciation of high art, the government of a modern western society spends public money on the creation and maintenance of museums and grants public subsidies to artists. It justifies this expenditure by claiming that a good society promotes what it believes is intrinsically valuable.

---

[16] "Non-autonomy-based perfectionist political action" is equivalent to the less cumbersome "type (2) perfectionist political action" as it was described in chapter 8.

Many would claim that the government acts correctly in this example. They believe that this use of public money would be justified because it is plausible to claim both that art is intrinsically valuable and that a good society promotes what is intrinsically valuable.

This is also my view. A full defense of it would need to show that the first claim, the claim that art is intrinsically valuable, is true. This would require a foray into aesthetics and value theory. I shall not attempt this here. Instead, I will just proceed on the assumption that art is intrinsically valuable, and I will try to defend the second claim, the claim that a good society promotes what is intrinsically valuable. This claim is clearly and straightforwardly a perfectionist claim.[17]

A potentially powerful argument against the public funding of art is that there are other values that have an equal or greater claim to public support. Under very poor economic conditions, it would be irresponsible for a government to spend scarce resources on art while many of its citizens starved. Less obviously, under some circumstances, it might be wrong for public money to be spent on art when it could be spent on other valuable projects such as space exploration. The force of this argument, however, cannot be gauged in the abstract. Its force depends on the particular context in which it is raised. To avoid this problem let us assume that in example 2, reasonably favorable economic conditions obtain and that there is no other value that has a clearly superior claim to public support.

Even with these qualifications, not everyone will agree with the view defended here. In chapter 8 I considered two arguments that are often brought against the public support of valuable pursuits. One argument holds that when the government supports some pursuits over others it tampers with people's opportunity costs and thereby violates their autonomy. The other argument appeals to the coercion minimization thesis in order to reach the same conclusion. Both arguments can and sometimes are pressed against the public funding of the arts. Yet it should be clear that the reasons for rejecting these arguments (offered in chapter 8) apply in this context. Neither argument shows that public funding of the arts is objectionable.

Some anti-perfectionists do not dispute this. They are willing to accept that the public funding of the arts is a legitimate function of government.

---

[17] Providing, of course, that what is taken to be intrinsically valuable is so taken because it contributes to the flourishing of humans. With respect to art, some, like G. E. Moore, have held that it has a value all its own, irrespective of its contribution to human flourishing. But even Moore thought that the organic unity that contains both art and the perception of art by humans is more valuable than art by itself. See *Principia Ethica*, pp. 135–36.

Echoing Rawls, they insist that their anti-perfectionism comes into play only at the level of constitutional essentials and basic justice. Since spending public money on art is not a matter of basic justice, it is permissible for governments to do it.[18] However, as I pointed out in chapter 3, this response is not fully satisfactory since no clear criterion has been put forward to distinguish matters of basic justice from other non-basic political matters.[19]

Still, even without a clear criterion, it is possible to make common sense judgments. Everyone would agree that traffic laws or garbage collection ordinances are not matters of basic justice and that laws protecting freedom of conscience are. It might be thought that public funding of the arts is like the former; it is clearly and uncontroversially a non-basic political matter. But this judgment is hard to sustain once it is borne in mind that (a) art expresses views about the meaning of life and endorses or rejects values and ideals that are frequently controversial; and (b) funding the arts is, on no plausible view, an essential function of government. A key tenet of anti-perfectionist political morality is that the state should not get behind values that are controversial, particularly when it has the option of keeping its hand clean. At the very least, this suggests that public funding of the arts is more problematic than clear-cut cases of non-basic political matters like traffic laws and garbage collection ordinances.

For these reasons, anti-perfectionists who support public funding of the arts would do well to provide a more principled defense of their views. One such defense is available and warrants comment. If sound, it provides a way to reconcile public support for the arts with anti-perfectionism. The defense in question builds on the thought that art can be understood as a public good that is underprovided by the market. On this view, the anti-perfectionist supports public funding of the arts not because he or she is intentionally favoring some valuable pursuits over others, but because he or she is trying to provide a solution to a collective action problem. There are two versions of this argument. The first one I will call the *crass version*, the second, the *elevated version*.

The crass version of the public goods argument begins with the observation that interest in the arts generates tourism. People come to

---

[18] Brian Barry is particularly clear on this point. Neutrality, he maintains, is applicable only with respect to the design of the constitutional framework. Within the framework, perfectionist policies can be pursued so long as they are settled upon by a fair political decision procedure. See *Justice as Impartiality*, p. 144 n.

[19] It is noteworthy that Rawls himself in *A Theory of Justice* explicitly rejected the idea that just governments could fund art on the grounds that it is intrinsically valuable. Funding for the arts, he held, is justified only if it is done through the "exchange branch" which requires unanimous consent. See *A Theory of Justice*, pp. 331–32, 282–84.

visit museums. When they do, they spend money, thereby increasing revenues. Since increased revenues benefit everyone in the community, the argument runs, everyone has a reason to support art. However, because of coordination problems the market does not provide an optimal level of support. Therefore, public funding is necessary.[20]

This argument has solid anti-perfectionist credentials. But, putting aside its plausibility for the moment, it is hard to believe that many who actually support the arts really believe it. Most people who defend public support for the arts sincerely believe that art is intrinsically valuable.[21] They do not think that art is on a par with other tourist attractions such as amusement parks. So this argument would conflict with the reasons that most people actually hold for supporting the arts.

This is not necessarily a reason for rejecting it. The best defense for a policy may be one that few espouse. But it does create a problem for anti-perfectionists who accept the third principle of restraint (see p. 32). On one interpretation of the publicity condition, there should be a correspondence between the reasons that people give in public argument and the reasons that actually motivate them. This suggests that the argument, even if it is plausible, may not be available to some anti-perfectionists.

But we can put this complication to one side. The important question is whether the argument is indeed plausible. Its plausibility turns on an empirical judgment – does funding of the arts generate more revenue than it consumes? This must be demonstrated in order for the crude version of the public goods argument to go through. I will not try to answer this empirical question here, but I will point out that even if it could be demonstrated that public funding of the arts generates more revenue than it consumes, this would not show that it was an efficient use of public money. For there might be some alternative project (say the construction of better amusement parks) that would generate even more revenue-per-tax-dollar-spent than the funding of the arts. Then, according to this argument, we would have every reason to fund it rather than the arts.

At the very least, it seems that, if we take the crude version of the public goods argument seriously, proposals to fund art should be accompanied by a serious effort to show that the money being spent is a

[20] A version of this argument is discussed by H. Brighouse in "Neutrality, Publicity and State Funding of the Arts," pp. 47–48. Note that this argument could be used to justify other publicly funded projects, e.g., the construction of football stadiums.

[21] Most, but not all. Some who support art may indeed have crass motives. The restaurant or shop owner may be a very vocal supporter for the proposed construction of a public museum down the street. But even here he or she will likely express his or her support in public by appealing to the intrinsic worth of art.

good investment. Taken seriously, this could have the effect that art would be supported not according to criteria relevant to its artistic value, but according to criteria relevant to its revenue-generating capacity. Without too much imagination, one can see that this would not likely improve the quality of art in one's society.[22]

The crude version of the public goods argument, then, might succeed in justifying some public support of the arts. But it would not likely justify the type of support that proponents of such funding have traditionally had in mind. And even what funding it does justify, it justifies only contingently, on the assumption that the funding is a good revenue-producing investment.

Consider now the elevated version of the argument. According to it, public funding of art is justified because it enriches the public culture. Publicly funded art exposes the public to new ways of thinking and seeing the world. As such, it benefits everyone, since it provides everyone with a richer range of cultural resources to draw on in thinking about their lives. Like the crude version, this version of the argument assumes that the market, by itself, would not provide the optimal type or amount of art. Although it is not clear how this is to be demonstrated, let us assume that it is true. The question, then, becomes, is this the type of public good that could be justified in anti-perfectionist terms?

The strength of the crude version of the public goods argument is that virtually everyone accepts that increased revenue is a public good. Such a judgment is not controversial. But matters are different when the public good in question is not revenue, but a good as amorphous as a richer public culture. Critics of public funding of the arts often complain that the art that is funded is hostile to traditional values and understandings of the world; and this judgment is confirmed when artists proclaim that the function of art is to shock, to disturb or unsettle conventional ideas. Of course not all art challenges traditional views; but, as artists themselves are quick to point out, art that does will fare less well in the marketplace. Hence, it is more dependent on public support.

When this complaint is made, it is hard to see how an appeal to the good of a richer public culture would be convincing. Critics of public funding can object that the arts do not give us a richer, but a more polluted, public culture or they can concede that the public culture would be richer, but maintain that it is better to live in a culture that is agreeable to their values. To these objections, proponents of public funding must reply that the critics are mistaken. They must insist that they have a false

---

[22] It is possible that the best way to get revenues from art would be to fund only good art; and governments might figure this out. If so, this objection could be met.

view about the arts and their importance to the public culture. These claims, however, are perfectionist claims and they do not sit well with anti-perfectionist commitments.

We are drawn to the following conclusion. The crude version of the public goods argument has solid anti-perfectionist credentials, but is implausible. The elevated version is plausible, but has poor anti-perfectionist credentials. Neither version, therefore, provides a successful anti-perfectionist defense of public funding of the arts.

I have claimed that the case for funding the arts is based on the claim that they are intrinsically valuable and that the government ought to support them for that reason. However, the failure of anti-perfectionist justifications does not show that we must accept this view. It has been suggested that public funding of the arts is justified because it contributes to a richer public culture *which, in turn, promotes personal autonomy*.[23] This argument seeks to show that public funding of the arts is another example of autonomy-based perfectionist political action and not an example of government action designed to favor particular valuable options.

Proponents of this argument must establish two points. First, they must show that the arts are not just a valuable option, but an option that is fundamental or integral to an autonomous life. Second, they must show that an unsubsidized cultural marketplace would fail to provide the type or amount of art necessary for people to lead autonomous lives. It is possible that both of these points are true, at least for some modern western societies. But neither point has been adequately established; and it is hard to see how the first point could be. An autonomous life requires a range of rich and varied options, but it does not require the presence of any one particular option. To state the obvious: many live sufficiently autonomous lives without acquiring an appreciation for the arts.[24]

For these reasons, the autonomy-based argument for public funding of the arts rests on unstable ground. We do better to justify public funding of the arts by claiming that a good society ought to spend a share of its resources on the promotion and celebration of intrinsically valuable

---

[23] See C. Taylor, "What is Wrong with Negative Liberty?"

[24] Maybe the argument is not that art is a crucial option, but that it promotes social attitudes that are necessary for an autonomy-promoting society. For example, it might be thought that art promotes tolerance, a respect for pluralism and a willingness to accept and celebrate innovation and that these attitudes must be cultivated in an autonomy-promoting society. This would help make sense of Taylor's remarks (in the paper cited in the above footnote) about the need for a society that cares about personal autonomy to attend to its "social matrix." But, even if this were right, it would not follow that these attitudes could not be sustained by other means or that public funding of art would be the most efficient way to sustain them.

goods. This argument not only captures the real reasons that motivate people to support art, it also is not vulnerable to the objection that it is based on dubious empirical assumptions or that it claims more for art than art can deliver.

The type of argument I have in mind has been advanced in a particularly stark form by Nagel. When it comes to art, he claims, "a good society should be anti-egalitarian, and committed to developing the maximum levels of excellence possible."[25] The reference to maximization makes the claim too strong, but Nagel is right to characterize his position on this issue as perfectionist.[26] And given that he is one of the more talented proponents of anti-perfectionism, the concession is revealing. It suggests that there is no principled anti-perfectionist defense of public funding of the arts. If such funding is, nevertheless, justified, it provides a good example of justified political action that promotes the good.

Discouraging the bad

Perfectionism concerns not only the promotion of the good, but also the discouragement of the bad. It is an unfortunate fact that in free societies some pursue lives of waste and ruin. Given the value and importance of autonomy, there are substantial limits to what governments permissibly can do to discourage such lives. But the limits, while substantial, may not rule out all efforts to discourage bad options.

> *Example 3* The government of a modern western society imple-
> ments regulations and restrictions[27] designed to discourage
> the consumption of a class of drugs that damage the interests
> of those who consume them. It takes into account the danger
> that its measures will be counterproductive, but concludes
> that the danger is worth taking. Some citizens object. They
> claim that the government has no right to tell them what they
> can and cannot do to their bodies. The government responds
> that it is taking steps to promote the well-being of its subjects
> and that this justifies its action.

Before discussing this example, a number of things should be said about it. The first thing to be said is that it raises important issues not raised in example 2. Here the government is drawing on its immense

---

[25] T. Nagel, *Equality and Partiality*, p. 135. (In addition to art, Nagel also mentions research and natural beauty as goods that ought to be publicly supported.)

[26] Ibid. p. 133.

[27] The regulations and restrictions that I have in mind include legal penalties and fines, restrictions on advertising, discriminatory taxation, public service announcements designed to discourage consumption and other publicly funded educational efforts.

power to discourage its subjects from engaging in certain types of conduct that they voluntarily wish to engage in. To make this point even clearer, let us suppose that at least some people in the society wish to use the drugs and fully understand the dangers of doing so. This means that the government cannot justify its measures by claiming that no informed person of sound mind would want to consume them.

The second thing to be said is that a good deal turns on the evaluative judgment that these drugs "damage the interests of those who consume them." Lacking extensive pharmacological knowledge of the probable effects of consuming different types of drugs, I deliberately have not specified any particular drug in the example.[28] Perhaps many recreational drugs currently targeted for legal regulation are not particularly dangerous, but I am assuming that there is a class of drugs that do significantly damage the interests of those who consume them. These are drugs which pose a severe risk to the physical and mental health of those who take them.

The final thing to be said about the example is that it refers to legal regulations and restrictions designed to *discourage*, not prohibit, the consumption of these drugs. This shows that the measures proposed in the example are less restrictive than the measures taken by many modern governments such as the current government of the United States. The case for prohibiting the consumption of recreational drugs, even dangerous recreational drugs, through the criminal law is harder to justify on perfectionist grounds than the types of measures contemplated in this example. In general, the criminal law is not a good instrument for advancing perfectionist goals. To see why, all one has to do is imagine some option or life-style that one considers to be unworthy and then compare it with time spent in prison. In most instances, people would be worse off in jail then they would be if they were left to engage in the unworthy pursuit.[29] It is particularly important to bear this in mind if the government action in question is justified on the grounds that it promotes the interests of those subject to it.[30]

---

[28] Not only do I lack the extensive knowledge, much of it does not seem to exist. D. Husak, for example, prefaces his study by claiming that "the empirical data about drugs and drug use . . . are inconclusive and subject to constant challenge and revision." See D. Husak, *Drugs and Rights*, p. 3.

[29] This point is made in the context of the drug legalization debate by D. Husak. See *Drugs and Rights*, p. 76.

[30] It is true that governments often use criminal prohibitions as a means to discourage conduct that is deemed to be unworthy. Here the justification is not that putting people in jail is better than letting them engage in the conduct, but rather that putting some in jail will discourage others from engaging in it. (See, e.g., J. Kaplan, "Taking Drugs Seriously.") There is surely merit to this type of justification. But I will not try to assess its limits here.

Thus the government action on offer in example 3 represents a moderate policy that lies between two extremes. These are, on the one hand, the policy of not seeking to influence the personal decisions of people to take or not take the drugs that they want to consume and, on the other hand, the policy of declaring war on drugs and calling into service the criminal law as the primary weapon for fighting the war.

I will argue that the government acts rightly in taking these measures. My defense of this view will be incomplete, for much depends on empirical estimates about the likely effects, both positive and negative, of such action and I cannot investigate such matters here. Still, it is possible to consider the plausibility of such a defense judged from the general standpoint of political morality.

All the measures in question are intended to increase the costs of using the targeted drugs. Most straightforwardly, these costs are economic, such as legal fines or higher taxation rates on consumption. But they are not limited to economic costs. The principal rationale behind public service announcements and other types of educational efforts that discourage the consumption of these drugs, as well as restrictions on advertising their sale, is to create and help sustain a social ethos that is hostile to their consumption. If such measures would be effective, and if the drugs targeted by them were indeed drugs that were genuinely dangerous to those who consume them, then the measures would be justified.

It may be objected that some who would be subject to these restrictions would not share the government's view about the undesirability of consuming the drugs. This no doubt would be true. But universal consent is not a necessary condition for justified political action.[31] The mere fact that some disagree would not, by itself, defeat the case for taking these measures. Of course those who disagree might have reasons for disagreeing. In particular, two lines of response might be pressed. First, it might be said that the drugs in question do not, in fact, damage the interests of *all* who consume them or, more weakly, that the government could never know that they damage the interests of all who consume them. Second, it might be said that even if the drugs did damage the interests of all who consumed them, it would still be impermissible for the government to take these measures because doing so would contravene people's interest in self-determination.[32]

---

[31] This is a bit quick. I give arguments for this claim in my "Lockean Anarchism from the Inside Out." See also J. Raz, "Government by Consent."

[32] See the papers by J. Narveson and W. Block in *Drugs, Morality and the Law*, edited by S. Luper-Foy and C. Brown.

The first response has considerable plausibility. Even if attention is restricted to a class of particularly dangerous drugs, it would probably be a mistake to assume that everyone who uses them would damage their interests. Not all people respond the same way to the same drugs. Some might be able to use them recreationally without impairing their general capacity to lead a valuable life. Moreover, even if this were not true, the government might have no way of knowing that it was not true. That is, the government may have no way of knowing that there is not at least one person for whom the targeted drugs would not damage his or her interests.

But these valid points do not defeat the case for undertaking the measures. The government must consider the interests of all those subject to its authority, not just those who are particularly well-suited to take dangerous drugs with relative impunity. This involves some trade-offs between the interests of different people, but this is not necessarily objectionable. In almost every area of public policy, governments must make such trade-offs.[33] Of course if the government is simply wrong in claiming that the targeted drugs damage the interests of those who consume them in general, then the case for the measures collapses. But in example 3 care has been taken to specify that the drugs in question are genuinely dangerous.

Does the second response fare better? At first blush, it is not at all plausible. Although people have a strong interest in self-determination, it does not follow that they have an interest in having access to any particular option, especially if the option is a bad one. As I argued in chapter 6, a sufficiently autonomous person must have access to a rich and varied range of options. It is not true that a range of options could not be sufficiently rich and varied if it did not contain the option to consume dangerous recreational drugs. This point has even greater force in the present context, for I have not said anything that implies that people would not have access to this option. My claim is that the government is justified in taking measures to discourage its citizens from choosing it. I have not claimed that the government is justified in using the criminal law to prevent its citizens from doing so.

However, the second response can be made to look more formidable. Sometimes it is argued that people own their bodies and that they, accordingly, have a right to do to them what they please, so long as others are not directly harmed in the process. The measures proposed in

---

[33] This is a consequence of the fact that the law must be cast in general terms. Even a law that is reasonable and just will not necessarily serve the interests of each person subject to it.

example 3 could be rejected because they do not fully respect this right. In this spirit consider the following claims by Feinberg.

By and large, a person will be better able to achieve his own good by making his own decisions, but even where the opposite is true, others may not intervene, for autonomy is even more important a thing than personal well-being. *The life that a person threatens by his own rashness is after all his life; it belongs to him and to no one else.* For that reason alone, he must be the one to decide – for better or worse – what is to be done with it in the private realm where the interests of others are not directly involved.[34]

Two points are noteworthy about this passage. First, it endorses the idea that people belong to themselves and uses it to reject paternalism. Second, it identifies this idea with the value of personal autonomy.

Whatever one thinks of the first idea, the second one ought to be rejected. If people belong to themselves and if they have a right to do to themselves what they please, then they have a right to destroy their own capacity to be autonomous. This means that if we care about respecting and promoting the autonomy of others it is possible, and indeed it is likely in some circumstances, that we will need to transgress this right. This forces a dilemma on us – should we transgress the right and protect their autonomy or should we respect the right and let their autonomy be diminished or destroyed?

The main problem with identifying the idea that people belong to themselves with the ideal of personal autonomy is that it makes it impossible to formulate this dilemma. And we need to formulate the dilemma in order to decide which is normatively more important, protecting autonomy or respecting the right of people to do to themselves what they please. I have not shown that the idea that people belong to themselves is mistaken. But I have argued at length that personal autonomy is a value of great importance. If that general argument is sound, then there is a good case for thinking that when, and if, personal autonomy comes into conflict with the right of people to do to themselves what they please, it ought to take precedence.

The second response, then, is unsuccessful to the extent that it identifies the idea that people belong to themselves with the value of autonomy. To repeat: this does not show that we do not have at least a *prima facie* right to do to ourselves what we please. Perhaps we have such a right; but it does sap much of the force out of the response. It also

---

[34] J. Feinberg, *Freedom and Fulfillment*, p. 92 (emphasis added). I am not sure whether Feinberg himself would object to the measures proposed in example 3. He might believe that his argument rules out only the criminalization of drugs. See his discussion of "dangerous drugs" in *Harm to Self*, pp. 127–34. But, whether or not he would press the argument further, others may be inclined to do so.

arouses the suspicion that the idea that people belong to themselves is not really a value at all. It may be an idea that derives its normative force from its mistaken identification with autonomy.[35]

Be that as it may, the case for the measures proposed in example 3 is not defeated by either the first or the second response. If a successful case is to be made against the measures, it must proceed by demonstrating that the targeted drugs are not as dangerous as the government claims they are.[36] If this could be demonstrated, then the measures could be rejected because they discriminate against those who choose an option that is not in general degrading or unworthy. However, example 3 is not far-fetched. There do exist drugs that are very damaging to the interests of those who consume them and governments ought to discourage their consumption if they can do so non-counterproductively.

The justification for these measures is perfectionist. In taking them the government discharges its duty to promote and sustain social conditions that promote the flourishing of those subject to its authority. As such, the measures provide an example of justified political action that discourages the bad.[37]

Before leaving this topic, one final objection should be confronted. This objection is noteworthy for its sweeping generality. If successful, it would rule out all government efforts to discourage particular options. The objection in question is pressed skillfully by Dworkin in his 1990 Tanner Lecture.[38] According to Dworkin, "the suggestion that people should be protected from choosing wasteful or bad lives not by flat prohibitions of the criminal law but by educational decisions and devices that remove bad options from people's view and imagination"[39] is a bad one. The reason Dworkin gives for this judgment is complex. It draws on his more fundamental argument that the value of a good life "lies in the inherent value of a skilled performance of living."[40] As such, living well,

---

[35] On this see G. A. Cohen's criticism of the identification of self-ownership with autonomy in *Self-Ownership, Freedom and Equality*, pp. 236–38. (In pressing this criticism Cohen works with a different understanding of autonomy than the one defended in this essay.)

[36] In thinking about how dangerous a drug is, the following questions are relevant: (1) What percentage of those who take it become addicted to it? (2) How severe are the withdrawal symptoms associated with addiction? (3) To what extent does consumption of the drug impair a person's ability to engage in valuable pursuits? and (4) To what extent does consumption of the drug damage a person's physical health?

[37] Once again, anti-perfectionists might claim that drug legislation is not a constitutional essential or a matter of basic justice. Therefore, they might argue, they could fully accept the moderate policy defended here. Perhaps this is right. But it is not clear why drug legislation is not a matter of basic justice. Critics of current drug policies often claim that the laws are not just foolish, but unjust. And even the enforcement of moderate drug policies often involves coercion.

[38] R. Dworkin, "Foundations of Liberal Equality."   [39] Ibid. p. 270.

[40] Ibid. p. 241.

he tells us, is "like painting well, it can be seen as responding in an appropriate way to one's situation" and the value of this response can be seen as "complete in itself," not contingent on its contribution to the world.[41] Working with this background conception of a good life, Dworkin explains what is wrong with the above suggestion:

[A] challenge cannot be more interesting, or in any other way a more valuable challenge to face, when it has been narrowed, simplified, and bowdlerized by others in advance, and that is as much true when we are ignorant of what they have done as when we are all too aware of it.[42]

A full response to Dworkin's argument would call for a detailed examination of his "challenge model" of well-being. I will not attempt this here; and since Dworkin himself concedes that the model is presently underdeveloped[43], it might be inappropriate to do so. Perhaps we should wait until Dworkin has completed the model before subjecting it to critical evaluation.

Nonetheless, I do want to argue that this particular argument against perfectionism is a bad one. My argument is simple. If Dworkin is right that perfectionist political action that discourages bad options is misguided because this action simplifies or narrows the challenge situation that people confront, then, at least in some circumstances, governments ought to *promote* bad options. Suppose, for instance, that two political communities are identical except that one has a problem with drug abuse. In this community the lives of thousands of people are destroyed because they become addicted to a particularly dangerous drug. The other community has no such problem. Its citizens remain blissfully ignorant of the existence of such a drug.

Given this supposition, if it is true that the first community should not undertake political measures to discourage the consumption of this drug because doing so would narrow and simplify the challenge situation that its citizens confront, then it follows, by parity of reasoning, that the second community has reason to take political measures to introduce or promote this drug, for doing so would widen and complicate the challenge situation that its citizens confront. But this is a manifestly absurd conclusion. It constitutes a *reductio ad absurdum* of Dworkin's argument.[44]

---

[41] Ibid. pp. 253, 247.   [42] Ibid. p. 271.   [43] Ibid. p. 196.

[44] In defense of Dworkin it might be said that his argument implicitly rests on a distinction between doing and allowing. On this interpretation, it would be wrong for a government to actively discourage bad options, but it would not be wrong for it to fail to promote bad options even if it was known that the latter would have the same consequences for the challenge situation of its subjects as the former. This interpretation rescues Dworkin's argument from my criticism. But it leaves Dworkin with the formidable task of providing a principled rationale for the proposed distinction. And in this context it is hard to see how the task could be successfully completed.

Perfectionism and culture

Thus far I have considered examples dealing with three issues of public policy. In each example I have defended a position that some critics of perfectionism would themselves be inclined to adopt. I have then tried to show that the position is more adequately justified within a perfectionist framework. In this section I consider one final issue. With regard to it, the position I defend is more controversial.

The issue in question concerns government policies that promote or favor one cultural way of life over others. This issue arises in a number of different contexts, but attention here will be concentrated on just one: government efforts to restrict immigration so as to sustain a particular national culture. By trying to answer the question of whether such efforts could be justified – and, if so, under what conditions – I believe a further weakness in anti-perfectionist liberalism can be exposed.

It should be plain that if restrictive immigration policies are ever justified, they are justified in virtue of the fact that people, or at least some people, have an interest in sustaining their national culture. So the first task is to be clearer about the nature of this interest. It is sometimes claimed that particular commitments and loyalties are constitutive of our personal identity. These commitments and loyalties, it is said, form the "evaluative framework" in which we make sense of the world in which we live.[45] It is also sometimes claimed that we have an interest in living in a public environment that is familiar, understandable and predictable. Only in such an environment can we feel at home in the world.[46] Finally, it is sometimes claimed that our self-respect is bound up with our membership in particular groups. To the extent that these groups fare well, our self-respect is enhanced.[47]

All of these claims express an underlying idea. While they explicitly refer to particular loyalties and commitments, they point toward a more universal truth about human beings; namely, human beings are creatures who need to have particular loyalties and commitments and whose flourishing is bound up with them. In the present context this idea is important. For it suggests that in order to justify political efforts to sustain a national culture people do not need to demonstrate that their culture is superior to all others. It may be sufficient if they can show that their national culture is one of the particular loyalties with which their well-being is bound up.

Let us refer to the idea that the above claims give expression to as the

[45] C. Taylor, *Sources of the Self*, pp. 25–52.
[46] Y. Tamir, *Liberal Nationalism*, p. 84.
[47] J. Raz and A. Margalit, "National Self-Determination," p. 134.

thesis that the *well-being of people extends beyond themselves*. This thesis can be explained as follows. The success of our lives hinges, in large part, on the success and value of the particular pursuits we engage in. These pursuits not only give meaning to our lives, they also provide us with opportunities for self-expression and self-development. Moreover, and importantly, a condition for participating in many valuable pursuits is coming to value the pursuits themselves. In this way, our well-being becomes tied to the success of things beyond ourselves.[48]

This thesis does not show that people must identify with and participate in a national culture to flourish. National loyalty is but one kind of particular commitment. People may engage in other pursuits and take on other loyalties. But it does support a weaker conclusion. To the extent that people identify with and participate in their national culture its preservation and success will affect their well-being. And this weaker conclusion, coupled with the fact that many people do, in reality, identify with their national culture, is sufficient to explain how people could have a genuine interest in sustaining it.[49]

Showing that people have such an interest is the first step toward justifying restrictive immigration policies. But to be justified these policies must also not impose excessive costs on those who do not identify with the national culture. Broadly speaking, these costs fall on two classes of people: those who do not live in the national territory, but have an interest in entering *and* those who live in the national territory, but do not identify with the national culture.

Reflecting on these costs, some have concluded that for modern western societies, as they now are and as they are likely to be for some time, restrictive immigration policies cannot be justified.[50] In what follows I will argue that this is not the case, although I will concede that for these policies to be justified a number of demanding conditions must be met. Then I will show that this position is not available to anti-perfectionists.

---

[48] For a clear statement of this thesis, see the discussion of friendship in J. Finnis, *Natural Law and Natural Rights*, pp. 141–44.

[49] Compare this line of thought with C. Taylor's argument that promoting the survival of a particular way of life can be a morally legitimate goal. See "The Politics of Recognition." Against this, it may be objected that while people may, as a matter of contingent fact, come to identify with their national culture in the relevant way, they should not do so. Such identification, it may be said, always breeds intolerance and aggression. Given the history of the twentieth century, this objection should not be taken lightly. But aggression and intolerance, while they may accompany sentiments of national identification, are not essential to it. Here I assume – although I do not try to prove – that there are some forms of national identification that do not give rise to these pathologies.

[50] See J. Carens, "Aliens and Citizens: The Case for Open Borders."

To better focus the discussion it will help, once more, to have before us an example.

> *Example 4* Taking pride in its past, and wishing to sustain its shared national identity, a modern western society adopts an immigration policy that favors those who are familiar with the national culture and discriminates against those who are not. The community justifies the measure not by claiming that its national culture is superior to all other cultures, but rather by claiming that the well-being of its members is tied up with the preservation of its distinctive national culture.

Does the community in this example act wrongly in adopting the restrictive immigration policy? Let me approach this question by making two artificial suppositions. First, suppose that everyone in the political community identifies with the national culture.[51] Second, suppose that there are no people who need to join the community, e.g. there are no non-members with a compelling interest in becoming a member. Given these suppositions and assuming that the national culture is valuable and that the political community is peaceful, it is hard to see why the policy would be wrong. Preserving the national culture would be justified for the reasons advanced above and no significant costs would be present to defeat the justification.

If this is right, there is a *prima facie* justification for the policy. The justification holds that the political community has a claim to restrict immigration so long as (a) doing so would help preserve or strengthen its national culture, (b) this national culture is not morally suspect and (c) its preservation promotes the well-being of its members. As indicated, this is only a *prima facie* justification. To see whether it could ever be conclusive we must now relax the artificial suppositions; for, clearly, they preclude the difficult questions. In the real world, nation-states contain national minorities and non-members often having a strong interest in joining them. In the face of these conditions, the justification of restrictive immigration policies is considerably more difficult. Still, the policies may be justified under some circumstances, and to know whether the community acts rightly in example 4 we need to know what the circumstances would have to be like in order for the policies to be justified.

Consider first the interests of non-members. The most compelling case for being admitted into another country is that one's life is at risk. People seeking asylum from oppressive governments ought to be allowed into a

---

[51] Note that a political community could be homogenous in this respect and heterogeneous in other respects.

nation-state if that is the only way they can save their lives. But normally such people are not seeking to become citizens of the states they are trying to enter. They seek refuge, not full membership.[52]

Others seek to immigrate into a country because they wish to be with family members. Here not only do they have a strong interest in joining the political community, but also the relatives who presently are members of the political community have a strong interest in their joining it. Given the importance of familial bonds to people's lives, they have a compelling interest in being allowed to immigrate.

Thirdly, and more commonly, people seek to immigrate into a nation-state in order to improve their economic prospects. This raises difficult issues of distributive justice. To what extent can a relatively affluent nation restrict immigration when doing so has the effect of maintaining its affluence at the expense of those who live in poorer countries? I will not try to answer this question here. But I will assume that nation-states have some leeway to pursue the interests of their own members at the expense of non-members and that when they are acting within this leeway the non-members seeking immigration for economic reasons do not have a compelling interest in being allowed to immigrate.[53]

Finally, people seek to immigrate into a country for a variety of idiosyncratic reasons. They like the climate, they like its culture, they are bored with their own country, etc. But while these reasons are real, they do not constitute a compelling interest. If these people are denied immigration, they do not have a strong complaint.

The preceding discussion suggests some conditions for a justified immigration policy. They are:

(a) Those seeking refuge from oppression are granted asylum if they have nowhere else to go;
(b) Those who wish to join family members who are presently members of the political community in question are allowed to immigrate; and
(c) The immigration policy does not unjustifiably favor the economic interests of members over non-members.

Since it is possible for these conditions to be satisfied and for a political community to adopt immigration policies that favor those who are familiar with the national culture, a due consideration of the interests of non-members does not show that the political community necessarily acts wrongly in example 4.

We have yet to consider the interests of national minorities. National

---

[52] Some hard questions arise with respect to who is to be counted as a refugee. I will not go into this matter here. But see A. Schacknove, "Who is a Refugee?".
[53] For the suggestion that nation-states have this leeway, see T. Nagel, "Ruthlessness in Public Life," p. 84, and S. Scheffler, *The Rejection of Consequentialism*, p. 34.

minorities are full members or permanent residents of the political community, but they do not identify with its national culture. For one reason or another, they are not at home in the country in which they live. But they too have an interest in living in a national culture that supports and sustains their self-respect and their sense of belonging. This points to a central tension in the justification of restrictive immigration policies: the same considerations which justify them also call them into question. For if the policies are successful, then the national culture will be preserved and perhaps strengthened. But if this occurs, it may only worsen the situation of national minorities. By protecting the self-respect and the sense of belonging of those in the majority, the policies may further diminish the self-respect and the sense of belonging of national minorities.

This tension is genuine. There is probably no way to resolve it completely.[54] But it would be a mistake to conclude that it rules out all restrictive immigration policies. To make that inference one would need to claim that the interests of national minorities – no matter how small a proportion of the national population they constitute – take precedence over the interests of those in the majority. And this claim is not plausible. In this context the numbers matter. The smaller the size of the national minority population, the weaker their claim to live in a national culture that reflects their shared ideals and commitments. This is why it is reasonable for nation-states to require immigrants to recognize and comply with government decisions on languages, public holidays and state symbols, all of which reflect the national culture. Conversely, the less substantial the national majority, the harder it will be for it to justify the adoption of restrictive immigration policies.[55]

However, even if a national majority is substantial enough to justify adopting such policies, it does not follow that no compensation is owed to national minorities if these policies are enforced. A range of measures may be available that would allow national minorities some autonomy in giving public expression to their shared ideals.[56] Which measures are

[54] It might be thought that the way to resolve the tension would be to move from the current system of nation-states to a system of small, self-governing units, each of which could then sustain its own distinctive culture. However, not only is it hard to see how we could get from our current system to this imagined alternative, it is not clear that the imagined alternative would resolve the tension. For within each smaller unit there would still be minorities and the tension would exist on a smaller scale. Of course one might stipulate that the units would be perfectly homogenous. But while this would resolve the tension, it would do so at the price of making the proposed arrangement utopian.

[55] This explains why it is harder to justify restrictive immigration in societies, like the United States, that have a long history of admitting immigrants from diverse backgrounds.

[56] See the variety of group-differentiated rights discussed by W. Kymlicka in *Multicultural Citizenship*.

appropriate depends on the particular circumstances of different political communities and we need not investigate this matter. The point to emphasize here is that if some measures are appropriate in a particular context, then in order for a restrictive immigration policy to be justified in that context, the measures must be undertaken. We now have two further conditions for a justified immigration policy.

(d) The numbers must be right, i.e. the national majority must be sufficiently substantial; and
(e) Where appropriate, compensatory measures must be taken to protect the interests of national minorities.

When these conditions are satisfied, a political community can adopt or enforce restrictive immigration policies without unjustifiably infringing the claims of national minorities. Taken in conjunction with conditions (a)–(c), they yield an account of justified immigration policy.[57]

Return now to example 4. If the preceding discussion is correct, the community acts rightly, or at least permissibly, so long as the five conditions outlined above are met. This shows how restrictive immigration could be justified in a modern western society.

It cannot be confidently asserted that anti-perfectionists would reject this judgment, since most have not addressed the subject of immigration at all. However, those who have addressed the subject have generally concluded that restrictive immigration policies are not justified. They are not justified precisely because their justification contradicts the spirit of anti-perfectionism.[58] As we have seen, these policies are intended to support particular values and ideals. They are intended to make a nation's public environment more hospitable to some ways of life and less hospitable to others.

Understood in these terms, restrictive immigration policies are inconsistent with what I have termed the second principle of restraint. This

---

[57] In her discussion of immigration Yael Tamir suggests a condition stronger than any advanced here. She claims that in order for a nation to be justified in adopting restrictive immigration policies it must fulfill "its obligation to assure equality among all nations." *Liberal Nationalism*, p. 161. Since "equality among all nations" does not exist today, nor has any prospect of existing anytime in the near future, this condition has the consequence of ruling out all actual restrictive immigration. This is an odd consequence for a theorist who is interested in justifying such policies. I believe that conditions (c) and (e), while vague and in need of greater specification, better capture the intuitions that prompted her to advance the equality condition.

[58] See, for example, B. Ackerman, *Social Justice and the Liberal State*, pp. 88–96. Ackerman rejects restrictive immigration policies out of hand, claiming that they contravene what he calls "the neutrality principle." He does concede that considerations of public order might justify some immigration restrictions, but stresses that this is the only valid reason for such restrictions.

principle states that citizens should refrain from acting with the intention to promote controversial ideals and values through political action. Given their background beliefs and commitments, national minorities could "reasonably reject" these policies. Notice, moreover, that in this context it is not plausible to claim that the policies in question do not involve basic justice and / or constitutional essentials. The questions of who is and who is not a citizen, and who is to be permitted and who is not to be permitted to enter the national territory, are fundamental, perhaps the most fundamental, political questions. If it is claimed that such questions are not fundamental, then the distinction between political matters that concern basic justice and constitutional essentials and those that merely concern secondary issues will look even less compelling than it already looks.

So anti-perfectionists who wish to hold on to the idea that it is permissible for states to restrict immigration to particular groups must confront another area in which their general theoretical commitments are in tension with their views on particular issues. But, as we have seen, it is open to them to reject this idea and take a hard line on the matter by insisting that it is wrong for states to adopt restrictive immigration policies, even when the five conditions listed above are satisfied. Indeed, this is the more consistent position for them to adopt.

For the reasons given here I believe this is the wrong position. However, this judgment cannot be affirmed without qualification. A complete and adequate justification for restrictive immigration would take us beyond the scope of this book. But a more modest judgment can be affirmed. Whether restrictive immigration policies could be justified, and whether the five conditions listed above are the right conditions, anti-perfectionism is deficient because it fails to take account of all the values relevant for a correct judgment on this matter. Given their theoretical commitments, anti-perfectionists must reject or substantially discount the claim that people have an important interest in living in a public environment that is hospitable to their way of life.[59] They must reject or discount this claim because it runs afoul of the principles of restraint which forbid governments from promoting controversial values.[60]

This, however, is a mistake. For many the preservation of their

---

[59] The tension between anti-perfectionism and government efforts to sustain a particular culture has been noted by others. See S. Perry, "Immigration, Justice and Culture," pp. 112–13.

[60] In a perfectly homogeneous society this might not be true. Here it could be said that the values in question were shared, not controversial. But almost all modern western societies are not culturally homogenous.

national culture has inherent value because it contributes to their well-being. This is a direct consequence of the general thesis that the well-being of people extends beyond themselves. Even if this interest should be overridden in many circumstances, it must be taken seriously in any adequate treatment of the subject of immigration policy.

Conclusion

In some respects, this chapter has been an addendum to the main line of argument in this book. At the outset I claimed that the central issue between liberal perfectionism and anti-perfectionist liberalism centers on which provides a better understanding of political morality. This is an important issue for political theory since we not only seek to know which substantive political judgments are correct, but also why they are correct. The arguments in this book have tried to show that liberal perfectionism is superior on this ground. This conclusion would not be imperiled if it turned out that the best understanding of perfectionist political morality and the best understanding of anti-perfectionist political morality yield the same substantive political judgments for modern western societies.[61]

Notwithstanding this point, this chapter has provided reasons for thinking that the two approaches point toward different political judgments with respect to at least some important public policy issues. It has also given reasons to think that the judgments supported by a perfectionist approach would be superior. Given the range of issues discussed and the detail in which they have been considered, it cannot be said that these reasons are conclusive. Still, the chapter has exposed weaknesses in (and limits to) a number of anti-perfectionist arguments. By so doing, it has provided a further measure of support for liberal perfectionism.

---

[61] "Yield" is probably too strong a verb for this sentence. Principles of political morality under-determine many, if not all, substantive political judgments about policy issues. So it might be better to say that these principles "provide support for" rather than yield such judgments.

Bibliography

Ackerman, Bruce. *Social Justice in the Liberal State*. New Haven: Yale University Press, 1980.
Arneson, Richard. "Freedom and Desire," *Canadian Journal of Philosophy* 15 (1985).
"Primary Goods Reconsidered," *Nous* 24 (1990).
"Neutrality and Utility," *Canadian Journal of Philosophy* 20 (1990).
Barry, Brian. *Theories of Justice*. Berkeley: University of California Press, 1989.
Justice as Impartiality. Oxford: Clarendon Press, 1995.
Beitz, Charles. *Political Equality*. Princeton: Princeton University Press, 1989.
Benn, Stanley. *A Theory of Freedom*. Cambridge: Cambridge University Press, 1988.
Berger, Peter. *The Sacred Canopy*. New York: Anchor Books, 1967.
The Capitalist Revolution. New York, Basic Books, 1991.
Berlin, Isaiah. *Four Essays on Liberty*. Oxford: Oxford University Press, 1969.
"Two Concepts of Liberty" in *Four Essays on Liberty*. Oxford: Oxford University Press, 1969.
Berlin, Isaiah and Williams, Bernard. "Pluralism and Liberalism: A Reply," *Political Studies* 42 (1994).
Berofsky, Bernard. *Liberation From Self*. Oxford: Oxford University Press, 1995.
Bond, E. J. *Reason and Value*. Cambridge: Cambridge University Press, 1983.
Braybrooke, David. "The Social Contract Theorist's Fanciest Flight Yet," *Ethics* 97 (1987).
Brighouse, Harry. "Neutrality, Publicity and State Funding of the Arts," *Philosophy and Public Affairs* 24 (1995).
Brink, David. *Moral Realism and the Foundations of Ethics*. Cambridge: Cambridge University Press, 1989.
Buchanan, Allen. "Revisability and Rational Choice," *Canadian Journal of Philosophy* 5 (1975).
Caney, Simon. "Anti-Perfectionism and Rawlsian Liberalism," *Political Studies* XLIII (1995).
Carens, Joseph. "Aliens and Citizens: The Case for Open Borders" in *Theorizing Citizenship*, edited by R. Beiner. New York: SUNY Press, 1995.
Christman, John. *The Inner Citadel*. New York: Oxford University Press, 1989.
Cohen, G. A. *Self-Ownership, Freedom and Equality*. Cambridge: Cambridge University Press, 1995.

Crowder, George. "Pluralism and Liberalism," *Political Studies* XLII (1994).

Dennett, Daniel. *Elbow Room*. Cambridge, Massachusetts: MIT University Press, 1984.

Devlin, Patrick. *The Enforcement of Morals*. Oxford: Oxford University Press, 1965.

Dobel, J. P. "The End of Ethics: The Beginning of Politics" in *Political Justification*, NOMOS XXVIII, edited by J. Roland Pennock and John W. Chapman. New York: New York University Press, 1986.

Dworkin, Gerald. *The Theory and Practice of Autonomy*. Cambridge: Cambridge University Press, 1988.

"The Concept of Autonomy" in *Theory and Practice of Autonomy*. Cambridge: Cambridge University Press, 1988.

"Is More Choice Always Better?" in *The Theory and Practice of Autonomy*. Cambridge: Cambridge University Press, 1988.

Dworkin, Ronald. "Why Should Liberals Care about Equality?" in *A Matter of Principle*. Cambridge, Massachusetts: Harvard University Press, 1985.

"Foundations of Liberal Equality" in *Equal Freedom*, edited by S. Darwall. Ann Arbor: The University of Michigan Press, 1995.

Elster, Jon. *Sour Grapes*. Cambridge: Cambridge University Press, 1983.

Solomonic Judgments. Cambridge: Cambridge University Press, 1989.

Feinberg, Joel. *Harm to Others*. Volume I of *The Moral Limits of the Criminal Law*. Oxford: Oxford University Press, 1984.

Harm to Self. Volume III of *The Moral Limits of the Criminal Law*. Oxford: Oxford University Press, 1986.

Harmless Wrongdoing. Volume IV of *The Moral Limits of the Criminal Law*. Oxford: Oxford University Press, 1988.

Freedom and Fulfillment. Princeton: Princeton University Press, 1992.

"The Child's Right to an Open Future" in *Freedom and Fulfillment*. Princeton: Princeton University Press, 1992.

Finnis, John. *Natural Law and Natural Rights*. Oxford: Clarendon Press, 1980.

Fundamentals of Ethics. Georgetown: Georgetown University Press, 1983.

"The Authority of Law in the Predicament of Contemporary Social Theory," *Notre Dame Journal of Law, Ethics and Public Policy* 1 (1984).

"The Legal Enforcement of 'Duties to Oneself:' Kant vs Neo-Kantians," *Columbia Law Review* 87 (1987).

Fletcher, George. "The Right and the Reasonable," *Harvard Law Review* 98 (1985).

Frankena, W. "The Ethics of Respect for Persons," *Philosophical Topics* 14 (1986).

Frankfurt, Harry. "Coercion and Moral Responsibility" in *The Importance of What We Care About*. Cambridge: Cambridge University Press, 1988.

Galston, William. "Two Concepts of Liberalism," *Ethics* 105 (1995).

Gaus, Gerald. *Justificatory Liberalism*. Oxford: Oxford University Press, 1996.

Gauthier, David. *Morals by Agreement*. Oxford: Oxford University Press, 1986.

Gellner, Ernest. *Conditions of Liberty*. New York: Penguin Books, 1994.

George, Robert. *Making Men Moral*. Oxford: Oxford University Press, 1993.

Gibbard, Alan. *Wise Choices, Apt Feelings*. Oxford: Clarendon Press, 1990.

Glover, Jonathan. *I: The Philosophy and Psychology of Personal Identity*. London: Penguin Books, 1988.

Gray, John. "On Negative and Positive Liberty" in *Liberalisms*. London: Routledge, 1989.

Berlin. London: Fontana Press, 1995.

Gregor, Mary. *Laws of Freedom*. Oxford: Oxford University Press, 1963.

Griffin, James. *Well-being: Its Meaning, Measurement and Importance*. Oxford: Oxford University Press, 1986.

"Against the Taste Model" in *Interpersonal Comparisons of Well-being*, edited by J. Elster and A. Hyland. Cambridge: Cambridge University Press, 1991.

Gutmann, Amy. "Civic Education and Social Diversity," *Ethics* 105 (1995).

Habermas, Jurgen. *Moral Consciousness and Communicative Action*. Cambridge, Massachusetts: MIT Press, 1990.

Justification and Application. Cambridge, Massachusetts: MIT Press, 1993.

Haksar, Vinit. *Equality, Liberty and Perfectionism*. Oxford: Oxford University Press, 1979.

Hampshire, Stuart. *Morality and Conflict*. Oxford: Blackwell, 1983.

Innocence and Experience. London: Penguin Press, 1989.

Hampton, Jean. "Should Political Philosophy Be Done Without Metaphysics?" *Ethics* 99 (1989).

"Immigration, Identity and Justice" in *Justice In Immigration*, edited by W. Schwartz. Cambridge: Cambridge University Press, 1995.

Hart, H. L. A. "Legal Rights" in *Essays on Bentham*. Oxford: Oxford University Press, 1982.

Haworth, Lawrence. *Autonomy: An Essay in Philosophical Psychology and Ethics*. New Haven: Yale University Press, 1986.

Hayek, F. A. *The Road to Serfdom*. Chicago: The University of Chicago Press, 1944.

Hobhouse, L. T. *Liberalism*. Oxford: Oxford University Press, 1911.

The Elements of Social Justice. London: George Allen & Unwin, 1922.

Holmes, Stephen. "Gag Rules or the Politics of Omission" in *Constitutionalism and Democracy* edited by Jon Elster and Rune Slagstad. Cambridge: Cambridge University Press, 1988.

Hume, David. *Dialogues Concerning Natural Religion* (1779), edited by R. Popkin. Indianapolis: Hackett Publishing Company, 1980.

Hurka, Thomas. *Perfectionism*. Oxford: Oxford University Press, 1993.

Husak, Douglas. *Drugs and Rights*. Cambridge: Cambridge University Press, 1992.

Kant, Immanuel. "On the Common Saying: 'That May Be True in Theory, but It Does Not Apply in Practice'" (1793) in *Kant's Political Writings*, edited by H. Reiss. Cambridge: Cambridge University Press, 1970.

The Metaphysical Elements of Justice (1797), translated by J. Ladd. Indianapolis: Bobbs-Merrill, 1965.

Kaplan, John. "Taking Drugs Seriously," *The Public Interest* 92 (1988).

Korsgaard, Christine. "Two Distinctions in Goodness," *The Philosophical Review* 92 (1983).

Kraynak, Robert. "John Locke: From Absolutism to Toleration," *American Political Science Review* (March 1980).

Kukathas, Chandran. "Are There Any Cultural Rights?," *Political Theory* 20 (1992).

Kymlicka, Will. *Contemporary Political Philosophy*. Oxford: Clarendon Press, 1990.

Multicultural Citizenship. Oxford: Clarendon Press, 1995.

Larmore, Charles. *Patterns of Moral Complexity*. Cambridge: Cambridge University Press, 1987.

"Political Liberalism," *Political Theory* 18 (August 1990).

The Morals of Modernity. Cambridge: Cambridge University Press, 1996.

Lehrer, Keith. *A Theory of Knowledge*. London: Routledge, 1990.

Locke, John. *A Letter Concerning Toleration* (1689), edited by James Tully. Indianapolis: Hackett, 1983.

Luper-Foy, Steven and Brown, Curtis. *Drugs, Morality and the Law*. New York: Garland Publishing, Inc., 1994.

Macedo, Stephen. *Liberal Virtues*. Oxford: Clarendon Press, 1991.

"Liberal Civic Education and Religious Fundamentalism: The Case of God v. John Rawls?," *Ethics* 105 (1995).

MacIntyre, Alasdair. *After Virtue*. Notre Dame: Notre Dame University Press, 1981.

Mason, A. "Autonomy, Liberty and State Neutrality," *Philosophical Quarterly* 40 (1990).

McDowell, John. "Might There Be External Reasons" in *World, Mind and Ethics*, edited by T. R. Harrison and J. E. J. Altham. Cambridge: Cambridge University Press, 1995.

Mendus, Susan. *Toleration and the Limits of Liberalism*. London: Macmillan, 1989.

Mill, John Stuart. "Essay on Coleridge" in *Utilitarianism and Other Essays*, edited by Alan Ryan. London: Penguin Books, 1987.

On Liberty (1859), edited by Elizabeth Rapaport. Indianapolis: Hackett Publishing Company, 1978.

Moon, J. Donald. *Constructing Community*. Princeton: Princeton University Press, 1993.

Moore, G. E. *Principia Ethica* (1903), edited by T. Baldwin. Cambridge: Cambridge University Press, 1993.

Mulhall, Stephen and Swift, Adam. *Liberals and Communitarians*. Second edition. Oxford: Blackwell, 1995.

Nagel, Thomas. "Moral Luck," *Proceedings of the Aristotelian Society* S.V. 50 (1976).

"Ruthlessness in Public Life" in *Moral Questions*. Cambridge: Cambridge University Press, 1979.

"Moral Conflict and Political Legitimacy," *Philosophy and Public Affairs* 16 (1987).

Equality and Partiality. Oxford: Oxford University Press, 1991.

"Personal Rights and Public Space," *Philosophy and Public Affairs* 24 (1995).

Nicholson, P. "Toleration as a Moral Ideal" in *Aspects of Toleration*, edited by J. Horton and S. Mendus. London: Methuen, 1985.

Nino, Carlos. *The Ethics of Human Rights*. Oxford: Oxford University Press, 1991.

Nozick, Robert. *Anarchy, State and Utopia*. New York: Basic Books, 1974.

Philosophical Explanations. Cambridge, Massachusetts: Harvard University Press, 1981.

The Nature of Rationality. Cambridge, Massachusetts: Harvard University Press, 1993.

Nussbaum, Martha. "Nature, Function and Capability: Aristotle on Political Distribution" in *Oxford Studies in Ancient Philosophy*, supplementary volume, edited by J. Annas and R. Grimm. Oxford: Clarendon Press, 1988.

Parekh, B. "Superior People: The Narrowness of Liberalism from Mill to Rawls," *Times Literary Supplement*, 25 February 1994.

Parfit, Derek. *Reasons and Persons.* Oxford: Clarendon Press, 1984.

Perry, Stephen. "Immigration, Justice and Culture" in *Justice In Immigration*, edited by W. Schwartz. Cambridge: Cambridge University Press, 1995.

Plato. *The Republic.* Indianapolis: Hackett, 1974.

Popper, Karl. *The Open Society and its Enemies.* New Jersey: Princeton University Press, 1962.

Quinn, Warren. "Rationality and the Human Good," *Social Philosophy and Policy* 9 (1992).

Morality and Action. Cambridge: Cambridge University Press, 1993.

Rawls, John. *A Theory of Justice.* Cambridge, Massachusetts: Harvard University Press, 1971.

"Kantian Constructivism in Moral Theory," *Journal of Philosophy* 77 (1980).

Political Liberalism. New York: Columbia University Press, 1993.

"The Law of Peoples" in *On Human Rights*, edited by S. Shute and S. Hurley. New York: Basic Books, 1993.

"Reply to Habermas," *The Journal of Philosophy* XCII (1995).

Raz, Joseph. *The Morality of Freedom.* Oxford: Clarendon Press, 1986.

"Autonomy, Toleration and the Harm Principle" in *Issues in Contemporary Legal Philosophy*, edited by R. Gavison. Oxford: Oxford University Press, 1987.

"Facing Up," *Southern California Law Review* 62 (1989).

"Government by Consent" in *Ethics in the Public Domain*. Oxford: Clarendon Press, 1994.

"Facing Diversity: The Case of Epistemic Abstinence" in *Ethics in the Public Domain*. Oxford: Clarendon Press, 1994.

"Authority, Law and Morality" in *Ethics in the Public Domain*. Oxford: Clarendon Press, 1994.

Raz, J. and Margalit, A. "National Self-Determination" in *Ethics in the Public Domain*. Oxford: Clarendon Press, 1994.

Rescher, Nicholas. *Pluralism: Against the Demand for Consensus.* Oxford: Oxford University Press, 1993.

Rousseau, Jean-Jacques. *The Social Contract* (1762) in *The Social Contract and Discourses*, translated by G. D. H. Cole. London: J. M. Dent, 1973.

Scanlon, T. M. "Rawls' Theory of Justice" in *Reading Rawls*, edited by N. Daniels. New York: Basic Books, 1975.

"Contractualism and Utilitarianism" in *Utilitarianism and Beyond*, edited by A. Sen and B. Williams. Cambridge: Cambridge University Press, 1982.

"The Significance of Choice" in *Equal Freedom*, edited by S. Darwall. Michigan: The University of Michigan Press, 1995.

Schacknove, A. "Who is a Refugee?" *Ethics* 95 (1985).

Scheffler, Samuel. "Moral Skepticism and Ideals of the Person," *Monist* 62 (1979).

The Rejection of Consequentialism. Oxford: Clarendon Press, 1982.

Human Morality. Oxford: Oxford University Press, 1992.

"The Appeal of Political Liberalism," *Ethics* 105 (1994).

Sher, George. "Liberal Neutrality and the Value of Autonomy" in *Contemporary Political and Social Philosophy*, edited by E. F. Paul, F. D. Miller, Jr and J. Paul. Cambridge: Cambridge University Press, 1995.

Sidgwick, Henry. *The Methods of Ethics* (1874). Seventh edition. Indianapolis: Hackett Publishing Company, 1981.

Stephen, James Fitzjames. *Liberty, Equality, Fraternity*. Indianapolis: Liberty Fund Inc., 1993.

Stocker, Michael. *Plural and Conflicting Values*. Oxford: Oxford University Press, 1989.

Tamir, Yael. *Liberal Nationalism*. Princeton: Princeton University Press, 1993.

Taylor, Charles. "Atomism" in *Philosophy and the Human Sciences: Philosophical Papers*, vol. II. Cambridge: Cambridge University Press, 1985.

"What is Wrong with Negative Liberty?" in *Philosophical Papers*, two volumes. Cambridge: Cambridge University Press, 1985.

"What is Human Agency?" in *Philosophical Papers*, two volumes. Cambridge: Cambridge University Press, 1985.

Sources of the Self: The Making of Modern Identity. Cambridge: Cambridge University Press, 1989.

"The Politics of Recognition" in *Multiculturalism and "The Politics of Recognition."* Princeton: Princeton University Press, 1992.

Tully, James. *Strange Multiplicity*. Cambridge: Cambridge University Press, 1995.

Unger, Peter. "A Defense of Skepticism," *Philosophical Review* 80 (1971).

von Humboldt, Wilhelm. *The Limits of State Action*, edited by J. Burrow. Cambridge: Cambridge University Press, 1969.

von Wright, G. H. *Norm and Action*. London: Routledge and Kegan Paul, 1963.

Waldron, Jeremy. "Legislation and Moral Neutrality" in *Liberal Neutrality*, edited by R. Goodin and A. Reeve. London: Routledge, 1989.

"Autonomy and Perfectionism in Raz's *The Morality of Freedom*," *Southern California Law Review* 62 (1989).

Liberal Rights. Cambridge: Cambridge University Press, 1993.

"Particular Values and Critical Morality" in *Liberal Rights*. Cambridge: Cambridge University Press, 1993.

"Theoretical Foundations of Liberalism" in *Liberal Rights*. Cambridge: Cambridge University Press, 1993.

Wall, Steven. "Public Justification and the Transparency Argument," *Philosophical Quarterly* 46 (1996).

"Lockean Anarchism from the Inside Out: A Comment on A. J. Simmon's *On the Edge of Anarchy*." Unpublished paper on file with author.

Walzer, Michael. "The Communitarian Critique of Liberalism," *Political Theory* 18 (1990).

Thick and Thin. Notre Dame: University of Notre Dame Press, 1994.

Wenar, L. "Political Liberalism: An Internal Critique," *Ethics* 106 (October 1995).

Williams, Bernard. "Introduction" to I. Berlin, *Concepts and Categories*. London: Oxford University Press, 1980.

"Internal and External Reasons" in *Moral Luck*. Cambridge: Cambridge University Press, 1981.

"Moral Luck" in *Moral Luck*. Cambridge: Cambridge University Press, 1981.

Ethics and the Limits of Philosophy. Cambridge, Massachusetts: Harvard University Press, 1985.

Wittgenstein, Ludwig. *Philosophical Investigations*. Oxford: Blackwell, 1958.

Young, Robert. "Autonomy and the Inner Self," *American Philosophical Quarterly* 17 (January 1980).

Index